Political & Social Economy

Edited by C. Addison Hickman
and Arthur M. Ford

Toward SOCIAL ECONOMY

HOWARD R. BOWEN

With a Foreword by
C. ADDISON HICKMAN
and an Afterword by the Author

SOUTHERN ILLINOIS UNIVERSITY PRESS
Carbondale and Edwardsville

Feffer & Simons, Inc.
London and Amsterdam

Library of Congress Cataloging in Publication Data

Bowen, Howard Rothmann, 1908-
  Toward social economy.

  (Political & social economy)
  Reprint of the ed. published by Rinehart, New York.
  Includes bibliographical references and index.
  1. Economics. 2. Welfare economics. I. Title.
II. Series. III. Title: Social economy.
HB171.5.B6925 1977   330.15'5   76-43973
ISBN 0-8093-0813-4

Table of Contents

v

List of Tables

vii

Foreword

by C. Addison Hickman

It is the lot of most books to have but one life, and often that life is short and brutish. *Toward Social Economy*, written by Howard R. Bowen, has had one life, and now manifestly deserves another. Originally published in 1948, the book was critically well received, was widely read, and had what appeared to be the normal life span of a few years. Created during a period when economic reconstruction, the malfunctioning of the market, and especially the spectre of unemployment were the central preoccupations of economists and of the public, the truly bold and original sections of the book, scattered throughout but mostly in Part IV, were not generally seen as the break-throughs which they are.

Yet now, a quarter of a century later, when we deal with such problems as appropriate social ends, the creation of social goods, the use of depletable resources between generations, and questions of income distribution and equity, we find ourselves going back to this now out-of-print book, only to find there the questions stated with astonishing clarity and simplicity and also to find some answers we had lost or never knew. Knowledge of this low-key classic has become a personal thing, as copies are cherished and become dog-eared through use. There has never been a time since 1948 when this book has not been in use at one or more major universities, to give new generations of students insights lost when economics veered in a more cautious, circumscribed, and technical direction.

The decision to bring out a new edition of *Toward Social Economy,* together with a new (1972) and even broader-gauged Afterword, was based in part on the belief that the book should again be read on its own merits, as a remarkably unified and penetrating analysis, with the date of 1948 of no moment. In this sense, *Toward Social Economy* could be read again with profit and new insight even if it pertained only to a long-lost early post-World War II era and had no special relevance to America or to economics in the late 1970s. Viewed in this light, the book is notable for its placement of economics and the economy within their institutional and systemic context, for its emphasis upon social ends in general and maximum aggregate satisfaction in particular, for its ingenious extension of market and pricing principles to whatever problems seemed amenable to such extension, and for equally vigorous analysis both of malfunctionings of the market and of sectors and problems that lie beyond the market. The book is distinctive methodologically because of the infinite care with which the often necessarily heroic assumptions that the author had to make were emphasized and made explicit. Indeed, the sweeping nature of some of these assumptions is often as revealing as are the models built upon them.

A word of caution. *Toward Social Economy* is so clear, so brief, and so modest and unassuming, that the unwary reader may be lulled into complacency. Ideas that are startling even in the late 1970s, let alone in 1948, are presented with no fuss and no fanfare. The style is aptly described by J. M. Keynes, in his remarks about Alfred Marshall's *Principles of Economics.* Keynes wrote (in his *Essays in Biography*) of the *Principles:* "It is elaborately unsensational and under-emphatic. Its rhetoric is of the simplest, most unadorned order. It flows in a steady, lucid stream, with few passages which stop or perplex the intelligent reader, even though he knew but little economics. Claims to novelty or to originality on the part of the author himself are altogether absent." Keynes goes on to point out that this style has its drawbacks. The clarity and simplicity can reach the point where the fresh insights and innovative ideas may be wrongly perceived as obvious and trite, and "Like a duck leaving water, he [the reader] can escape from this douche of ideas with scarce a wetting."

As a possible antidote to overly-casual reading, it might well be noted at this juncture that this book has innumerable insights, many ideas still fresh and original, and startling relevancy to the world of the late 1970s. Indeed, it might be argued that this book, after a Rip Van Winkle dormancy, is more relevant now, to our society, to our economic system, and to economics than it was when it was originally published in 1948.

Many of the issues now agitating economists, public officials, and the public in the late 1970s are anticipated and confronted in *Toward Social Economy*. What social ends are we really trying to achieve, and what are our priorities? Is capital really scarce, with a looming capital shortage, or is it potentially abundant? Are we making adequate investments in human or nonmaterial capital? Is there really a social imbalance between our production of things sold in the market and social goods, and if so, how do we know? In a nation that professes both free enterprise and democracy, how can social decisions as to the output of social goods be made? What is the optimal amount of leisure, both for the individual and for society? Should chronically decreasing-cost industries be nationalized, regulated, or left alone? How can optimal income distribution be determined? How much inequality in income distribution is justified by incentive considerations? Do we really have free consumer choice? How can a society determine how much capital should be accumulated for the benefit of subsequent generations? More to the point, currently, how can a society decide how much land and natural resources, especially depletable minerals, should be set aside for the use of such generations? Is chronic unemployment an intrinsic and inherent feature of capitalism, as some believe that Keynes argued, or can it be prevented within capitalism? Bowen offers no nostrums and no slide-rule formulas, but he casts a piercing light in *Toward Social Economy* upon each of these questions.

The Afterword, "Toward a Humanistic Economics," is both an extension and an updating of *Toward Social Economy*. In this epilogue, originally given as the C. Woody Thompson Memorial Lecture at the 36th Annual Meeting of the Midwest Economics Association, Bowen reflects the new environment of the 1970s and his own further reflection and research during the period since the book first appeared. Always a social scientist and a social philosopher as well as an economist, he expands the already broad compass of *Toward Social Economy* in new and exciting ways.

"Toward a Humanistic Economics" contains, in addition

to thoughtful sections on equality and on the necessary role of social critics, at least two distinct advances beyond the earlier book. First, the implications of the view of the economic system found in *Toward Social Economy* for the discipline of economics, and especially for its breadth and range of vision, are here made crystal-clear. In spelling out these implications, Bowen offers a withering critique of the "new" (now standard) welfare economics, which he believes has sacrificed relevance and usefulness for logical purity and a vain attempt to be value-free. He offers, in the place of this precise but narrow and perhaps arid version of welfare economics, a humanistic theory of welfare which offers "life" as the object to be maximized.

The second advance beyond *Toward Social Economy* is thus in the choice of social ends. The book assumes maximum aggregate satisfaction as the end toward which economic behavior is directed. This end is not so much advocated by Bowen as it is assumed, largely as an inheritance from classical and neo-classical economics. Bowen is very conscious, in the book, of the limitations of this postulated end, and he is equally aware of the hedonistic, materialistic, and utilitarian way in which this end can be and often has been construed. Nevertheless, in 1948 Bowen had little choice but to predicate his analysis upon this social end. He thus proceeded to work out the principles of social economy, and to employ the price system where this proved possible and social choice where it did not so prove. The end result was a very revealing body of analysis, as notable for its self-conscious and explicitly stated limitations as for its new insights and innovative thrusts. In the process, he cast new light, implicitly, both upon the viability of a market-centered approach and upon the adequacy of maximum aggregate satisfaction as an end.

In "Toward a Humanistic Economics" Bowen goes the added mile that both time for reflection and awakened interest by economists and others in alternative social ends make possible. During the past decade, there has been a notable increase in interest in a very old idea, newly regarded as an attractive and viable social end—enhancement of the quality of life. In the Afterword, Bowen opts for this social goal and proceeds to define it in a way that remains uniquely his. As the Afterword reveals, he believes that life is maximized when time (the truly scarce and basic means) is allocated in such fashion that human values, not necessarily exclusively economic in character, are most fully attained. He is also concerned that life as a whole, from birth to death, be maximized. This preoccupation with time is, incidentally, a thread running through the book as well as in this Afterword. It might be possible to redefine maximum aggregate satisfaction so broadly as to be similar to maximizing or enhancing life, but Bowen wisely breaks the ties and encumbrances of history and of long usage and simply postulates a new social end.

In this process, new problems of measurement are encountered and acknowledged. Bowen is not intimidated by these problems, however, partly because he believes that rough-and-ready interpersonal comparisons at least by classes is feasible, and partly because of his confidence in our ability to devise new and effective methods of measurement—such as the development of social indicators.

It is hoped that those readers who have earlier encountered *Toward Social Economy* will read this edition, with its provocative Afterword, with a new sense of excitement and rediscovery. Most of all, it is hoped that a new generation of readers, in large part without prior access to this book, will discover herein an insightful new way of looking at our society, our economic system, and economics.

PART I

Introduction

Chapter 1

THE ECONOMIC SYSTEM

E conomics is about the economic system. The first step in the study of economics is to obtain a clear conception of what the economic system is and what it does.

The economic system may be defined as the framework of institutions by which the use of the means of production and of their products is socially controlled. The purpose of this chapter is to clarify this definition. The nature of the "means of production" will be discussed first, then the need for social control over these means of production will be indicated, and finally the specific functions of the economic system will be described.

Means of Production

Virtually all human ends are achieved through the action of human beings within an environment.[1] The sole means available for the attainment of human ends are thus, (1) human beings with all their characteristics and potentialities, and (2) the various features of their environment. Not all of these means, however, can be regarded as means of production, otherwise the economic system would encompass all human activities and interests. The means of production are distinquished by two qualities: (1) the capacity to contribute to the production of transferable goods [2] and (2) scarcity.

---

[1] Cf. Alfred Marshall, *Principles of Economics,* 8th ed., London, 1930, p. 139: "In a sense there are only two agents of production, nature and man. Capital and organization are the result of the work of man aided by nature, and directed by his power of forecasting the future and his willingness to make provision for it. If the character and powers of nature and of man be given, the growth of wealth and knowledge and organization follow from them as effect from cause."

[2] Goods are defined to include both physical things and services which are wanted by human beings.

Only those human beings are regarded as means of production who are capable of contributing to the production of transferable goods, i.e., goods which can be enjoyed by other individuals. Thus, an individual capable of contributing to the production of food, books, clothing, medical service, dramatic performances, or any of a host of similar goods, is regarded as a means of production. This implies that certain individuals (e.g., invalids, infants, and "unemployables") are excluded from the category of means of production. Their activities (e.g., sleeping, eating, getting exercise, playing) yield enjoyments which are restricted to themselves and do not add to the satisfaction of others.[3] The distinction between human beings who are capable of producing transferable goods and those who are not is important, because the productive power of those who possess this capacity is of direct interest not only to themselves but also to the members of the social group generally. The capacity of an individual to yield transferable goods makes him a part of the reservoir of available social resources.

Anything in the environment which can produce a good for any one person could produce the same good for another person. Hence, all environmental means are capable of producing products that are transferable in the sense of not being inherently personal to any one individual. Even if the good cannot be separated from the means, the means itself can be transferred from one person to another. Thus, the capacity to produce transferable goods is not significant in identifying the environmental means of production.

Only those human and environmental means are regarded as means of production which are scarce relative to the amount of them which could be used to advantage. The exclusion of freely available means is to be explained not by the unimportance of such copious goods as air or natural gas in certain areas, but by the fact that the use of these means is a matter of almost complete indifference—a matter to which men need give

---

[3] The activities of a child or of an invalid may bring pleasure to other persons. If so, the resulting goods are technically transferable and such individuals must be regarded as means of production. However, certain goods which are technically transferable are usually prevented from coming into the market by legal or other institutional barriers.

little attention.[4] The utilization of scarce means, on the other hand, requires care, frugality, foresight, and administration, because the employment of these means for any one purpose is always at the sacrifice of some valued alternative use. The very attribute of scarcity implies that all possible uses cannot be achieved, that some uses must be foregone, and that the actual use must be selected after a comparison of possible alternatives. The administration of scarce means, which is called *economizing*, is a matter of great social importance.

Scarcity, as a criterion of the means of production, is chiefly relevant to the environmental means. Human beings, if capable of producing transferable goods, are generally scarce in the sense that more of them could be used advantageously if available. This does not imply, however, that they are in fact always so used—as all of us who have lived through the 1930's know.

To summarize, the means of production include those human beings and features of the environment which, because they are capable of yielding transferable goods and are scarce, are of vital social concern and must be administered with care and frugality.

Primary Means of Production

Ultimately, everything that man is able to accomplish is attributable to (1) human beings with their basic "biological" or "natural" characteristics, capacities, and propensities (whatever these may be), and (2) such elemental features of the environment as air, climate, and the surface of the earth. These are the primary means—the raw materials—of human existence on this planet. In so far as these means are scarce and are capable of contributing to the production of transferable goods, they constitute the primary means of production.[5]

---

4 Frequently some things are so abundant as to become a nuisance or even a danger, for example, water during a flood. In such cases, the abundance leads not to indifference but to an attempt to curb a menace, and economic calculation is required to secure freedom from the nuisance.

5 Professor Cassel (*Theory of Social Economy*, New York, 1932, p. 89) refers to the primary means of production as "those means of production which cannot themselves be increased by production." The inclusion of human beings together with their biological attributes as a primary means may be criticized on the

These elemental resources are to be distinguished from those means of production which have been themselves produced through the use of the primary means of production and which are, therefore, intermediate. These intermediate means include (1) all the characteristics, capacities, skills, and propensities of human beings that are culturally derived—i.e., "produced" or learned, and (2) such "artificial" features of the environment as buildings, machinery, ships, materials in process of production, automobiles, clothing, stocks of food, and many others. The intermediate means—usually called *capital goods*—may be regarded as means of production, since they yield transferable products and are scarce. They are intermediate since their existence is dependent upon the antecedent use of the primary means of production.

It may be useful for most purposes, though perhaps illogical, to include as primary means certain existing environmental features which, though originally the result of man's handiwork, are nondepreciating and therefore permanent.[6] Examples are concrete dams, canals, road cuts and fills, and harbor developments. Such works, unless deliberately altered by human action, remain indefinitely as one of the given and unchanging conditions of human existence. They may be classified, therefore, as primary means.

In a sense, the accumulated knowledge of a society—particularly its technology—may be regarded as a means of production similar in nature to those permanent environmental features which are the result of man's handiwork. Knowledge is a means of production quite as fundamental as laborers and land. Moreover, it is relatively permanent in the sense that once discovered ("produced"), it is usually carried on as part

---

ground that the population itself is "produced." For example, Marshall stated that it is convenient and traditional "to include some account of the growth of population in numbers and character as a part of the general discussion of production." (*Principles of Economics, op. cit.*, p. 139.) It seems expedient, however, to assume that people are not produced as means but only as ends in themselves. Consequently, the size and character of the population can be regarded as a "given" element, unless in the analysis of certain problems it is useful to make other assumptions.

6 The word "permanent" is used in a loose sense to mean unchanging within any period that would be of importance in human calculations or plans. A permanent environmental feature would be one for which no depreciation allowance would be required for physical wear and tear.

of the cultural heritage. Thus, it might logically be classified as a subdivision under land. However, the knowledge accumulated by a society is not properly regarded as a means of production because it is not scarce. Though the acquisition and use of knowledge and skills by any individual may involve considerable effort, the knowledge itself, regarded as part of the social heritage, is not scarce. The use of a given bit of knowledge by one person in no way lessens the possibility of another person's using that same knowledge. Scarcity becomes an attribute of knowledge chiefly through artificial restrictions on its dissemination or application, as when knowledge is held in secrecy by the initiated, or when its use is restricted through patents.[7]

Another special problem of classification is created by the existence of certain environmental means which, though found in "nature" and nonproducible,[8] are depleting. These include mineral deposits and in some cases underground water. These means are certainly primary since they cannot readily be produced, but partake of the nature of intermediate means since they are exhaustible.

Need for Social Control

For two reasons the use of the means of production must inevitably be controlled in some way through social processes or agencies.

First, the scarcity of the means of production frequently leads to conflicts of interest among individuals and groups. The possession of these means (or their products) by any one person or group necessarily lessens the amount available to others. This conflict of interest, which may range from mild rivalry to armed strife, must, in the interests of peace and security, be resolved by some form of social control over individuals. Conflict arises not only in regard to the use of land, forests, minerals, fishing rights, and water-power rights, but also in regard to the use by some individuals or groups of the services of other individuals

---

7 Cf. J. M. Clark, *Studies in the Economics of Overhead Cost*, Chicago, 1923, p. 119 *et seq.*; F. A. von Hayek, "Economics and Knowledge," *Economica*, February, 1937, pp. 33-54; W. H. Hutt, "The Sanctions for Privacy under Private Enterprise," *Economica*, August, 1942, pp. 237–244.

8 At least, under present technology.

or groups—as in slavery, serfdom, imperialism, or employer-employee relationships.

Second, efficient use of the means of production requires organized, coordinated, and cooperative action on the part of virtually all persons in society. Though production could be carried on by each individual for his own use in the manner of Robinson Crusoe, cooperation makes possible division of labor and specialization. Cooperative production is, therefore, technically superior in the sense that greater output is possible with a given supply of the means of production. Division of labor implies that each productive agent is used for only one or a few types of operations in the production of any given product. This requires that the means of production be organized so that each may perform its service in the right way, at the right time, and to the right extent. Specialization, on the other hand, implies that the production of each good is carried on in separate organizations or even that different stages in the process of producing each good are carried on separately. Some arrangement must be made, then, to ensure that each line of production is pursued in the right way, at the right time, and to the right extent. In short, in order to achieve the technical advantages to be gained from division of labor and specialization, it is necessary that the social group arrange for organizing, guiding, and controlling the productive process so that the essential coordination and teamwork can be achieved. Any society that wishes to gain the advantages of cooperative production must provide or evolve a system of controls over the use of the means of production. Even the so-called "laissez-faire system," which attempts to maximize individual freedom in the use of the means of production, is based on highly developed and socially sanctioned rules regarding the use of these means. These rules, of course, are largely identified with the system of "private property" with all its implications.

The scarcity of the economic means combined with the technical superiority of division of labor and specialization makes of production a social and cooperative process, and necessitates some form of *social control* over the use of productive means. Consequently, any advanced society which hopes to be cohesive, stable, and efficient, must possess customs, laws, or other socially sanctioned usages for regulating the use of its means of production. These institutions, taken together, constitute its economic system.

Functions of the Economic System

In controlling the use of the available productive means, the social group must have a mechanism for determining: (1) what individuals shall be empowered to exercise control over the means of production, (2) to what extent the means of production shall be used, (3) what specific goods shall be produced, (4) how the means of production shall be used in the productive process, and (5) how the product shall be distributed and consumed.[9] The performance of these five functions constitutes the task of the economic system.

First, the particular individuals who are to control the means of production must be chosen. Some arrangement must be made for selecting these individuals and for vesting them with the power to administer the means of production available to the group.

Second, the extent to which the means of production shall be used must be determined. The decision must be made, for example, as to how much labor shall be expected from each laborer, or how much land use shall be obtained from each piece of land.

Third, it must be decided what goods shall be produced. This problem arises from the fact that the means of production have innumerable alternative uses; hence, it must be decided for what specific purposes they shall be used—whether for the production of butter, guns, recreation centers, hats, skates, medical service, clothespins, dynamos, operas, radios, or any of

---

[9] This classification of the functions of the economic system partially follows that of Professor F. H. Knight. In his *Risk, Uncertainty and Profit*, New York, 1921, pp. 57-58, Professor Knight divides the "task of organization" into three parts: (1) the guidance of production, (2) the organization of production, and (3) the decision as to what portion of productive effort shall be devoted to provision for future wants. In the present classification, this third item is regarded as a subclass under item (1). In a later paper (in the University of Chicago Syllabus, *Second Year Course in the Study of Contemporary Society*, 4th edition, Chicago, 1935, pp. 189-192), Professor Knight has expanded his classification into five functions: (1) control of production, (2) organization of production, (3) distribution, (4) provision for economic progress, and (5) control of consumption in the short run.

a thousand other things. Shall more swords and fewer plow-shares be produced? More wheat and less corn? More skis and fewer swimming suits? These and thousands of like questions must be answered in some way until all available means of production have been assigned to specific uses.

Fourth, decisions must be made as to how the means of production shall be combined, organized, and superintended in carrying out the decisions as to what shall be produced. The technical methods of producing any particular good are seldom rigidly definite; instead, there are usually several or many possible alternative methods, each requiring a different combination or organization of resources. Wheat, for example, can be produced on many different kinds of land, with different types of labor, and with different methods of tillage. If wheat is to be produced, a decision must be made as to precisely how the means are to be applied for accomplishing the desired result. For other products a like decision must be made. Such decisions will be conditioned by the fact that when the means of production are employed in different combinations, varying results will be achieved in terms of quantity of product. In short, physical results depend upon the amounts and the proportions in which the various means are employed.[10] If, in producing wheat, we combine one acre of land and ten days of labor, the result will likely be different from what we shall obtain if we combine two acres with five days of labor. And every difference in the combination employed, within wide limits, will likely yield a different result in terms of bushels of wheat.

Finally, fifth, it must be determined what use shall be made of the goods that flow from the productive process, in particular, how these goods shall be distributed among the individuals whose ends are being considered. In a patriarchal society the problem of distribution might be solved by rationing the product among individuals. In a capitalistic society distribution is accomplished by fixing prices on the services of the means of production, and disbursing incomes to individuals according to these prices in return for the services of the means under their control—these incomes constituting the purchasing power of the individuals for the social product. In a com-

---

10 See Chapters 6 and 7.

munistic society the product is presumably distributed more or less equally among all individuals or "to each according to need." In short, every society must make some provision for deciding how the social product shall be divided among individuals. Moreover, once the problem of personal distribution of the products is arranged, decisions as to how the goods are to be used by the individuals to whom they have been allocated must also be made. Should individuals be free or should they be subject to various forms of social control in the use of these goods? If social control is exercised, what manner of control and to what end?

To summarize, every society—wherever located and however constituted—must have some mechanism for solving these five basic problems. The social institutions by means of which this is accomplished comprise the *economic system.*

There are, of course, many possible kinds of economic systems. Some of the more common types are suggested by such words as "feudalism," "socialism," "communism," and "capitalism." As different as these systems are, they are alike in that they all provide *some* solution to the problem of how economic resources shall be used.

The use of resources in any society is, and must be, controlled through a set of institutions known as the economic system. The precise manner in which the society uses its resources will depend, therefore, upon the nature of its economic system. For instance, the use of resources in a capitalistic society might be changed considerably if that society should adopt communism. Even minor institutional changes within the general framework of capitalism would have influence upon the use of resources, for example, the adoption of minimum-wage laws, steeper graduation of income taxes, prohibition of alcoholic beverages, enforcement of religious taboos on certain types of consumption, the spread of ascetic attitudes, increase of the typical school-leaving age, reduction in working hours, and changes in fashion. Thus, the various influences that shape the character of economic systems are, in a sense, the ultimate determinants of the use of resources.

PART II

Institutions and the Economic System

Chapter 2

ECONOMIC RELATIVITY

To the ordinary person the surface of the earth appears as something uniquely permanent and unchanging. People live and die, wars are fought, new technologies are adopted, but the hills and valleys remain, the rivers flow ceaselessly on, and the oceans obey the tides. The geologist, however, knows that the surface of the earth is anything but unchanging, and that the illusion of its permanence is attributable to the brevity of the lifetime during which any one individual sees it. If time is reckoned in thousands of years, the earth's surface, far from being static, is characterized by the most profound changes. Wind, water, gravity, friction, heat, steam, chemical action, and many other influences are capable of completely transforming the landscape.

Likewise, the ordinary person tends to view the society of which he is a part as a more or less fixed and unchanging organization.[1] The religious, familial, political, educational, economic, and other institutions appear to him to be almost as stable as the Rocky Mountains. In so far as he thinks about them at all, he feels that present institutions have always existed and always will. Here again, however, the view of the individual

---

[1] This attitude, according to Professor Walton Hamilton, has been particularly prevalent in the United States. "From time out of mind the value and permanence of 'fundamental' institutions have been questioned. The escape in America from a discussion of problems so basic has been largely due to the newness of our society. The open frontier, the wide distribution of industrial opportunity, the lack of formal class lines, and a spirit of self-reliance have centered our attention upon the more immediate problems of applying a machine-technique to a new continent and collecting the golden returns. So closely have we been absorbed in this that we have regarded our institutions as a part of the immutable universe itself, as unalterable as the path of the stars." *Current Economic Problems*, rev. ed., Chicago, 1924, p. 751. Professor Hamilton explains, however, that awareness of our institutions is developing with our growing "consciousness of maturity," and the rise of certain social problems.

is limited by the brevity of his experience. The sociologist and historian, in their study of the development of society, regard the period of a single lifetime as a mere moment in the history of mankind, and are able to demonstrate the enormous changes in social institutions which take place with the passage of time. They point out that society has not always been just as we see it today; moreover, that there is no reason to suppose that it will always continue in its present state. Society and its institutions are in a constant state of evolution, and no particular condition of society may ever be regarded as final.

At times the surface of the earth undergoes sudden and terrific alterations, as when it is subjected to flood, earthquake, volcano, or landslides. The effect of such events is clearly, if not painfully, discernible to human beings. Similarly, changes in social institutions are sometimes executed with breath-taking rapidity, so that living individuals are able to witness and consciously participate in great social transformations. The twentieth century has thus far been a period of drastic social change. Individuals living today have witnessed, within a period of thirty years, the collapse of monarchy, the establishment of communism, the rise and fall of fascism, and the world-wide adoption of increased political control over economic activities. These fundamental and far-reaching institutional changes, changes which have taken place before our very eyes, proclaim the transiency of institutions.

These changes also demonstrate vividly that the precise character of the economic life at any moment of time is strongly conditioned by the nature of the institutions in operation at that time. For example, the economic life of modern Russia with its social ownership of the means of production and its centralized control of the productive process stands in sharp contrast to the economic life of, let us say, nineteenth-century England where private property, freedom of enterprise, and freedom of consumer choice were the order of the day. Similarly, economic arrangements in medieval Europe where social position, occupations, incomes, and rights were assigned to individuals by the authority of tradition and custom varied from those in modern America where these matters are determined to a considerable extent through the operation of free individual choice and competition within a market.

The great importance of institutions in differentiating various types of economic systems should not, however, blind us to the existence of certain underlying realities which are common to all economic systems no matter where located or how organized. One of the most important tasks of economic science is to distinguish clearly between those aspects of economic life which are institutional, i.e., relative to the particular form of social organization that exists at any time or place, and those aspects which are common to all systems. This distinction is peculiarly important at a time like the present when far-reaching institutional changes are being widely advocated, and when, as a matter of fact, the institutional pattern is undergoing changes of the most violent and disturbing character.

Veblen once remarked that "economic theory can be regarded as a monographic treatment of the logical implications of one set of economic institutions." This is a fair description of the brand of economic theory which has become traditional in England and America. Anglo-Saxon economics, because it attained full flower during the rise of capitalism, has attempted chiefly to describe and analyze the economic life of a society characterized by the capitalist institutions of private property, free enterprise, free consumer choice, etc. This type of theory has been useful, on the whole, in developing an understanding of the economic process and in providing a basis for economic policy within the world with which it was concerned. It has been severely limited, however, by the fact that it has taken capitalistic institutions for granted, and has studied the economic process without attempting to distinguish those elements which are peculiarly capitalistic and those which are common to all systems. As a result, orthodox economics has become less useful—even confusing—when applied to the economic life of the modern world, and it is likely that its usefulness will be still further impaired at a time when words like "planning," "fascism," "communism," "socialism," and "industrial democracy" are bandied about in the daily vernacular. By assuming a *given social framework,* classical economics has effectively ignored the area in which real social problems arise. This by no means implies, however, that traditional economics has completely outlived its usefulness or that it is now of mere antiquarian interest. Rather it suggests that economists must extend the frontiers of their interest beyond the limits of classical capitalism, and give increasing attention to the role of institutions in the economic process. Thus economic principles which are basic and "universal" must be distinguished from those which are "relative" and transitory. The body of doctrine resulting from this approach will provide a secure foundation for the more detailed and specific studies of particular types of economic systems.

The following chapters of Part II present a brief description of the characteristics, origins, and development of social institutions in general and an analysis of the nature and functions of the particular institutions that comprise the economic system.

Chapter 3

SOCIAL INSTITUTIONS

The term "social institution" is variously defined. In the present context it refers to any practice which is socially accepted and widely prevalent. Thus any mode of action, way of thinking, procedure, observance, or convention which is more or less common to the members of the social group may be regarded as an institution.[1] However, for a pattern of action to become sufficiently stereotyped to be considered an institution, it generally (though not always) must be backed up by some form of sanction or enforcement. Consequently, as a counterpart to most institutions some form of control exists which ensures the conformity of individual conduct to the institutional pattern. Thus, institutions usually include the folk practices and social rules and also the machinery to control the practices and administer the rules. In the language of William Graham Sumner, an institution consists of "a concept plus a structure." The *concept* is a set of attitudes, ideas, or beliefs which define the functions of the institution for the society; the *structure* refers to the organization of material equipment and personnel by means of which the concept becomes effective.

Institutions are the molds within which individual conduct is shaped. They are controls over the actions of the individuals in almost every department of his life.[2]

---

[1] An institution is defined by Veblen as "a widespread social habit," by Professor Walton Hamilton as "a cluster of social usages," and by Professor C. H. Cooley as "a definite and established phase of the public mind." See Walton Hamilton, "Institution," *Encyclopaedia of the Social Sciences*, Vol. VIII, pp. 84-89; W. G. Sumner, *Folkways*, Boston, 1907, p. 53; C. R. Noyes, *The Institution of Property*, New York, 1936, pp. 9-10; T. Parsons, *The Structure of Social Action*, New York, 1937, pp. 399-408; F. S. Chapin, *Contemporary American Institutions*, New York, 1935, pp. 319-320; F. S. Chapin, *Cultural Change*, New York, 1928, pp. 44-50; C. Panunzio, *Major Social Institutions*, New York, 1939, pp. 25-27.

[2] "But it is this same individual who, by some usually indirect collaboration, composes and conforms [to] the social organization with its institutional habits

The individual regards most of the institutions of his group as part of the given and fixed conditions of his existence almost on a par with the laws of physics or biology. He finds that he must conform to the rules of property or marriage or religion almost as strictly as he must conform to the physical law of gravitation. He adjusts his behavior to both, and knows that any attempt to act in a way contrary to either will entail some form of unpleasantness. Indeed, in many cases he behaves according to the precepts of existent institutions merely because he is so completely imbued with the culture of his group that it never occurs to him to act otherwise.[3]

Institutional Control over Individual Behavior

The control of institutions over individual conduct is exercised both positively and negatively. On the positive side, the individual learns, through education and imitation, to act in ways that are socially prescribed. At the same time, he acquires the prevalent ethical attitudes toward the accepted modes of behavior so that he not only *acts* according to the social pattern, but *desires* to act in that manner.[4] In other words, the group

and ways and its relations. Once organized this collectivity becomes a negative constraint, if not a positive stimulus, to the individual. He is now a part of a whole and to a certain extent not only is his freedom of action limited, but there seems to be created some impetus and inertia under which the group acts as its component individuals would not act separately. The single man is caught up in the current of the crowd. Thus while individuals collectively grow institutions, the institution adds thereafter something more than the sum of the individual sources of behavior. At least it does so in directing and determining behavior, if not in initiating it. For that reason there appears a collective regularity which is different from the statistical regularity of a group of discrete units." C. R. Noyes, *The Institution of Property, op. cit.,* p. 6.

3 Cf. Ruth Benedict, *Patterns of Culture,* New York, 1934, p. 236: "If we are interested in human behavior, we need first of all to understand the institutions that are provided in any society. For human behavior will take the forms those institutions suggest, even to extremes of which the observer, deep-dyed in the culture of which he is a part, can have no intimation."

4 "(1) A society depends for its existence on the presence in the minds of its members of a certain system of sentiments by which the conduct of the individual is regulated in conformity with the needs of the society. (2) Every feature of the social system itself and every event or object that in any way affects the well-being or cohesion of the society becomes an object of this system of sentiments. (3) In human society, the sentiments in question are not innate but are developed in the individual by the action of the society upon him." A. R. Brown, *The Andaman Islanders,* p. 233.

confers upon him not only a pattern of behavior but a system of values by which to guide his behavior and to judge the actions of others.[5] A thoroughly socialized individual will thus be conditioned so that he will react (and will want to react) to each situation in the accepted manner. For him genuine problems of conduct arise only in those relatively few situations where there are no socially prescribed modes of action. Individuals who are not so conditioned are regarded in all societies as outcasts, criminals, or psychopathics, though the kind of behavior which is antisocial in one group may be highly "respectable" in another. On the negative side, institutions exert control over individual conduct by penalizing violations of the accepted modes of behavior. The individual in society is soon convinced of the expediency of "correct" behavior when he learns that failure to conform to the institutions of his group, even to the more trivial of them, almost invariably involves a penalty whether in the form of inconvenience, ostracism, scorn, derision, fines, imprisonment, or even death. Some institutions are so strongly sanctioned that infraction by an individual is regarded as a cardinal sin calling for the utmost penalties; others are more or less mildly enforced, while still others have little moral authority behind them. In general, however, any practice which is of sufficient generality to be dignified by the name "institution" will be enforced by at least a modicum of moral pressure. The severity of enforcement depends upon two factors. First, it depends upon the relative importance of the social end for which the institution is an implementation. The more important the end, the more rigorous will be the enforcement of the institution. For example, in our society, the right of the individual to live is regarded as highly significant; therefore, murder is a cardinal sin calling for an extreme penalty. On the other hand, the practices relating to dress are considered less vital; hence, for a man to attend a formal ball in overalls would call forth a mere psychological penalty in the form of derision or ostracism. Second, the severity of

---

5 "The problem of society is to produce the right attitudes in its members, so that the activity will take a socially desirable form . . . If the members of a certain group react in an identical way to certain values, it is because they have been socially trained to react thus, because the traditional rules of behavior predominant in the given group impose upon every member certain ways of defining and solving the practical situations which he meets in his life." W. I. Thomas, *The Unadjusted Girl*, Boston, 1923, p. 233.

enforcement depends upon the closeness of relation between the action to which the institution refers and the social end or value which gives the institution its sanction. The closer this relation, the greater will be the moral authority of the institution.[6] Thus murder, which is a direct violation of the principle "Thou shalt not kill," is an extreme sin; whereas adulteration of food, which may bring untimely though less immediate death, is a relatively minor transgression. Or highway robbery is a serious offense because it is a direct violation of property rights; whereas the exploitation of workers is often largely ignored because it is only indirectly related to the prohibitions against stealing.

Classification of Institutions

The major institutions of society may be classified into eight principal types according to their functions, each type corresponding to a fundamental division of man's activities.[7] As with most classifications, the divisions among the several categories are somewhat blurred and indistinct. First, the *familial* institutions include the established practices regarding sexual behavior, care of the young, and affectional relationships among the various members of the kin group. Second, the *language* includes all practices having to do with the communication of ideas between individuals. Third, the *educational* institutions include all of those practices having to do with the transmission of the culture from one generation to the next, the dissemination of ideas within the group, and the discovery of new ideas. Fourth, the *religious* institutions comprise those practices or observances relating to the supernatural or to the attempt of men to achieve communion with the universal. Fifth, the institutions of *aesthetic expression and appreciation* include such practices as carving, painting, drawing, music, and poetry, and the enjoyment of the results of these activities. Sixth, the *recreational*

---

[6] Talcott Parsons, *Structure of Social Action,* New York, 1937, pp. 401-402.

[7] Cf. Clark Wissler, *Man and Culture,* New York, 1938, p. 74. See also B. Malinowski, "Culture as a Determinant of Behavior," *Scientific Monthly,* November, 1936, pp. 440-449. "Every culture," says Professor Malinowski (p. 442), "must be analyzed into the following aspects: economics, politics, the mechanism of law and custom, education, magic and religion, traditional knowledge, technology and art."

institutions include all the practices relating to play, sports, and games. Seventh, the *military* institutions include the practices of the group in dealing with enemies of the group. Finally, eighth, the *economic* institutions comprise all the practices having to do with the use of means of production and of their products. It may be thought that this classification omits one of the most significant forms of social organization, namely, government. As a matter of fact, government has been included by implication. Government in the strict sense does not have special functions of its own, separate from those of the above eight types of institutions. Rather, it represents part of the apparatus by which individual behavior is controlled in conformity with the institutional patterns. It includes only those practices which are concerned with enactment, administration, and enforcement of formal controls over individuals, including the resolution of conflicts among individuals. Thus, a government which legalizes marriage becomes part of the familial institutions, a government which forbids gambling at race tracks becomes part of the recreational institutions, a government which enforces property rights becomes part of the economic institutions, etc.

The interrelationships among these various classes of institutions are so numerous and tangled that it may be doubted whether any important purpose is served by a classification. For example, within the family important economic and educational functions are carried on. Similarly, the church, which is primarily a religious institution, may exercise control over economic activities, education, or recreation. The apparent difficulties of classification are largely dispelled, however, if the *functions* of institutions are distinguished from the apparatus, organization, or "structure" by means of which these functions are carried out.[8] For example, the modern family as a concrete form of social organization does not logically fall into any *one* class; rather, it is partly a familial, partly an economic, and partly an educational institution. Therefore, in any list of, let us say, the economic institutions, certain aspects of family organization would necessarily be included. Similarly, other aspects of the family would be classified as part of familial and educational institutions.

---

[8] Cf. F. H. Allport, *Institutional Behavior*, Chapel Hill, 1933, p. 23.

The Social Utility of Institutions

It has been indicated that the behavior of individuals in all departments of life is preponderantly subject to guidance and regulation through the social institutions, and it has been implied that the area of conduct is relatively small which does not conform to the institutional matrix. A question rather naturally follows as to whether this social tyranny over the actions of the individual—applicable to every nook and cranny of his life—serves any useful purpose. The answer to this question is clearly in the affirmative. If it were not for social controls over individual behavior, life would be intolerable, perhaps impossible. If the individual were without established patterns to guide his actions, he would be hopelessly encumbered by the sheer difficulty of deciding upon his own plan of behavior. If he were to struggle valiantly with this enormous task, he might with good fortune survive, but he could hardly be expected to achieve modes of action as efficient, as satisfying, or as unobnoxious to his fellow men, as those which have evolved out of the experience of the race. This is true for a number of reasons. First, the attainment of many individual ends requires the coordinated efforts of many individuals, the success of which cannot be achieved unless the actions of the various cooperating individuals are guided according to predetermined and definite rules. Second, if individual action were not controlled according to established and well-recognized patterns, each individual would find himself completely uncertain regarding the likely future behavior of *other* persons and hence would lack a secure basis for planning his own actions.[9] Third, without socially imposed controls there would be no workable arrangement for reconciling the incompatible interests of different individuals, or when such control is not possible, for preventing actual physical combat among rivals. Finally, fourth, without social control the individual could not always be counted on to act rationally even with reference to his *own* ends, particularly in those cases where the ends are attainable only in the distant future.[10] For all these

---

[9] See Walton Hamilton, *Current Economic Problems,* rev. ed., Chicago, 1924, pp. 758-761.

[10] Talcott Parsons, *Structure of Social Action, op. cit.,* pp. 435-436.

reasons social control over individual behavior leads to the greater attainment of individual ends, on the whole, than would otherwise be possible. In this sense, the institutions through which control is exercised may be regarded as means to the attainment of *individual* ends.

Chapter 4

INSTITUTIONAL DEVELOPMENT

Recognizing that institutions are the principal determiners of detailed individual conduct and that institutions are indispensable to the orderly functioning of society, a vitally significant question remains, namely, What determines the precise form and character of the social institutions in existence at any given time? Is the institutional pattern of a particular time and place the outcome of pure chance or sheer accident, or can it be explained in terms of well-defined principles? A definite answer to this question is not available for the reason that empirical investigation in this field involves great difficulty. Nevertheless, one possible answer—an answer that is at least plausible and suggestive—will be presented. This view, stated briefly, is that the institutions of a society tend, in the long run, to develop so that the behavior patterns prescribed by the institutions are more or less conformable to the *ends* of the individual members of the group (within limits set by the extent of available resources and technical knowledge); and that the *ends* to which the institutions tend to become adjusted derive from the basic "nature" of human beings.

Before discussing this theory of institutional evolution, however, it is well to be clear as to just what is meant by the term "ends."

Ends

The role of *ends* in human action is one of the most controversial, yet basic, problems of the social sciences. On the one extreme, it is held that all or most human behavior can be interpreted as related to ends that are part of the consciousness of the individual actors; and at the other extreme is the view that the idea of "end" is a meaningless, or at best useless, concept.[1] Although much of the controversy is a war of definition, nevertheless there is a genuine area of disagreement that is not easily resolvable. It is my opinion, however, that the concept *end* not only can be defined meaningfully, in the sense that it can be given empirical content, but also that it is an indispensable tool for the study of society.

There are at least three possible definitions of *end*. First, an end may be defined simply as the result or outcome of an act. In this sense, every action may be said to have an end, since every action has consequences. Second, an end may be defined (as in everyday usage) as a *conscious* aim or motive which leads to action. When action is related to an end in this sense, the end becomes part of the initial situation leading to the action; the end, of course, may or may not correspond exactly to the final situation which, in point of fact, is reached, depending upon whether the action is appropriate. Finally, third, an end may be defined as a final situation which, if achieved, will terminate a given line of action, will resolve tension, or perhaps will yield satisfaction. This concept includes the second case, where the individual "knows what he wants and goes after it," but also

---

[1] The following quotations are illustrative of the differences of opinion on this subject. Mr. J. A. Hobson, for example, has stated, ". . . human conduct differs from every other known sort of organic conduct in that the operative units entertain, and are immediately influenced in their activities by advance images of 'the desirable,' termed ideals." *Economics and Ethics,* New York, 1929, p. 125. And Professor Lionel Robbins states, "The conception of purposive conduct in this sense does not necessarily involve any ultimate indeterminism. But it does involve links in the chain of causal explanation which are psychical, not physical, and which are, for that reason, not necessarily susceptible of observation by behaviorist methods." *The Nature and Significance of Economic Science,* 2nd ed., London, 1935, p. 90. Cf. also, A. B. Wolfe, "On the Content of Welfare," *American Economic Review,* June, 1931, p. 221. On the other hand, Professor John Dewey finds that it is not possible to separate ends and actions. He says, "A motive does not exist prior to an act and produce it. It is an act *plus* a judgment upon some element of it, the judgment being made in light of the consequences of the act." *Human Nature and Conduct,* New York, 1922, p. 120. Or again, "Ends are foreseen consequences which arise in the course of activity and which are employed to give activity added meaning and to direct its further course. They are in no sense ends of action. In being ends of *deliberation* they are redirecting pivots *in* action." *Ibid.,* p. 225. In somewhat the same vein, Professor Louis Wirth holds that ". . . the ends of action are never fully statable and determined until the act is finished. . . ." Introduction to Karl Mannheim, *Ideology and Utopia,* New York, 1940, p. xxiv. See Talcott Parsons, *The Structure of Social Action,* New York, 1937, for an extended discussion of this point.

includes another case where the individual feels a state of unease or tension but does not "know" what will yield satisfaction. In this situation he may have no conscious end other than vague feelings of unrest, or he may have conscious ends which he thinks will put an end to his unease but which, as a matter of fact, will fail to yield the expected satisfaction even if attained. Under these conditions the individual is likely to embark upon a persistent series of experimental or random actions until through a process of trial and error he reaches the "end," a condition where tension is, in point of fact, resolved. It is this third concept of *end* which is most useful for present purposes.

Under this definition, it will be noted, it is not necessary that the individual be aware of the goal he is seeking.[2] If he is aware of his end, then it is possible for him to act rationally with reference to that end, i.e., to pursue that line of action which so far as he knows is most appropriate to the achievement of his aim. If he is not aware of his end, on the other hand, but only feels a vague sense of want or unease, he will not be able to pursue a rational line of action but will experiment and "mill about" until by accident he has attained his goal and tension has been relieved.[3] Thus, not only rational but also much nonrational action may be interpreted as related to ends.

Having defined the concept *end,* the next question is, Where do individual ends come from? What determines the character of these ends? Traditionally, there has been an almost irresistible temptation on the part of social scientists to explain ends in terms of certain primary "forces" that are regarded as natural and inherent to man.[4] These forces have been vari-

---

[2] The nature of the end must be decided by the observer and not the actor.

[3] The most difficult scientific problem in connection with the study of human ends is: How can an observer know what are the ends of any given individual? Obviously, ends cannot be inferred exclusively from acts; such inference would be tantamount to assuming that all action is logically related to ends. The observer is faced, then, with the necessity of obtaining information by piecing together data from a variety of sources: (1) introspective reports of the individual under controlled conditions, (2) psychoanalytical conversations with him, (3) incidental statements by him, (4) his overt behavior, (5) reports of his friends and acquaintances, (6) his life history, and (7) analysis of the individual's situation in terms of a general theory of human ends and needs.

[4] The following are some examples. "It is universally acknowledged, that there is a great uniformity among the actions of men, in all nations and ages, and that human nature remains still the same, in its principles and operations. The same motives always produce the same actions: The same events follow from

ously labeled "instincts," "desires," "needs," "urges," "drives," "wants," "impulses," "prepotent reflexes," and "wishes." These concepts have been used as devices for explaining action in terms of the inner requirements of the organism, just as physicists sometimes describe motion in terms of "forces." On the whole, it is perhaps legitimate to assume that human beings do have certain basic characteristics which give rise to a number of fundamental needs—fundamental in the sense that they are common to men at all times and places.[5] It seems clear, for example, that all persons (except suicides or radical ascetics) have the biological need of food, sexual gratification, protection from the elements, and activity. Moreover, there is reason to conclude, from the data of anthropology, that a great preponderance of individuals in all human societies have felt the need of companionship, of social approval, of a secure status in society, and of relief from monotony. These social needs of the

---

the same causes. Ambition, avarice, self-love, vanity, friendship, generosity, public spirit; these passions, mixed in various degrees, and distributed through society, have been, from the beginning of the world, and still are, the source of all the actions and enterprizes, which have ever been observed among mankind." David Hume, "An Enquiry Concerning Human Understanding," in *Essays Moral, Political, and Literary*, ed. T. H. Green and T. H. Gross, Vol. II, p. 68. Compare also the following statement of the modern psychologist Professor E. L. Thorndike: "It would be useful to present an inventory of the wants, interests, and attitudes which belong to the human species as products of its genes and of the 'forward' influence of each of them, of each feature of them that may operate separately, and of each group of them (or of features of them) which may operate together. Ever so inaccurate and inadequate an inventory as could be drawn up in the present state of knowledge would be valuable. From these original propensities all wants that any individual ever acquires somehow develop. In spite of the selection, repressions, and transmutations caused by modern physical and social environments, they may persist and crop out with important consequences." *The Psychology of Wants, Interests and Attitudes*, New York, 1935, p. 15. See also Clark Wissler, *Man and Culture*, New York, 1938, pp. 251-280.

5 Of course the precise line of demarcation between those needs that are "fundamental" and those that are socially superimposed is not clearly known. For present purposes, however, it is unnecessary to make this distinction with precision. Professor J. F. Brown suggests that "hereditary" traits may be defined operationally as those which are (as yet) not susceptible to manipulation; and "environmental" traits as those which can conceivably be manipulated. *Psychology and the Social Order*, New York, 1936, pp. 262-273. However, Professor Brown states (p. 273) that, "one may as well say there is no such thing as original human nature, that the age-old quest for a definitive list of traits common to humans as humans is a hopeless quest for constants which do not exist." Even the "tendency to self-preservation and race-preservation" is not, he says (p. 274), a part of human nature; otherwise how account for homosexuals and suicides?

individual have been classified by Professor W. I. Thomas as the four "social wishes," namely, the wishes for (1) response, (2) recognition, (3) security, and (4) new experience.[6] In addition, it is likely that most men feel the need of a set of valued goals toward which their activities can become meaningful.[7] In fact, *striving* itself may be one of the most fundamental needs of man; without striving life would probably be devoid of content.[8] As Professor Mannheim has said, "Would not this elimination of all tension mean the elimination also of political activity, scientific zeal—in fact of the very content of life itself?" [9]

Though there may be some controversy as to the proper classification of the basic needs of human beings, it can be fairly stated that mankind, wherever he exists and wherever he has been known, is endowed with certain needs which have given rise to certain corresponding ends.[10] These ends, to be sure, are extremely indefinite and amorphous. They do not call for special kinds of satisfactions. Rather, they are ends of a broad and

---

[6] W. I. Thomas, *The Unadjusted Girl*, Boston, 1923, p. 4 *et seq.* See also W. I. Thomas and Florian Znaniecki, *The Polish Peasant in Europe and America*, New York, 1927, Vol. I, p. 73. Cf. B. Malinowski, "Culture as a Determinant of Human Behavior," *Scientific Monthly*, November, 1936, p. 447: "How can we link up religion, magic, sorcery and divination as cultural phenomena with our whole system of interpretation in which we conceive of culture as the vast apparatus for the satisfaction of human needs? We have seen that the fundamental needs of the human organism, those of food, reproduction, safety, freedom of movement, are satisfied under culture by *ad hoc* systems of organized activities. Culture thus establishes the quest for food and the industries, technical constructiveness, courtship and marriage, kinship schemes and military organizations.

"We have seen how this cultural roundabout way of indirect satisfaction imposes secondary or derived needs. These are not innate drives of the organism but highly derived implications of man's cultural response to innate urges. Thus economic desires, values, standards, legal inhibitions and the consciousness of one's rights and privileges, social ambition and kinship sentiments, political prestige and submissiveness are essentially human characteristics. But they are imposed by the circumstances of human existence in organized communities and not by reflex or instinct of any factor of innate endowment."

[7] Professor Thomas would probably classify this under the wish for recognition.

[8] This might be classified under the wish for new experience.

[9] Mannheim, *Ideology and Utopia, op. cit.*, p. 231.

[10] Cf. Kimball Young, *Social Psychology*, New York, 1930, p. 73. "More important than the mere enumeration of unlearned reactions is the recognition of the fact that human behavior rests fundamentally upon physiological needs of the organism, and that personal-social and cultural pressures are from the outset of life constantly modifying and enlarging the scope of activities in reference to these biological demands."

general nature that are capable of satisfaction in a great variety of ways. For example, the need for food can be satisfied by any one of a myriad of different diets; or the need for recognition by artistic skill, athletic prowess, pecuniary acquisitiveness, success in the hunt, or number of wives. "Wants, attitudes, and interests not only influence behavior and modify the behavior of organisms; they also are themselves changed. They are strengthened and weakened by the course of inner development and by the experiences of life. They may be shifted in respect of their attachments so that different situations call them forth." [11]

The Conformity of Institutions to the Primary Ends

The modes of achieving these indefinite primary ends vary among different societies and at different times within any one society. The degree to which these ends are achieved and the precise manner of achieving them is determined, at any given time and place, by the institutions then and there prevailing. Through induction into the culture, the individual learns (in fact, is required) to achieve his ends through those modes of behavior that are socially acceptable. In this sense, the primary or innate ends of the individual are given specific form and content within the framework of the accepted institutions of his society. In the long run, however, the specific modes of behavior prescribed by the institutional pattern must conform reasonably to the primary needs or ends of human beings. Otherwise, tension and unrest will develop within the group until finally a new order will be evolved within which men can be tolerably comfortable. This does not imply that institutions are always— or even at any time—completely conformable to primary ends, but rather that through institutional change this conformity tends to be approached.[12]

---

11 E. L. Thorndike, *The Psychology of Wants, Interests and Attitudes, op. cit.,* p. 5.

12 "But society in the broader sense, even though conceived not as an 'organism' but merely as an organisation, must be regarded as existing for various sorts of human purposes. For the impulses to form societies are rooted in broad instincts of gregariousness and of sexual and racial feeling, which are best described as organic, and, though these instincts become spiritualised and rationalised with the progress of the human mind, they never cease to carry biological import." J. A. Hobson, *Work and Wealth,* New York, 1914, p. 14.

Acceptance of the theory here expounded, that there is a close relationship between the primary ends of human beings and the character of institutions, does not commit one to the view of the eighteenth-century philosophers that there is a certain "natural" and preordained system of social organization that is uniquely compatible with the inherent nature of man.[13] The possible modes of achieving the primary ends are so infinitely diverse as to rule out this view. Nor is it to be concluded, at the opposite extreme, that man can become accommodated to *any* institutional pattern. The more tenable position lies between the two extremes: on the one hand, no particular type of system can be regarded in all its details as peculiarly consistent with the nature of man; but, on the other hand, the nature of man does place limits, in the long run, upon the possible variability of the social structure.

Assuming that in the long run the character of the institutions of any society must conform more or less to the primary ends of the individuals in the group, the problem still remains of explaining the particular institutions in effect at any given time and place, i.e., how they came to be what they are. Undoubtedly the character of institutions depends in large part upon the character of the natural environment and upon the state of technical knowledge. Modes of behavior will tend to be established which are appropriate to the environment in so far as knowledge permits. For example, one would hardly expect the African native to live in an igloo; neither would one expect the modern American, with his industrial technology, to live in an igloo if he should settle down in arctic regions. But environment and technology are not sufficient to explain fully why the institutions of a given time and place have come to be what they are. A full explanation must take into account the fact that any given set of institutions is the product of a historical development, that it is the outgrowth of earlier institutional systems, and that part of the explanation of the given institutions is to be found in the nature and functioning of earlier ones.[14] It is, of course, obvious that a society imposes upon its

---

[13] "The philosophers' ideas about Nature are now recognized as erroneous, their natural institutions being nothing but slight modifications of those of their own time." Edwin Cannan, *Wealth*, London, 1914, p. 90.

[14] "In fact as an aspect of a continuous social process an institution has no

individual members not only certain specific modes of behavior but also a detailed and comprehensive system of ends or values that are more or less consistent with the prescribed forms of behavior. Some of these ends may be mere expressions of the primary ends; but others may be distinct from and quite unrelated to the primary ends. These latter ends, though completely external to the primary ends, may nevertheless occupy a highly significant position in the value system of individuals. In fact, the members of the group may be entirely unable to distinguish the two types of ends. Whenever individuals are unable to attain their ends as defined for them by the social group—whether these ends are primary or merely cultural—frustration and tension leading to institutional change is the likely result. Curiously, however, in the process the specific ends themselves are likely to be revised, so that the new adjustment terminates with a change both in institutions and in ends or values—except that ultimately the institutions and the value system must conform reasonably to the primary ends of human beings. Accompanying the change in institutions and in ends is also a change in ideas and systems of thought. This is thoroughly discussed by Karl Mannheim in *Ideology and Utopia*. In short, the institutions, the ends, and the ideas of a group are interrelated and may be regarded as part of a single cultural system.[15]

It may be concluded, despite the limitations upon institutional change due to human nature, that the range of possible institutional systems is enormous, and that one must consider well before assuming that any particular institution—even the most important or the most revered—is natural or inevitable.

The Evolution of Institutions

The history of mankind consists largely of an unending but spasmodic series of institutional changes. One of the most baffling problems in the study of society, a problem which has espe-

---

origin apart from its development. It emerges from the impact of novel circumstances upon ancient custom; it is transformed into a different group of usages by cultural change." Walton Hamilton, "Institution," *Encyclopaedia of the Social Sciences*, Vol. VIII, p. 84.

15 ". . . an ethical attitude is invalid if it is oriented with reference to norms, with which action in a given historical setting, even with the best of intentions, cannot comply." Karl Mannheim, *Ideology and Utopia, op. cit.*, p. 84.

cially intrigued great social thinkers such as Marx, Pareto, Veblen, Spengler, Toynbee, and others, is how to explain the course of this institutional development. Up to the present, despite the enormous amount of attention given to the subject, no theory of history has been developed which is adequate for predicting the extent and the direction of changes implicit in any particular social situation. Nevertheless, certain of the phenomena generally associated with institutional change are well known. It is the purpose of this section to outline very briefly these facts.

Whenever the institutions of a group are in reasonable harmony with the ends of individuals, an equilibrium tends to be established so that there is little tendency toward modification of these institutions. Each change in the situation or condition of the group, however, is likely to disturb this equilibrium, and is likely to bring about social change. Such disturbance may be initiated, for example, by war, technical discoveries, advancement of knowledge, migration, climatic changes, exhaustion of natural resources, or contact with other societies. As a result of one or more of these changes, new ways of doing things and new modes of behavior are likely to be adopted. For example, as a result of mechanical discoveries new techniques may supplant time-honored methods of production; or, as a result of migration new types of dwellings or new diets may be adopted. On the other hand, some well-established institutions may carry within them the seeds of change, since they logically lead to a situation that is in conflict with other group interests. For example, a society that places a high value on large families may be forced, through the inevitable growth of population, to modify its familial institutions; or, in a society where the distribution of wealth and income tends cumulatively to become less equitable, a revision of the property system may be ultimately necessary.

The evolution of institutions, of course, does not take place automatically. It requires active and often strenuous efforts on the part of individuals and of organized groups. In general, the failure of adjustment between institutions and ends may be recognized when considerable numbers of individuals show signs of frustration or groping unrest. These individuals may have no inkling of the real reason for their exasperation, i.e., they may be unaware of their ends. In this condition, however, they are easy prey for any leader who presents a plausible program that is congenial to the temper of the dissatisfied classes. Thus, the combination of dissatisfaction and the willingness of popular leaders to exploit this dissatisfaction as a means of achieving power produces organized social movements which operate openly or subterraneously, depending upon the degree to which freedom of speech and organization is possible.[16] These movements may range from transitory "crazes" and "cults" to great social organizations of a semipermanent character. At the same time, there may be many competing movements, each with its leaders, its organization, and its program, each contending that it offers the only real solution for the world's ills. Moreover, within each of these movements will develop a body of thought, ideas, or rationalizations to provide a quasi-intellectual basis for the program.[17] The role of social movements in the process of social change is well illustrated in the contemporary world when our political and economic institutions are undergoing profound change. Not only are there fascism and communism, but also a host of minor movements such as the Townsend Plan, American Liberty League, militant trade unionism, nationalism, the planning movement, "soak-the-rich" and "share-the-wealth" campaigns, technocracy, the Oxford movement, social credit, "Jew-baiting" and "red-baiting," Social Justice, and many others.

Each of the various movements growing out of the popular unrest exerts an influence on the current scene, and as a result of the combined agitation of all of them the established institutions are revised. Often, however, the newly created situation proves to be anything but a satisfactory and final solution; thus additional new movements develop to bring about further

---

16 So long as the system is working "well," no attempt is made to change it. Indeed, the individuals of the group conform to the institutional pattern without thought, for the simple reason that it is the "thing to do." When, however, there is a serious blockage, when the institutions fail to give adequate outlet for the satisfaction of individual needs, then unrest becomes manifest, and through the phenomenon of leadership, dissatisfaction becomes focused in social movements. Only then do individuals become truly conscious of institutional control.

17 Professor Mannheim refers to thought as a "particularly sensitive index of social and cultural change." *Ideology and Utopia, op. cit.,* p. 74. See also Hadley Cantril, *The Psychology of Social Movements,* New York, 1941.

changes. Finally, by a slow and awkward process of trial and error, the society progresses toward a new and more or less stable institutional adjustment which is sufficiently in line with the ends of the group to obviate the major sources of irritation and unrest.[18]

Most established institutions are so solidly entrenched that they cannot be easily and immediately dislodged. Any movement to bring about a change in institutions will likely encounter the resistance of a substantial portion of the community. This resistance has several sources. First, individuals tend to become accommodated and habituated to their traditional way of life and are reluctant to modify their behavior according to new and unaccustomed patterns. Second, each institution becomes encrusted with the interests of those individuals who will be harmed in some way by the change. A change in religious institutions will be resisted by the clergy and the devoted followers; a change in educational practices will be fought by the teachers who will lose their jobs or who will be forced to undertake additional training; the adoption of steam shovels will be resisted by ditch diggers; etc. Third, institutions—especially the more potent of them—exercise their control over individuals through the power of sanctity. The individual is taught that the institution is sacred and that to defile, oppose, or question the rightness of the institution is a moral wrong. Individuals under the spell of this sacrosanctity will, of course, oppose any change because the institution has become an end in itself and is valued for its own sake. This type of control renders such institutions as the church, property, state, and marriage, highly resistant to change. Moreover, each of these institutions tends to be justified on quasi-intellectual grounds by means of an ideology. For example, the church has its theology, capitalism its classical eco-

---

[18] This ultimate equilibrium toward which the institutional structure approaches—but perhaps never attains—must not be thought of as a state of affairs in which all unrest and tension are completely eliminated and in which all individuals are completely sated. Striving for meaningful and valued goals is itself an end of individuals. The "happiness" of the individual by no means implies complete satiation of all wants or inactivity. Rather "happiness" is a relationship of the individual to his situation (present and expected) such that the activity necessary to the satisfaction of his wants is pleasurable in and of itself rather than endured merely for the sake of attaining ends beyond this activity. Happiness is not a wantless state. It is, rather, a condition in which the ratio of wants to satisfactions is at an optimum.

nomics, communism its Marxist doctrine, the state its "natural right" or "social contract" theories, the tax system its "benefit theory." On the basis of these rationalizations, powerful arguments of wide appeal can be constructed to "prove" that the existing order is the only possible or moral order.[19]

The impetus to institutional change, then, is almost universally confronted with stubborn resistance. If the "conservatives" or proponents of the *status quo* hold the majority of power and influence, then the attempted change will be checked. If the "radicals" or the proponents of change are able to have their way, the change will be effected. If there are strong elements on both sides, as is frequently the case, the institution will undergo gradual modification as a result of compromise. The reluctance on the part of people to change their habits and the active efforts of those persons having interests in the preservation of the *status quo* tend to cause a lag in the development of institutions behind the changes in the forces giving rise to institutional development. History is thus largely an account of the process by which new institutions are developed out of the conflicts between adherents to the old order and seekers of new arrangements. And the many conflicts of modern society can be explained in terms of the problems of institutional change. Fascism, communism, liberalism, capitalism, trade-unionism, etc., are all terms that suggest to any twentieth-century individual the conflicts associated with the evolution of some of our most fundamental institutions.[20]

In the process of evolution strange things can happen to institutions. Some may lose all significance and die, as pagan religions, polygamy, or handicraft methods of production. Some may lose all significance but live on in mere form without content or purpose, as the vestigial tail of a dress suit or Halloween. Some, having originated for a given object, may then be diverted to an alien purpose, as a club which is organized for the discus-

---

19 The thinking of an individual tends to be so bound up with the interests of his class that he is usually unable to recognize these ideological constructions as rationalizations and defense mechanisms. Indeed, as frequently as not the individual who is satisfied with the existing order looks upon it as something absolute and eternal, and he is completely impervious to the notion that there might be another satisfactory order or even that the present order is susceptible to change.

20 The conflicts associated with institutional change are sometimes regarded as struggles, between classes or factions, for social predominance.

sion of intellectual problems and later becomes a mere gathering for the purpose of social diversion or for conveying prestige upon its members. Some institutions, on the other hand, may gradually adapt themselves to changing conditions; in fact, the survival power of an institution is probably in inverse ratio to its capacity for progressive adaptation.

As pointed out, a change in the situation or condition of a society will tend to bring about modifications of the institutions directly affected by the change. However, modifications of these institutions will, in turn, tend to bring about changes in other institutions which are not directly influenced by the initial change. In short, the various institutions are complexly interrelated, so that changes in any one will be reflected in changes in the others. To illustrate this intertwined and tangled nature of the institutional system it is necessary only to recall the trite fact that a thoroughgoing revision of the whole social fabric has been wrought by the Industrial Revolution. The influence of this great movement, originating as a change in techniques of production, has extended to all the major institutions, including the state, the family, property, education, and even religion.[21]

On the whole, the process of institutional change is an awkward and cumbersome process. Important modifications are generally possible only when the institutions in question have become so thoroughly outmoded as to precipitate a virtual breakdown in the social order, and then only after serious (and usually bloody) conflict between the proponents of the new order and the guardians of the *status quo*. Moreover, even when the impetus to change is sufficiently forceful to upset the established order, the movement toward a new order occurs through a process of trial-and-error gyrations and without planned direction. When sensitive and thoughtful individuals have viewed this process of social adjustment, they have been prone to ask if it might not someday be possible to substitute intelligence and planning for random collective behavior with its inevitable accompaniments of "needless" injustice, insecurity, suffering, and inefficiency. Plato's proposal of rule by "philosopher kings"

---

21 Another more immediate example of the multiform changes resulting from a variation in one institution is provided by the introduction of the automobile. This is amusingly illustrated by E. B. White, *Harper's Magazine*, March, 1940, pp. 443-444.

and the doctrine of the modern "planners" are alike in that both are based upon optimism regarding the possibility of *directed* social change.[22]

---

[22] ". . . the new teachings of the conscious control of the rational will of man over human institutions and therefore over the 'laws' which regulate the working of these institutions, (is) the most important outcome of ordered psychology in the field of the social sciences." J. A. Hobson, *Economics and Ethics, op. cit.,* p. 121.

Chapter 5

ECONOMIC INSTITUTIONS

Having described the characteristics of social institutions and the process of institutional development, we are now ready to examine those particular institutions—the economic institutions—which together comprise the economic system.

It was pointed out in Chapter 1 that the function of the institutions included within the economic system is to control and regulate the use of the means of production, more specifically, (1) to select the personnel who are to exercise control over the means of production, (2) to regulate the supply of the factors of production, (3) to determine what specific goods shall be produced, (4) to control the manner in which the factors of production shall be organized, and (5) to regulate the use of the goods produced. It is the purpose of this chapter to describe the kinds of institutions by means of which these five functions are performed.

Institutions Relating to the Selection of Individuals to Exercise Control over the Means of Production

Since it is the task of the economic system to control the use of the means of production, some provision must be made in any society for selecting the individuals who are actually to exercise this control and for empowering these individuals to carry out this responsibility. In this regard the practices of various groups vary enormously. The control may be exercised by many separate individuals, each acting independently and on his own initiative as in laissez-faire capitalism, by various groups of individuals acting jointly or cooperatively, by the entire group acting through the body politic, by a monarch or oligarchy, or, as is

37

most usual, by a combination of several of these. In any case, the question of who shall control the means of production is a matter of the greatest significance, because the exercise of this power carries with it control over the entire productive process.

The control over the means of production includes control not only over *things* (environmental means) but also over *human beings*. In considering the institutions relating to the selection of personnel for controlling the means of production, it is convenient to discuss the human means separately from the environmental means.

Control over the human means of production (laborers) may be exercised in a number of different ways. Under the system known as "free labor," each individual has the exclusive right to use or dispose of his labor power in any way that he sees fit; in a slave society, on the other hand, certain free individuals are permitted to own and control other individuals, the latter being slaves; in systems of complete state control over laborers, the labor of each individual is subject to disposal through political authority; etc. Historically, the most usual form of control over laborers has been a combination of these, with part of the control exercised by heads of households and even by religious leaders. Under feudalism, for example, there was an element of slavery, of individual control, of political control, of religious control, and of familial control. Today, though slavery has largely disappeared and religious and familial controls have diminished, we are still some distance from a system of "free labor." The control of the individual over his own labor is narrowly circumscribed by political authority and by other less formal—though nonetheless important—institutional forces. For example, the individual is denied the opportunity to engage in such occupations as prostitution, production of narcotics, and bootlegging; under certain conditions gainful employment of children and women is prohibited. The position in the family of the child, and indeed of the wife, is often that of serf or semi-slave in so far as freedom of control over his or her own labor power is concerned. The number of hours per day and the number of days per week are regulated. If the individual works on Sunday, he may violate religious doctrine. A condition of selling one's labor is that he comply with the requirements of trade-unions or professional associations. There are strict laws regulating the activities of physicians, druggists, barbers, undertakers, lawyers, and many other professional groups. In case of war, the individual is conscripted or his labor is directed by the state. The prestige attaching to certain occupations means that young persons are encouraged, if not forced, into these occupations by ambitious parents, and the desire of the typical father to have his son associated with him in business is a factor limiting the freedom of the son over his own labor power. Even when an individual obtains employment, he finds it unavoidable to submit to the authority of his employer. True, he is formally free to terminate his employment at any time, yet the difficulty of securing another job often means that he has no practicable choice but to follow the dictates of his master. In short, even in a society which purports to have "free labor," the disposal of labor power is controlled in accordance with a whole complex of practices by persons other than the laborers. As a result, the individual finds that he possesses only a fraction of the total power of control over his labor, and that a large part of this power is vested in other persons who are selected according to certain socially approved customs or practices.

The selection of persons to control the use of environmental means may also be accomplished in a number of ways. Under the system known as "private property," the control is diffused among many individuals, each acting independently and on his own initiative and each free to do with "his" means as he pleases. In this system it is implied that each individual is entitled to exclusive control over all things of which he can in any way, except through fraud or duress, obtain possession, and that control includes the right of the individual to use, sell, rent, bestow, bequeath, destroy, or otherwise dispose of any of these things.[1] Under the system known as "state socialism," control over the

---

1 "But what is meant by the rights of property? In ordinary use the phrase means just that system to which long usage has accustomed us. This is a system by which a man is free to acquire by any method of production or exchange, within the limits of the law, whatever he can of land, consumable goods, or capital; to dispose of it at his own will and pleasure for his own purposes, to destroy it if he likes, to give it away or sell it as it suits him, and at death to bequeath it to whomsoever he will. The state can take a part of a man's property by taxation. But in all taxation the state is taking something from a man which is 'his,' and in so doing is justified only by necessity." L. T. Hobhouse, *Liberalism*, New York, 1911.

environmental means of production is vested in certain public officials. In other societies, dignitaries of the church or heads of families may have this authority. In most societies, however, control over land and capital goods is exercised simultaneously by a number of functionaries, each having certain duties and responsibilities. In modern America, for example, control over the environmental means is vested only partially in individual owners. The power of the individual to dispose of his means of production is strictly limited by political authority. He is not permitted to use these means in any way regarded as detrimental to the interests of other individuals. He may not drive his motorcar except according to certain rules. He is allowed to construct only certain kinds of buildings in certain places, and these must conform to established specifications. A manufacturing establishment must provide facilities for sanitation and "proper" working conditions. An individual is not allowed to create a public "nuisance." All owners are liable to taxation, the right of eminent domain, and conscription of wealth. In fact, an examination will show that a very substantial, if not the major, part of modern legislation represents some form of restriction on the right of the individual to exercise control over his wealth, thus representing an infringement on the property "rights" of the individual and a virtual exercise of certain of these rights by functionaries of the state. Moreover, in a growing number of instances the state is acquiring control over land and capital goods by outright ownership. At the same time, in the United States the control of the individual over "his" property is being greatly weakened through the growth of corporate enterprises in which preponderant control is lodged in the hands of directors or of managements. Thus, the control of environmental means in the United States is vested partly in individual owners, partly in public officials, and partly in corporate officials. This, of course, represents only one possible manner of distributing control over the environmental means of production. At other times and places other arrangements have existed.

Once it is settled what persons in the group are to administer the means of production, there is still the problem of how these functionaries shall make use of the means under their control. It might be supposed that the persons selected to administer the means of production would be empowered to use these with perfect arbitrariness. This, however, is far from the truth. The conduct of these administrators is, in almost every case, guided by the prevailing customs, practices, folkways, conventions, usages—the institutions—of the group. Their decisions are, in the main, mere expressions of prevailing institutions, and only to a minor degree or in exceptional circumstances are they the result of arbitrary choices. This will become abundantly clear as we discuss the various institutions that determine what shall be the supply of the factors of production, what specific goods shall be produced, how the factors shall be organized, and how the product shall be used.

Institutions Relating to the Supply of the Factors of Production

Assuming that the supply of the means of production is given, the basic problem in the use of these means is to determine what shall be the supply of the *factors* of production. This problem is of little significance with reference to land (primary environmental means), because in general there is no reason for withholding from use any existing land. Thus, the supply of the factor *land use* ordinarily corresponds closely to the supply of *land*. It is possible, however, that the culture of a society might require the withholding of land from productive purposes for any of a number of reasons. For instance, land might be withheld for "leisure" uses such as for wild game preserves, or certain territory might be restricted from use because of its religious significance, or land might be set aside so that its productivity would be preserved for future generations. Thus, the institutions of the group might even determine at least partially the extent to which the available supply of land would be used.

The supply of labor, on the other hand, is always subject to institutional control, since in all societies there are important "leisure" uses of human time. Thus, every society is faced with the fourfold problem of determining (1) what proportion of its people shall work and what proportion shall be idle, (2) how the time of those employed shall be divided between leisure and labor, (3) what shall be the relative supplies of labor of different types, and (4) how intensely people shall work. The decision as to what proportion of the population shall be idle depends upon the institutions of the group with respect to such matters as old-age retirement, formal education, employment of women and children, slavery, prison labor, attitudes toward leisure, monasticism, distribution of income, etc. The decisions as to the working time of those employed are similarly determined by the institutions of the group relative to the length of the working day, the observance of holidays, and vacations. Moreover, assuming that the supply of labor in general is given, the supply of different types of labor is determined to a considerable degree by the institutions of the group regarding the recruitment of persons for various occupations and the training of workers. Finally, the decision as to the intensity with which labor is to be carried on is made largely according to the custom of the group or of particular occupations. The principal limitation upon institutional factors as determinants of the supply of labor is that enough persons must work sufficiently long hours with whatever intensity is necessary to support the group on at least the level of bare subsistence.

The supply of capital is also determined institutionally, in this case by those institutions which influence the amount of production that is devoted to future rather than immediate ends. In our society the supply of capital is regulated largely by the decisions of individuals who are motivated by such (institutional) factors as (1) the prevailing attitude toward thrift and toward the provision for future personal contingencies, (2) the degree to which life and personal property are safeguarded from violence, (3) the distribution of income, and (4) the prospects for pecuniary return from capital. In other societies different arrangements may exist. The supply of capital may be determined by decisions of the group acting through the body politic, by the will of a dictator or a priesthood. The only limitation upon the decisions regarding the supply of capital is that imposed by the amount of the productive power available, a certain portion of which must be reserved to provide goods for the immediate sustenance of population.[2]

---

[2] It is conceivable that a society might devote so much of its resources to the accumulation of capital as to leave an insufficient residue of product even for the bare subsistence of the population. It is said, though I have no authoritative verification for this statement, that the central authority in Russia, during the first

Institutions Relating to the Decisions as to What Specific Goods Shall Be Produced

No matter what individuals or groups possess control over the use of the means of production, it is clear that the kinds of goods which will be produced through the use of these means will be determined largely by the customs, habits, and practices of the group in the consumption of goods. In other words, the goods produced must largely be those which the people are accustomed to consume. A dictator, a ruling class, or even a democratic government may direct that the means of production be used to produce goods of a type slightly different from those customarily enjoyed by the people. Yet, even the most powerful ruler would scarcely attempt to bring about arbitrary and drastic changes in the consumption of the masses. Thus, the consumption practices of the group constitute one of the most powerful forces determining the use of the available means of production.

Consumption patterns have varied greatly at different places and at different times. The costumes of a Chinese coolie, a Brazilian planter, an American businessman, a Tyrolian peasant, and an African native are all distinctive. Similarly, the diets of a Parisian and of a Londoner are totally unlike. The Parisian eats snails which are disgusting to the Londoner; the Londoner, on the other hand, eats Yorkshire pudding, which the Parisian despises. Similarly, the average Italian likes opera to which many Americans are indifferent. The Frenchman or Italian regards his wine (or the German his beer) as a necessity; whereas the American prohibitionist regards consumption of alcoholic beverages as a positive moral wrong. One could enlarge upon these differences ad infinitum, but these illustrations are sufficient to demonstrate the institutional and relative character of any given consumption pattern.

Five-Year Plan, directed so much of that country's productive power into the construction of dams, railroads, factories, and other fixed plant, that insufficient productive power was left over to provide for the immediate needs of the people. As a result, thousands of people are said to have starved. Whether or not this was true of Russia, there is no doubt that such an orgy of capital accumulation is conceivable.

In some communities the individual is allowed considerable latitude in forming his own consumption habits. Within limits he may, for example, choose from among a wide variety of different commodities and usually may select from a wide variety of different types or styles of any given commodity. This, however, by no means implies that the individual is a free agent in deciding his own consumption pattern. For example, a businessman would hardly dare to appear at his office in pajamas or in a swimming suit. It is the *practice* to be attired when at work in a conventional and uncomfortable business suit consisting of trousers, waistcoat, and jacket. Moreover, the suit must not be "out of style" or too "showy" or "loud." One may choose the color of the suit from among several dark and dull shades, one may choose the type of lining, but one may not choose the length of the trouser legs, the width of the cuffs, the number of superfluous buttons on the sleeves, or the shape of the lapels. These things are dictated, as surely as is the law against improper parking, and are much more effectively enforced. In the same way, the type of houses, the style of furniture, the model of automobiles, and the character of recreations are cast in rigid institutional molds—leaving only the merest details to individual discretion and personal taste. On consideration, it becomes obvious that the consumption practices of a society are thoroughly institutionalized. This does not necessarily imply that individuals are forced by the dictates of social convention to consume things which they do not want. It may mean, rather, that their "wants" are determined largely within the culture. "Consumer sovereignty," or freedom of consumer choice as it exists in modern society, is thus seen to be somewhat illusory.

The institutions of consumption, of course, are subject to evolution. Styles or practices change regarding the use of commodities. New commodities or services are adopted, and old ones discarded. The process of altering our consumption practices, however, generally meets with considerable resistance, and is therefore usually a slow and laborious process. For example, the introduction of the automobile was accompanied by tremendous opposition on the part of the general public. New clothing styles for women are often resisted on the ground of "indecency." There was a time when silk hose, short skirts, and bobbed hair were considered "daring." After the discovery of potatoes in America, their use in the diet was impeded for many years because potatoes were thought to be poisonous. The introduction of the cigarette in this country was opposed on moral grounds both when adopted by men during the early part of the century and when adopted by women twenty years later. Many other examples of resistance to changes in consumption habits can be found. However, one of the unique characteristics of modern society, a characteristic that distinguishes it sharply from primitive groups, is that consumption is relatively dynamic, that people are on the whole readily receptive to new practices, and that each individual is allowed a certain degree of freedom in shaping his own consumption pattern. Nevertheless, we must not lose sight of the fact that the accepted practices of the community exert a powerful influence over the consumption of its individual members. Moreover, whatever degree of freedom exists for the individual in this connection *is* one of the practices or institutions of the society.

To explain fully the consumer behavior of a society, it is necessary to introduce the principle of diminishing marginal utility. This principle may be stated as follows: Other things being equal, as an individual increases his consumption of any good (expressed as a rate per period of time), the increment of satisfaction added by each successive unit of the good tends to decline. Or, to state the same thing in behavioristic terms, as the rate of consumption of any good increases, the less of other things will the individual be willing to give up in order to acquire additional units of the good.[3]

This principle helps to explain the fact that the consumption of an individual or a group tends to be spread over many different goods. For example, an individual who is formally free to adjust his pattern of consumption as he chooses (within the limits of his means) will start by providing that good which promises to satisfy the most urgent need or to yield the greatest satisfaction. As he begins to acquire this good, however, he

---

[3] In the modern theory of demand, the virtual equivalent of diminishing marginal utility is the principle that indifference curves shall be convex to the origin. See J. R. Hicks, *Value and Capital*, Oxford, 1939, Chapter I, especially pp. 20-23.

finds that successive units yield less and less satisfaction, and that it then pays him to devote some of his means to the good of second urgency. As he obtains some of that good, he again experiences diminishing marginal utility and finds it worth his while to begin acquiring some of the good next in line of urgency, etc. In this way his consumption tends to be spread over many different goods. If it were not for the phenomenon of diminishing marginal utility, the consumption of an individual would likely be limited to whatever good he might begin at first to acquire. Since successive units of it would be just as valuable to him as the first unit, there would be no reason for him to stop acquiring this good until he had devoted all of his means to it.

The principle of diminishing marginal utility helps to explain the diversity in the socially accepted consumption pattern of a group. The consumption institutions of a society are the product of a long evolution. They have evolved out of the experiences of the group and represent, to a greater or less degree, an adjustment to the needs of the individuals, and to the potentialities of the environment. Thus, since individuals are subject to diminishing marginal utility, the accepted consumption patterns of societies are likely to provide for considerable variability in the consumption of individuals.

Institutions Relating to the Technical Organization of the Factors

One of the functions of the economic system is to provide for the selection of the particular technical methods to be employed in the productive process—to determine how the factors of production are to be organized. These decisions are also dependent upon the institutions of the group, particularly upon those habits, customs, and practices that are followed in production.

The task of producing any particular good may be carried on by various technical methods. For example, a pair of shoes can be made by simple direct handicraft methods, by any one of several machine methods, or by a combination of methods. Moreover, the source of energy to operate the machines may be human beings, animals, direct water power, steam, steam-electricity, hydroelectricity, or internal combustion. Transportation of the raw materials and shoes may be effected by human beings, horses, railways, automobiles, aeroplanes, canoes, rafts, or steamboats, and the storage and transfer of these materials may be accomplished by any of a number of methods.[4]

The sum total of the actual methods used in the various processes of producing shoes constitute the practices of the community in making this commodity. Similarly, in making each other commodity or in the rendering of each type of direct personal services (e.g., by physicians, barbers, actors), the methods used constitute the practices of the community in providing these various goods, and the sum total of all the practices employed in the production of all the different types of goods used in the society make up the *institutions of production.*

In most societies of which there is historical or anthropological record, the ways of producing goods have been established by custom and tradition, and have not been subject to easy or rapid alteration. Sometimes, indeed, the technical methods of production have actually been incorporated into the sacred rites of the group, and have therefore become almost completely ossified.[5] It is, therefore, one of the remarkable characteristics of the modern era that men have shown unprecedented willingness to adopt an attitude of comparative

---

4 In modern society, each type of industry tends to develop its own peculiar customs regarding the extension of credit terms to customers, methods of sale, methods of buying, etc. For example, the life insurance business has selling methods quite different from those of investment banks. In some lines of business it is customary to extend credit on ten-day terms, others thirty days, and others as long as six months or one year. In some industries there are many middlemen between raw material producer and final consumer; in others, almost none.

5 "In many parts of Oceania an art practiced by a special group of craftsmen is not a mere technical performance but has a definitely religious character and may be regarded as a long series of religious rites. It is not enough to be able to make a canoe but you must also know the appropriate rites which will make it safe to use it for profane purposes without danger from ghostly or other supernatural agencies." W. H. R. Rivers, "The Disappearance of Useful Arts," quoted from University of Chicago, *Syllabus and Selected Readings* for Social Science I, 6th ed., August, 1936, pp. 282-283. Mr. Rivers continues (p. 283), ". . . in studying the history of culture we must be prepared for changes not to be accounted for by the likes and dislikes of the civilized and almost incredible from the utilitarian point of view. We must be very cautious in assuming that elements of culture are so useful or so important that they would never be allowed to disappear."

rationality toward their techniques of production, and have shown a disposition to employ whatever modes of production seem suited to the attainment of their ends. According to Mr. Durbin:

> The typical condition of technical processes in a pre-capitalistic economy is that of irrational tradition. The processes of sowing, gathering and reaping in agriculture; of spinning, weaving and dyeing in the textile industries; of mining, smelting and refining in the metallurgical industries; are not determined by scientific experiment and discovery, or by the rational adjustment of means to ends, but by the compulsion of slowly acquired traditions and criteria of excellence established through the accident of local memory. It is said, for example, by economic historians that towards the end of the medieval period in this country every technical detail in the manufacture of woolen cloth was legally prescribed by Parliament. This may be an extreme case, but even in cases where the technique of production was not protected by the severe sanctions of the law, the idea of "appropriate technique" was that of "the good way in which our fathers worked" rather than the economizing of means or the maximizing of output. The grip of tradition was everywhere strong, and no one who knows the technical "conservatism" of a pre-capitalist peasantry today—in India or Russia—will doubt the predominance of such forces in a medieval economy.
>
> What is new in the Industrial Revolution, at the time when the capitalist order is brought into existence, is not the *discovery* of mechanical devices. On the contrary, the knowledge of many of them existed long before any Industrial Revolution occurred. The machinery used in a medieval clock or the sideshows of a medieval fair was far more complicated than the simple mechanical devices employed in the first machines of an Arkwright or a Watt. The new principle is the idea that processes of reason, science and mechanics should be applied to the technique of industrial production; that machines could and should be used to raise output. A medieval society looks upon machines as *toys*. A capitalist society looks upon them as instruments of production. What has changed is not knowledge, but a habit of thought. What has really altered is an emotional judgment.[6]

Because modern society has acquired a relatively rational attitude toward its methods of production, it does not follow that these methods are completely outside the institutional

---

[6] E. F. M. Durbin, *The Politics of Democratic Socialism*, pp. 78-79.

complex of modern society. In the first place, the rational behavior is itself a widely prevalent habit of action and *is* therefore one of the institutions of modern society. Moreover, it must not be supposed that the particular techniques of production in effect at any time are always totally lacking in the widespread uniformity and the permanence which would characterize them as institutions.

Once the productive practices of the community have been adopted and have become entrenched, they possess important survival power even beyond the time when the continuation of these practices is no longer consistent with the ends of the community. Each method of production develops its vested interests and hangers-on, and these groups tend to exert pressure, sometimes powerful, to resist the incursion of new ways of doing things. Labor groups, for example, have traditionally resisted the adoption of "labor-saving" machinery. The term "sabotage," as a matter of fact, is derived from the practice in the nineteenth century of French workers to throw their wooden shoes (*sabots*) into the new machinery; and the resistance of modern labor groups to the introduction of new machinery is well known and easily understandable. Owning groups likewise resist the adoption of new methods whenever the value of their existing investment is thereby jeopardized. Corporations are known to delay the adoption of new methods, and even to buy up patents for the express purpose of preventing a new method from being used. Farm groups have sometimes shown unwillingness to accept new methods, and are often vociferous in their demands for subsidies to protect their wonted way of life. Even the general public is inclined to look askance at the introduction of new techniques. It is a prevalent notion, not entirely without foundation, that the displacement of workers by machines leads to permanent unemployment and is a social evil; again, many people are reluctant to see ancient skills die out because these skills are viewed as arts which are considered good in themselves; similarly, the displacement of the independent merchant by the chain store is regarded as an evil and resisted even by discriminatory taxation. It is said that the introduction of the steam locomotive was opposed on moral grounds, and it was a commonplace until recently to hear the dictum that "the automobile is ruining the country." Hand-made commodities are often preferred to those of machine manufacture. And it is common to bemoan the substitution of large-scale for small-scale industry "on general principles." It must be concluded, however, in spite of these and many other illustrations of irrational attitudes toward technical methods, that the survival power of the institutions of production in modern society is probably less than that of other institutions since the techniques of production are seldom clothed with moral or religious sanctions. This group of institutions is hence somewhat more dynamic than those having more powerful sanctions, and is consequently perhaps the most active source of social change.

Institutions Relating to the Distribution of Product among the Members of the Society

Each society must, as pointed out in a preceding chapter, provide some solution to the problem of how the economic goods that emerge from the productive process shall be used. This problem resolves largely into the question of how the product shall be divided among the members of the group. There are numerous possible solutions. The most obvious one would be a sort of catch-as-catch-can method whereby each person would be allowed to enjoy whatever goods he could obtain by purchase, violence, stealth, chance, or otherwise. The inevitable disorderliness and uncertainty of this method, however, would practically necessitate the laying down of certain social rules to govern the process, the character of these rules depending upon the form of economic organization. If production were carried on in self-sufficient households, with little exchange among households, distribution would be largely a matter of rationing the product among the members of the household. Even today, distribution *within* the family partakes somewhat of this form. In case the means of production were under state control, the problem could also be solved by simple rationing whereby each person would be allowed a specified share of the social product. The rationing might be on the basis of perfect equality among individuals or it might involve unequal treatment of individuals, depending upon the particular practices and traditions of the group. The process of distribution might be accomplished as an incidental part of the system of private control over the means of production. This is the technique used in modern America where each individual receives an income in return for the services of those means of production which he owns or controls. Under this plan, each person's share in the social product is determined by the prices which he can obtain for the services of the means at his disposal. The outcome of the market process is, however, substantially modified by a number of other institutions relating to distribution. For example, taxation and the expenditure of public funds result in the redistribution of income whenever the benefits from governmental services are not apportioned according to the contributions of individuals made in support of these services. Collective bargaining and minimum-wage laws sometimes influence the portion of the social product going to labor. The system of charities, philanthropies, and other voluntary contributions has redistributional effects. The practice of charging the rich higher prices than are paid by the poor (e.g., in medical treatment) is still another example. Thus, the institutions determining the distribution of the social product are, in modern America, far broader in scope than the mere pricing mechanism whereby each individual receives an income according to the prices he can get for "his" means of production.

Conclusion

In the two preceding chapters the role of institutions in the guidance of human conduct was discussed. It was shown that the institutions of a society are the molds within which individual behavior is based and that institutions exercise control over individuals in almost every department of their lives. In this chapter an attempt has been made to show that the particular branch of human activity relating to the use of the means of production—economic activity—is no less subject to institutional control than any other aspect of human conduct.

The five main functions of the economic system are performed through the instrumentality of the *economic institutions*. These have been classified into five groups corresponding to the five functions of the economic system: (1) institutions relating to the selection of the individuals who are to exercise control over the means of production, (2) institutions relating to the supply of the factors of production, (3) institutions relating to the decisions as to what specific goods shall be produced, (4) institutions relating to the technical organization of the factors, and (5) institutions relating to the use of the goods produced. This is not an exhaustive classification, however, since it omits certain auxiliary economic institutions such as money and credit, organized exchanges, the customs and conventions of buying and selling, the law of contracts, and many others.

Since the activities of individuals in the use of the means of production are regulated, at any given time and place, through the institutions then and there prevailing, the precise manner in which a society will use its means of production will depend upon and be determined by the character of its economic institutions. For example, a change in the practices relating to inheritance of wealth will alter the distribution of control over the means of production and change the distribution of income. The enactment of legislation for the regulation of electric power enterprises will likely result in altering the quantity of electricity produced, or the incomes of the owners of the affected properties. The development of collective bargaining in labor relations will probably influence the supply of labor, the technical organization of production, and the distribution of income. The adoption of a code of professional ethics by physicians will influence the availability of medical service to various classes and the income of physicians. Free public education with numerous scholarships for the less well-to-do will tend to alter the distribution of incomes. The introduction of widespread consumer credit will increase the consumption of relatively expensive durable goods. The imposition of progressive taxes will reduce the rate of capital accumulation. The substitution of "central planning" for private enterprise will alter the relative quantities of goods produced. A religious taboo will reduce the consumption of affected articles. The custom of generous philanthropy will increase the amount of means devoted to religion, scientific research, education, or art. The sanctification of particular methods of production will prevent the adoption of more efficient methods and restrict the amount of the total social product. The social disapproval of leisure, combined with asceticism, will make for rapid accumulation of capital. A strong spirit of nationalism will encourage the application of a large portion of the means of production to military purposes. These and many other possible illustrations indicate how completely the use of the means of production is determined by the customs, conventions, and practices—the institutions—of the group, and how any institutional change is likely to bring about a change in the use of the means of production.

The almost complete dependence of the economic process upon the character of the extant institutions means that economics is primarily a study of institutions and of their workings. Even traditional classical economics is of this type, its particular subject matter being the institutions associated with one or more of the variants of laissez-faire capitalism.

The economic process varies, from one time or place to another, to the extent that economic institutions are different. At different periods of history and in different parts of the world, economic systems have varied in almost every detail. There is little in common, for example, between the economic systems of a Melanesian native group, the Aztec empire, a Greek city state, an English medieval manor, modern America, or modern Russia. Each of these economic systems represents a configuration of institutions almost totally unlike that of any of the others, yet each has a practicable means by which the fundamental tasks of the economic order have been accomplished. A close study of these systems would reveal, moreover, that no one of them has ever been completely static, and that each emerged as a result of an evolutionary process. It is only reasonable to suppose, then, that the various systems in operation today will gradually become modified until they, too, will have been transformed into new and different systems.

It is customary to refer to specific types of economic systems by such words as "feudalism," "capitalism," "fascism," and "socialism." Each of these words represents an ideal concept of an economic system composed of certain particular institutions. Feudalism implies an agricultural society in which each individual is assigned to his station in life according to birth and custom, and in which workers are attached to the land and are subject to lords who are responsible for providing protection and justice. Laissez-faire capitalism is regarded as a system in which there is private ownership of wealth, free labor, freedom of contract, freedom of enterprise, freedom of consumer choice, a system of prices, and a minimum of formal regulation over economic activities. Fascism is similar to capitalism except that control over the means of production rests more largely in the state even though "ownership" and detailed control remain nominally in the hands of private individuals. Socialism is a system characterized by free labor, free consumer choice, state "ownership" of land and most capital goods, and state direction of the productive process. There has, perhaps, never been an economic system to which any one of these terms, as defined, could be applied with perfect accuracy. There have been systems which were predominantly feudalistic, capitalistic, fascistic, or socialistic, but never have we had any one of these types in a pure form. To illustrate this it is necessary only to note how far modern America departs from ideal capitalism, or modern Russia from ideal socialism.

PART III

Production and Capital

Chapter 6

THE PRODUCTIVE PROCESS

The means of production have been defined as those persons and features of the environment which are scarce and are capable of yielding transferable goods. These means, however, are only potentially productive—they serve no end unless actually used, and their mere existence in no way ensures their use. Thus, one may distinguish between the *means of production* and the services of these means; the latter will be referred to as the *factors of production*, or simply *factors*. Accordingly, a human being (laborer) is a means of production, but the service of this human being (labor) is a factor of production. Similarly, a plot of ground (land) may be a means of production, but the use of this plot as building site, railroad right of way, or a cabbage patch (land use) is a factor of production.

Primary and Intermediate Factors

Just as one may distinguish analytically the primary from the intermediate *means* of production, so one may differentiate between the primary and intermediate *factors* of production. A primary factor consists of the services of a primary means of production, and an intermediate factor of the services of an intermediate means. Actually, most persons and pieces of land represent an almost inextricable mixture of primary and intermediate elements; consequently, most factors are correspondingly hybrid. The services of a plumber, for example, are attributable partly to his "natural" endowments and partly to his education and training; or the services of a piece of farm land are attributable partly to the "original and indestructible powers of the soil" and partly to the prior efforts of man in grading, draining, fencing, and fertilizing the land. However, it is useful for analytical purposes to assume that the primary

56

and intermediate elements are distinguishable. Thus, the primary factor of production, *labor*, is defined as those services of human beings which are attributable to their natural endowments. This definition is more restricted than the everyday concept of labor in that it excludes that portion of human services which is attributable to education and training. Correspondingly, *land use* is defined as the services of the primary environmental means of production. This, too, differs from the ordinary concept of land use. A large portion of what is ordinarily called land is both producible and depreciating and, therefore, not a basic or "given" element. Moreover, certain things which have been produced but are permanent can usefully be regarded as primary means and are, therefore, classed as land.

Though the primary factors may be separated into the two broad classes, labor and land use, each of these classes may be further subdivided into many different types—as many as there are different kinds of laborers, and of land. "We may arrange," said Marshall, "the things that are required for making a commodity into whatever groups are convenient, and call them its *factors of production*."[1] Thus, when one speaks of a factor of production (in the singular), he refers to a given *type* of labor or of land use. A factor of production thus consists of a certain type of services all the units of which are exactly alike in the sense that any one unit is a perfect substitute for any other unit.

Production a Physical Process

Production may be defined simply as the application of the factors to the achievement of human ends. It includes a wide variety of activities which may be classified as follows:

1. The transformation, fabrication, or manufacture of things
2. The transportation of things and persons
3. The storage of things
4. The purchase, sale, exchange, or transfer of things (or persons)
5. The performance of direct services by things (houses, automobiles) or by persons (doctors, teachers, barbers)

---

[1] Alfred Marshall, *Principles of Economics*, 8th ed., London, 1930, p. 339.

Production is essentially a *physical* process. It requires that physical quantities of labor be combined or organized with the services of physical units of land in the provision of physical quantities of economic goods. The kinds and amounts of goods resulting from the use of the factors are determined by the laws of mechanics, chemistry, biology, etc. Different applications of labor and different uses of land yield different results. Variations in the physical conditions of the process are likely to bring about changes in the physical quality or quantity of the product.

Specialization and Division of Labor

The factors of production can serve more effectively if employed within *specialized* productive units in which a minute *division of labor* is practiced. Modern production carries out this functional application of the factors to the nth degree. For example, the production of a simple everyday commodity such as a loaf of bread extends literally over the length and breadth of a continent and requires thousands of people. The wheat may be produced on a Kansas farm, hauled to a local elevator, shipped by rail to a Kansas City flour mill, ground into flour, sent to a warehouse, shipped to a baker, mixed with other ingredients, baked into bread, trucked to retail grocers, and sold and delivered to final consumers. These particular incidents in the metamorphosis of a loaf of bread include, however, only a small portion of the productive activities involved. The production of the wheat on the Kansas farm requires the use of plows, harvesters, tractors, trucks, and other farm equipment—all of which must be produced. Thus the iron miner, the blast furnace, the logger, the sawmill, the farm-implement factory, and the distributor of farm supplies are all brought into the task of producing bread. At the same time, such supplies as jute bags, binder twine, lubricating oil, and gasoline are necessary. The service of the railroad requires a host of different commodities ranging from ties to snow plows, and from telegraph instruments to roller bearings. The flour mill must be constructed by carpenters, masons, and steelworkers, and the machinery must be fabricated. And virtually all the persons involved in this complex process must be trained for their tasks. Moreover, each of these many separate operations is carried on by groups of individuals organized within plants where minute division of labor is practiced.[2]

Time and Production

At any particular stage in the production of a loaf of bread, various types of labor and land use, primary factors of production, are employed. In addition to these, however, each operation requires the use of intermediate means of production that have been derived from prior productive efforts. Examples are machinery, buildings, semifinished goods, fuel, or the skill of workers. The production of each of these intermediate means, in turn, requires the employment not only of labor and land use, but also of intermediate means derived from still more remote productive efforts. However, if a complete catalog were made of all the steps in the production of a loaf of bread, no matter how far removed, the entire process could be traced ultimately back to the primary factors of production, namely, labor and land use. Thus, a loaf of bread, or any other similar final commodity, may be regarded as the physical outcome of applying the primary factors of production in certain proportions and in given time sequences. All of these applications of labor and land use reach their intended destiny when, through the use of the bread, a human end is attained. In a sense, then, the bread may be regarded as the embodiment of all the factors which contributed to its usefulness.

From this discussion it is clear that production is a time-consuming process, and that a large proportion of productive activities are not intended to lead immediately to the realization of human ends, but rather to aid indirectly in their attainment. Such methods of production are often described as "indirect" or "roundabout," because in providing goods it is necessary first to produce the things and train the persons used in the production of the goods.

---

[2] To compare the organization of production by human beings with that of certain insects is instructive. See H. H. Ewers, *The Ant People,* trans. C. H. Levy, New York, 1927; Maurice Maeterlinck, *Life of the Bee,* trans. A. Sutro, New York, 1936; Caryl P. Haskins, "The Social Animal," *Atlantic Monthly,* February, 1946, pp. 109-117.

Production as a Continuous or Repetitive Process

The indirect or roundabout method of production may be thought of most usefully as a continuous or repetitive process, having no definite beginning or end. Each type of product emerges from the process in a continuous stream, and each of the stages or operations involved in its production is continuously taking place. At various stages, the results of productive efforts at earlier stages are steadily being depreciated or destroyed; hence these earlier operations as well must continue unceasingly. Thus given physical materials enter into, pass through, and emerge from the productive process, but the process itself goes on more or less continuously, with new materials replacing the old at virtually every stage. In the production of meat, for example, animals are constantly being raised, sent to market, slaughtered, and processed; meat is constantly being sold to retailers, sold to consumers, cooked, and finally used in the satisfaction of wants. The process is unending. The equipment and operations of the meat industry on any one day will be much the same as on any other day. There will always be a stream of animals "going in at one end," and meat available for consumers "coming out at the other." Other industries share this repetitive continuity—with due allowance for seasonal variations and for the exhaustion of nonreproducible raw materials. The production system as a whole appears as a sort of giant sausage grinder with raw materials entering at one end, going through various processes, and emerging as finished goods at the other. The kinds of products emerging may change from time to time, there may be fluctuations in amounts produced and in methods of production, but the process goes on forever—so long as man has ends which he strives to attain through the use of limited means.

The concept of production as a continuous or repetitive process must be qualified in three minor respects. First, that portion of productive activity which is devoted to the development of permanent improvements is nonrepetitive. This includes such operations as the leveling of land, the building of dams, and the construction of breakwaters. These permanent improvements, even though "produced," are classified as land.

Second, productive activities designed to bring about modification of the culture are nonrepetitive. These include the work of inventors, research workers, reformers, politicians, publicists, and others. Most changes wrought in the culture as a result of these activities—especially accretions to the body of knowledge —are usually made once and for all. Ordinarily the process need not be repeated periodically.[3]

Finally, if production uses up exhaustible resources, the process cannot be perfectly repetitive. As the supply of these resources diminishes, the methods of production will necessarily be subject to progressive change. To the extent that these resources are capable of being "produced" through the discovery of new deposits, however, "prospecting" becomes a regular part of the process of production, and this case would no longer be an exception.

Quantitative Measurement of Factors and Goods

Production has been defined as the process by which physical quantities of economic factors are combined and organized in the provision of physical quantities of economic goods. In the process the factors represent *input* and the economic goods represent *output*. The theory of production is concerned with the functional relationship between inputs and outputs. Consequently, as a prelude to the theory, it is essential to find quantitative units in which to measure physical amounts of the factors and physical amounts of the products.[4]

The factors of production are generally measured in units of which *time* is a dimension. Labor is most conveniently measured in man-time units. A particular type of labor may be measured in terms of man-hours, one man-hour representing the amount of service which is customarily[5] rendered in one

---

3 Production devoted to the modification of the culture is unique in that the product is not ordinarily scarce unless made so by artificial restrictions on the application of the new cultural development. See pp. 5–6 above.

4 For a thorough and able discussion of the problem of measuring quantities of the factors, see Fritz Machlup "On the Meaning of the Marginal Product," in *Explorations in Economics: Notes and Essays Contributed in Honor of F. W. Taussig*, New York, 1936, pp. 250-263.

5 Obviously, the man-hour unit is not wholly satisfactory because it ignores variations among individuals in intensity of labor. The only suitable measure of

hour by one man of given primary traits. This definition of a unit of labor, of course, includes only that portion of the services of the man which is attributable to his natural or biological characteristics. The remainder, attributable to his training or to his cultural attributes, is regarded as the services of factors employed previously for training him and for initiating him into the culture. Land use is usually measured in terms of area-time. Quantities of a particular type of land use may be expressed in terms of acre-years, one acre-year representing the services for one year of one acre of primary land of a given type. That class of land which consists of depleting and non-reproducible materials, however, is usually measured in purely physical terms without time dimension (e.g., tons of coal, barrels of petroleum).

The units available for measuring quantities of economic goods produced (outputs) are somewhat less suitable than those employed in measuring quantities of factors. Economic goods may be defined, strictly, as the human satisfactions [6] resulting from the use of the means of production. However, economists almost universally regard as economic goods not the actual satisfactions obtained by human beings, but rather the *final means* to these satisfactions. These means consist of nondurable commodities capable of providing direct satisfactions, and of the direct services both of durable commodities and of persons. The term "economic good," then, ordinarily refers not to actual but to potential satisfactions, since there is no guarantee that final means, even when available, will actually yield the satisfactions for which they were ostensibly intended. In accordance with this definition, an economic good (in the singular) may be defined as a particular class of final means, each unit of which is exactly like each other unit.

In measuring economic goods quantitatively, the kinds of units to be employed may depend upon the class of economic

labor intensity, however, is in terms of units of output, and is therefore useless because the present problem, which is to discover the relation between units of input and units of output, cannot be solved if input and output are measured in identical terms. The man-time unit may be justified on the ground that, in practice, an hour's labor of a given type of worker does represent a more or less definite quantity of labor as evidenced by the fact that the man-time unit is used preponderantly as a basis for paying wages. Admittedly, it is not a precise measure.

[6] Or, avoidances of dissatisfactions.

good to be measured. Nondurable commodities are invariably measured in terms of physical units such as loaves or pounds or quarts. On the other hand, the direct services of durable commodities or of persons, if measurable at all, are expressed in various types of units. In some cases these economic goods may be measured in terms of standard units. For example, the service of a barber may be expressed in number of haircuts or the services of an automobile in miles traveled. Frequently the direct services of durable commodities can be measured in terms of time units. For example, the services of a given type of house are expressible in months available for occupancy. For many direct personal services, however, there is no practicable unit of measurement. The services of a teacher or clergyman, for instance, cannot be measured except in terms of more or less vague estimates of "effectiveness." The only alternative is to use time as a quantitative measure of these services, but this begs the question inasmuch as time also measures the quantity of factors involved.

Chapter 7

INPUT-OUTPUT RELATION

The purpose of this chapter is to discuss the theory of production, or the principles governing the relation between the input of factors and the output of product.[1]

The Production Function

Two of the basic laws of production are obvious. First, the production of different types of goods involves different types and combinations of the factors. In other words, the process of producing automobiles differs from that of producing fur coats, pickles, sheet music, or light bulbs. Second, in the production of any particular good, different combinations of the factors yield different results in terms of physical *quantity* of output. That is to say, the quantity of any product is functionally related to the quantities of the factors employed in its production.[2] Neither of these propositions is surprising or pro-

---

[1] Some of the more important and useful nonmathematical discussions of the subject matter of this chapter are: F. M. Taylor, *Principles of Economics*, 9th ed., New York, 1920, pp. 122-145; T. N. Carver, *The Distribution of Wealth*, New York, 1928, pp. 53-101; P. H. Wicksteed, *Common Sense of Political Economy*, London, 1910, pp. 527-549; J. B. Clark, *The Distribution of Wealth*, New York, 1914; H. C. Taylor, *Agricultural Economics*, New York, 1922, pp. 132-153; Paul H. Douglas, *Theory of Wages*, New York, 1934, pp. 17-67; J. M. Cassells, "On the Law of Variable Proportions," in *Explorations in Economics: Notes and Essays Contributed in Honor of F. W. Taussig*, New York, 1936, pp. 223-236; E. H. Phelps Brown, *The Framework of the Pricing System*, London, 1936, Chapter III; George J. Stigler, *The Theory of Competitive Price*, New York, 1942, pp. 116-146.

[2] The laws of production are physical laws; therefore, they apply not only to the factors of production but also to the services of abundant means. For example, air (a noneconomic factor) is often a part of the physical input of productive processes, for example, in the carburetor of a motorcar. The laws expressing the physical relation between the input of air and the output of product are precisely of the same nature as for economic factors such as petroleum, land, or labor. Of course, economy requires that a free good like air always be employed in such quantities that its contribution to product would be the maximum possible.

found. It is useful, however, to elaborate upon the second in order to show in some detail the *manner* in which changes in output result from changes in the application of the factors.

For most goods there is no definite or stereotyped technical method of production; instead, the factors usually may be combined in various proportions and in various time sequences. The production of bread, for example, may be carried on by any one of perhaps thousands of different methods, ranging from the simple household technique of raising wheat, grinding it into flour, and baking bread, to the complex, highly specialized, and lengthy process described in the preceding chapter. Each different method—involving a different combination of the factors—yields different results in terms of quantity of physical product. Moreover, within each general type of method it is possible to alter the combination of the factors usually with a resulting variation in quantity of product.

The functional relation between quantity of input and quantity of output, called the *production function*, may be expressed in two empirical propositions.

The first of these may be stated: If the proportions in which the factors are combined remains constant, a variation in the quantity of the factors will lead to a proportional change in the quantity of product. This implies that a doubling of the quantity of all factors employed in a given process will lead to a doubling of product. For example, if the product of 100 acres of a given type of land combined with 75 days of a given type of labor is 2,000 bushels of wheat, then the product of 200 acres of the same kind with 150 days of the same kind of labor would be 4,000 bushels, assuming that labor and land are the only factors employed and that the method of production remains unchanged.[3]

The second proposition is somewhat more complex: When several factors of production are combined in a given process, if the amount of any one factor *applied in a given way* be varied, assuming all the other factors to be held constant, (1) an increase in the variable factor will result in a more than propor-

---

[3] In many productive operations, of course, a change in the level of output may unavoidably be accompanied by a change in the proportions of the factors. The proposition stated here applies only if the quantities of *all* factors are increased in the same proportion.

tional increase in the physical product (increasing returns) up to a critical point which is designated the point of diminishing returns,[4] (2) further increases in the variable factor beyond this point will result in a less than proportional increase in physical product (diminishing returns), until finally (3) additional increases in the variable factor will add nothing to product or even cause it to diminish (constant or decreasing total output).[5]

This second principle, usually called the *law of diminishing returns* (or the law of variable proportions), states the general form of the production function. It describes the effects upon the output of a given product when the *proportions* in which the factors are combined are changed.[6]

There is nothing surprising about this law. It is based upon empirical observations of actual productive processes; it is fully confirmed by experience in a wide variety of situations; and it conforms with common sense.

---

[4] In this discussion the point of diminishing returns for a given variable factor has been defined as that combination of the factors in which a small increment of the variable factor (all other factors held constant) will lead to a proportional increase in product. There are, however, at least three other ways of defining the point of diminishing returns, all of which lead to precisely the same result. First, the point of diminishing returns may be designated as the point where the total product divided by the number of units of the variable factor employed is at a maximum, i.e., where the average product per unit of variable factor is at a maximum. Second, the point of diminishing returns may be defined as that point where the marginal product of the variable factor (see p. 76 below) is equal to the average product per unit of that factor. Third, the point of diminishing returns may be defined (by means of a curve showing the relation between the quantity of the variable factor and the quantity of product) as the point where a straight line drawn from the point of origin is tangent to the curve. For a more detailed statement of these relationships, see J. M. Cassells, *op. cit.*

[5] The point of diminishing returns may be stated algebraically as the point at which $\dfrac{\triangle Y}{Y} = \dfrac{\triangle Q}{Q}$

where: $\triangle Y =$ a small increment of the variable factor.

$Y =$ the quantity of the variable factor.

$\triangle Q =$ addition to product resulting from the small increment of Y.

$Q =$ the total output produced with Y.

Similarly, diminishing returns applies whenever $\dfrac{\triangle Y}{Y} > \dfrac{\triangle Q}{Q}$.

[6] The nature of the production functions, as summarized in the law of diminishing returns, holds true only if the postulated changes in the combinations of the factors are not accompanied by radical changes in the method of production employed.

The principle may be illustrated by the hoeing of a vegetable garden. If the garden were untouched during the growing season, it would produce little other than a chaos of weeds. If hoed once during the season, a dramatic increase in production would probably result. A second hoeing might lead to another sharp increase. A third and successive hoeing (though perhaps worth the effort) would inevitably result progressively in smaller increases in product, until, finally, hoeing beyond the fifteenth, twentieth, or perhaps thirtieth time would lead to no appreciable increase in product. In fact, such intensive cultivation might lead to an absolute decrease in product because the process of hoeing might, if carried to excess, actually reduce production by disturbing the plants. The plausibility of the law of diminishing returns is indicated by the classic remark that if it were not for this principle, the entire food supply of the world could be raised in a flowerpot.[7]

The literature of agricultural experimentation is replete with empirical investigations illustrating the law of diminishing returns as applied in the production of farm crops and livestock.[8] For example, one comprehensive study shows the effect of increasing applications of irrigation water (assuming all other factors held constant) upon the yield of potatoes (Table I). Within the range of the experiment, the application of water is clearly subject to diminishing returns, because, as shown in Table I, successive increments of water yield less than proportional increases in product. However, if the application of water were progressively increased, ultimately a point would be reached where any further addition of water would result in no addition to product and even in an actual decrease in total output.

---

[7] Traditionally, the law of diminishing returns has been extended to show the effect of changes in population (labor supply), assuming given natural resources, upon output. Applied in this way, the corollary is reached that beyond the point of diminishing returns, further increases in population will lead to less than proportional increases in product, assuming given technology and capital supply.

[8] The results of many of these studies and the general laws derivable from them are presented in the illuminating paper by W. J. Spillman and Emil Lang, *The Law of Diminishing Returns* (New York, 1924). Another important paper is H. R. Tolley, J. D. Black, and Mordecai Ezekiel, *Input as Related to Output in Farm Organization and Cost of Production Studies.* (United States Department of Agriculture Bulletin No. 1277, Sept. 18, 1924.) See also, "Economics of Planting Density in Rubber Growing," *Economica*, May, 1946, pp. 131-135.

TABLE I

Effect of Variations in Amount of Irrigation Water upon Yield of Potatoes*

Inches of Water per Acre	Yield of Potatoes per Acre (bu.)	Percentage Increase in Water	Percentage Increase in Yield
6	132	. . .	. .
12	199	100	51
18	246	50	23
24	270	33⅓	10
30	289	25	7
36	299	20	3

* W. J. Spillman and Emil Lang, *op. cit.*, p. 4. This study was originally reported in Bulletin No. 339 of the United States Department of Agriculture.

Though most of the empirical studies on production functions relate to agriculture, the identical principles apply as well in manufacturing, mining, trade, office work, and, so far as is known, all other branches of production.[9]

An important characteristic of the production function is that when any one factor is employed at the stage of increasing returns, the other factor (or factors) is subject to decreasing

---

[9] Empirical studies relating to nonagricultural production generally compare different methods from the point of view of money cost per unit of output rather than from the point of view of physical quantity of factor input per unit of output. Such studies, however, can easily be converted into physical terms if the prices per unit of the factor inputs are known.

The weaving processes in the textile industry provide an instructive illustration of the effects of varying combinations of factors. It is customary in this industry for one weaver to tend several automatic looms. When the number of looms per weaver is small, a considerable portion of the weaver's time is idle. As the number of looms per weaver is increased, the time of the weaver becomes increasingly occupied in mending breaks in the threads and in performing other functions. As the ratio of looms per weaver is further increased, however, the time of the weaver becomes so fully occupied that some of the looms must be idle awaiting the weaver's attention, especially when "breaks" occur on several looms simultaneously or in quick succession. Thus, in varying the proportions between looms and weavers, the usual relationship holds that the principle of increasing returns is applicable up to a certain point, that beyond that point the principle of diminishing returns becomes effective, and finally, if the number of looms per worker is increased excessively, that a point of decreasing total output is reached.

A study by one firm in the silk and rayon industry, regarding the effect of varying the ratio between looms and weavers, yielded the results shown in the

total output. In fact, increasing returns is the obverse of decreasing total output. This relation is explained by the fact that when one factor is subject to increasing returns, additions to the product may be obtained not only by increasing the quantity of that factor but also by reducing the quantity of the other factor. This suggests an important practical principle relative to the organization of production: It is always more economical [10] to employ the factors in such proportions that the principle of diminishing returns applies simultaneously to all the factors employed. If any one factor is employed under conditions of increasing return, some other factor is being employed under conditions of decreasing total output, and output can be increased merely by using less of the latter factor. Also, if any one factor is employed under conditions of decreasing total output, production can be increased merely by using less of this factor.

A numerical illustration of this relationship between increasing returns and decreasing total output is presented in the Appendix to this chapter.

Qualifications

The preceding discussion of the theory of production has been intentionally simplified in three important respects.

First, the discussion has been based chiefly upon the supposition that only two factors of production are employed. Obviously the production of a typical good requires not two, or three, but literally thousands of different factors. Moreover,

---

following table, as reported by Professor L. P. Alford ("Looms per Weaver," *Textile World,* January, 1936, pp. 72-73). It was assumed that each loom is idle 15 per cent of the time due to stoppages.

Number of Looms per Weaver	Approximate Product per Loom Expressed as Per Cent of Maximum Attainable	Index of Approximate Total Product per Weaver
2	85	170
3	82	246
4	78	312
5	73.5	367.5
6	68.5	411
7	63	441
8	57	456
9	50	450

10 See Chapter 13 for a discussion of the meaning of "economical."

these factors are not combined simultaneously within a single enterprise but are utilized in a time sequence covering a period of years and involving numerous productive establishments. These facts, however, do not vitiate or even materially alter the basic theory of production. It is still true that the amount of product is functionally related to the quantity and the combination of factors employed; the principle of diminishing returns still holds for each factor, assuming that all other factors are held constant. Moreover, these principles hold true not only of the entire productive process but also of any part of the process. Thus, in the production of bread, the laws of production apply separately to the raising of wheat, the milling of flour, the provision of transportation, the smelting of iron for machinery, the baking of the bread, or to any other steps in the process, so long as the output at that particular step in the process is regarded as the "product," and the input within that step as "factor." Thus, for any selected portion of the process the output may not be final goods and the input may not be primary factors of production. When, however, a productive process is viewed in its entirety, the input consists of primary factors and the output consists of final goods irrespective of how the various stages of the process may be separated in space or time. The final product is regarded as a synthesis of all the many types of primary factors used directly or indirectly in its production, and the laws of production relate ultimately to the effect of variations in the input of primary factors upon the output of final goods.

Second, it has been assumed in the discussion of the laws of production that it is always possible to find a quantitative measure for product. Particularly in the case of personal services, this is not always possible; hence, in some cases, the laws of production are not practically demonstrable.

Third, the discussion of the laws of production have led to the inference that it is always technically possible to employ the factors in an infinite variety of combinations. As a matter of fact, in the everyday world it is frequently impossible, or at least impracticable, to combine the factors in any desired proportions. The factors, or their intermediate products, cannot always be applied in the quantity desired because they are not always divisible into infinitesimal units. Therefore, certain combinations of the factors cannot in practice be attained. For example, if a railroad is required to connect a mine and a smelter, it is necessary to construct a right of way, to lay tracks, etc. Though it is possible to vary the nature of the completed railroad according to the amount of traffic to be carried, yet there is an irreducible minimum necessary if any rail transport is to be provided. Thus, it is not possible for the mining enterprise to achieve any desired combination of the factors. Rather, it must submit to the technical fact that the provision of even the smallest amount of rail transport necessitates a certain minimum investment of resources. Similarly, an electric transmission system requires a minimum investment irrespective of the load it is to carry. Or if a manufacturing establishment requires a certain type of lathe for a given task, though the model of the lathe may be varied according to the amount of work to be done, nevertheless a certain minimum of investment must be made if the particular task is to be done at all. Examination of actual production will readily demonstrate that industry abounds in cases where, for technical reasons, the factors cannot be obtained in desired quantities and consequently cannot be combined in the most advantageous proportion. This situation is referred to as "lumpiness" of the factors.

If it were not for this lumpiness of the factors, many of the problems relating to the achievement of productive efficiency would be eliminated. One of the most significant managerial tasks is to achieve, in light of existing technology, the most efficient combination of factors. Moreover, were it not for this lumpiness, the size of the productive establishment would be a matter of relative indifference from the point of view of productive efficiency. The great significance attaching to the size of firms is due largely to the fact that variations in size make possible variations in the *combinations* of the factors. The great advantage of the large firm, so characteristic of modern industry, is to be accounted for in large measure by the fact that large-scale operation makes possible the full utilization of lumpy factors whereas small-scale operation necessitates utilization of some factors at less than "capacity." [11]

11 See Chapter 30. Cf. F. H. Knight, *The Ethics of Competition,* New York, 1935, pp. 186-236; also George J. Stigler, *Production and Distribution Theories,* New York, 1941, pp. 72-76.

Again, under certain circumstances it is not possible to vary at will the combinations of the factors because technical considerations may require that the factors be used in fixed proportions. In the production of a chemical compound by a synthetic process, a fine adjustability in the combination of the factors is precluded, since the constituent elements, at least, must be combined in invariable proportions.[12]

The practical impossibility within many productive situations of combining the factors in any desired proportion does not, however, alter the laws of production. It is still true that different combinations and quantities of the factors, wherever they are possible, lead to different physical quantities of product, and that any increase in a variable factor, holding all other factors constant, will up to a certain point lead to increasing returns, beyond that point to diminishing returns, and finally to constant or decreasing total output.

Appendix

The character of the principle of diminishing returns may be explained by means of a hypothetical example. The accompanying schedule (Table II) is designed to illustrate the effect upon the output of a given commodity of changes in the quantities of factors employed. In the left half of the table it is assumed that the quantity of factor X is held constant and the quantity of factor Y is varied; in the right half, factor Y is held constant and factor X varied. The table is so arranged that the *proportion* of X to Y for each combination as shown on the left half is identical to that for the corresponding combination as shown on the right half. For example, the combination 2-1 (2 units of factor X to 1 of Y) is shown on the left half as 100 units of X and 50 units of Y, and on the right half as 200 units of X to 100 units of Y—the only difference between the two combinations being that on the right half, the amount of both X and Y is just twice that as shown on the left half. Consequently, the amount of product forthcoming from the combination 2-1 shown on the right half is just twice that shown on the left half.

---

12 Professor T. N. Carver has shown that even synthetic chemical processes are subject to the principle of diminishing returns. In such a process not all of any one element is used up, but by increasing the amount of one element used, the per cent of the other that will be absorbed is increased. *Principles of Political Economy,* New York, 1919, p. 367.

The device of presenting the factors arranged in identical proportions enables one to compare simultaneously the effect of variations in factor Y (holding X constant) with the effect of variations in factor X (holding Y constant). This is useful, because in the study of the laws of diminishing returns only the combination of the factors—not their absolute amounts—is important.

TABLE II

Hypothetical Schedules Showing Functional Relation between Quantity of Factors and Quantity of Product

COMBINATION OF THE FACTORS: RATIO OF FACTOR X TO FACTOR Y	FACTOR X HELD CONSTANT AT 100 UNITS; FACTOR Y VARYING				FACTOR Y HELD CONSTANT AT 100 UNITS; FACTOR X VARYING			
	1	2	3	4	5	6	7	8
	Quantity of Factor Y	Product	Percentage of Increase in Factor Y	Percentage of Increase in Product	Quantity of Factor X	Product	Percentage of Increase in Factor X	Percentage of Increase in Product
4–1	25	20	....	....	400	80	33	....
3–1	33½	41	33	103	300	123	50	....
2–1*	50	74	50	81	200	148	100	3
1–1	100	144	100	95	100	144	100	41
1–2	200	204	100	42	50	102	50	44
1–3*	300	213	50	5	33⅓	71	33	45
1–4	400	192	33	....	25	48	....	....

* Approximate point of diminishing returns and decreasing total output.

Refer now to the left side of Table II, where the quantity of factor X is held constant at 100 and the quantity of factor Y is varied. For each combination the quantity of product is indicated in column 2. With successive increases in the quantity of factor Y, the product increases at first more than in proportion until, approximately at combination 2-1, the point of diminishing returns is reached. Beyond this point further successive increases in factor Y lead to less than proportional increases in product, until approximately at combination 1-3, further increases lead to an actual decrease in product. These relations can be seen most clearly by reference to columns 3 and 4 in which are shown the successive percentage increases in factor Y and in product. Increasing returns applies so long as the percentage increase in product is greater than the percentage increase in Y. Beyond this, *diminishing returns* applies so long as the percentage increase in product is less than the percentage increase in Y. Finally, *constant* or *decreasing total output* applies when further increases in Y yield no further increases or decreases in product.

Turn now to the right side of Table II where the quantity of Y is held constant and the quantity of X varied. Successively increasing amounts of factor X may be noted *reading from bottom to top* in column 5, and corresponding amounts of product may be noted in column 6. The percentage changes in factor X and in product are shown in columns 7 and 8 which should be read from bottom to top. Reading from the bottom of columns 7 and 8, increases in X are associated with more than proportional increases (increasing returns) in product up to the combination 1-3. Beyond this point additional increases are associated with less than proportional increases in product (diminishing returns) until combination 2-1 is reached. Beyond this point further increases in X are associated with decreases in total output (constant or decreasing total output).

Comparing the two sides of the table, the point of diminishing returns on one side corresponds approximately with the point of constant or decreasing total output on the other side. The limits of the range of diminishing returns are approximately the same on both sides. On the left side, the point at which diminishing returns sets in is *approximately* at the combination 2-1; correspondingly, on the right side, the approximate point at which decreasing total output sets in is also at combination 2-1. Similarly, on the left side the point of decreasing total output is approximately at combination 1-3; and on the right side diminishing returns sets in at about the same point. This correspondence is not accidental, but rather in accordance with the general principle. In fact, the failure of the table to demonstrate the *exact* coincidence of these points is due solely to the fact that with large incremental units the points of diminishing returns and decreasing total output cannot be located precisely. If, however, schedules were expanded so that the incremental units of variable factors would be infinitesimal, then it could be demonstrated that the point of diminishing returns (when Y is the variable) would be at precisely the same combination as the point of decreasing total output (when X is the variable).[13]

---

[13] The following is a fairly simple method of estimating the precise position of the point of diminishing returns. As pointed out above (p. 66 footnote) diminishing returns for a given factor sets in at that point where the average product per unit of the factor (total product divided by number of units of the factor employed) is at a maximum. Thus, if the total product is known for all values of factor Y, assuming the quantity of all other factors to be fixed, the point of diminishing returns for the factor lies where the average product per unit of the factor is at a maximum. To illustrate, interpolating in Table II, it is found that the precise point of diminishing returns for Y is at the combinaton where Y is 59 and X is 100. This is the combination 1.695-1. Moreover, the point of decreas-

The coincidence between the point of diminishing returns and the point of decreasing total output means that the *range* of combinations subject to diminishing returns is precisely the same for both factors. Beyond these limits one of the factors is subject to increasing returns and the other to decreasing total output. Moreover, the correspondence in the range of diminishing returns for the two factors implies that increasing returns for one factor is *related* to decreasing total output for the other. This may be illustrated by reference back to Table II. For example, at combination 4-1, when 100 units of X are combined with 25 units of Y, the product is 20. When Y is increased to 33⅓ (combination 3-1), the product is then 41, the increase in product being more than proportional to the increase in Y. However, the adoption of combination 3-1 could be achieved, instead of by increasing Y, by decreasing X. If this were done, the combination would be 75 units of X to 25 units of Y; the proportions of the factors would still be 3 of X to 1 of Y but the amounts of each of the factors would be just ¾ of that shown in the table for combination 3-1. The product would, therefore, be just ¾ of 41 or 30.75. This is greater than the product derived from using 100 units of X and 25 units of Y; hence, the product would be increased by *reducing* the quantity of X when Y is held constant. Experimentation will show that, if one of the factors is being employed under increasing returns, the product can always be increased by using less of the other factor.

ing total output for X is at precisely the same combination. The computations for obtaining these results are shown in the following table:

Combination of the Factors: Ratio of Factor X to Factor Y	Factor X Held Constant at 100 Units; Factor Y Varying			Factor Y Held Constant at 100; Factor X Varying	
	Quantity of Factor Y	Product	Average Product per Unit of Y	Quantity of Factor X	Product
2.000–1	50	74.0	1.4800	200.0	148.00
1.961–1	51	75.9	1.4882	196.1	148.82
1.923–1	52	77.8	1.4962	192.3	149.62
1.887–1	53	79.6	1.5019	188.7	150.19
1.852–1	54	81.3	1.5056	185.2	150.56
1.818–1	55	83.0	1.5091	181.8	150.91
1.796–1	56	84.7	1.5125	178.6	151.25
1.754–1	57	86.3	1.5146	175.4	151.40
1.724–1	58	87.9	1.5155	172.4	151.54
1.695–1	59	89.5	1.5169	169.5˙	151.70
1.667–1	60	91.0	1.5167	166.7	151.67
1.639–1	61	92.5	1.5164	163.9	151.64
1.613–1	62	94.0	1.5161	161.3	151.61

Chapter 8

MARGINAL PRODUCT AND COST OF PRODUCTION

According to the general laws of production discussed in the previous chapter, variations in the input of the factors in a given productive operation lead to variations in product. Thus it is empirically possible to determine the effect upon output of the addition or withdrawal of various amounts of a *particular* factor. Indeed, if it were not possible to determine the effect of changes in the amount of various factors employed, there would be no rational basis for deciding how the factors of production should be organized in relation to any particular set of ends. As Professor F. H. Knight has stated, "Organization is called for, is possible, and is carried out only through the fact that the separate contributions of separate agencies to a joint product can be identified." [1]

The Marginal Product

In ascertaining the productive contributions of particular factors, the concept of *marginal product* is useful. The marginal product of any one factor (in a given process of production) may be defined as the amount by which output would be reduced if one unit of the factor were withdrawn, all other factors and conditions being held constant. This may be illustrated by an example: Suppose that the combination of 5 units of factor X and 8 units of factor Y yields a product of 20, and that when one unit of factor X is withdrawn (holding the quantity of factor Y constant) the product is reduced to 17. The marginal product of factor X is then 3. On the other hand, if with the withdrawal of one unit of factor Y (assuming the quantity of factor X to be

---

[1] *Risk, Uncertainty and Profit*, New York, 1921, p. 103.

held constant at 5) the product is reduced from 20 to 18, the marginal product of Y is 2. Moreover, since all the units of either one of the factors are presumably alike, the marginal product refers not to one *particular* unit of the factor but rather to *any unit*. Strict consistency requires that the units in which the factors are measured be of infinitesimal magnitude. With such units, it is a matter of indifference whether the marginal product of a factor be defined as the reduction in product occasioned by the withdrawal of one unit or as the addition to product that would be forthcoming if another unit of the factor were employed.

The concept of marginal product is significant, of course, only when the quantity of a factor employed can be increased or decreased by small increments or decrements. In situations where the factors are lumpy or must be combined in fixed proportions, the marginal product of any one factor cannot be ascertained.

The Principle of Imputation

Since the marginal product of a given factor refers to *any* unit of that factor, the portion of the total product attributable to all the units of the factor employed might be assumed to be equal to the marginal product of the factor multiplied by the number of units employed. Indeed, it can be demonstrated that if the amount of the product imputed to each of the factors employed is calculated in this way, the sum of the imputed products will be exactly equal to the total product resulting from the combination of the factors. This may be called the *principle of imputation*. Stated algebraically, it is:

$$MxX + MyY = Q$$
where: Mx = Marginal product of factor X
X = Number of units of factor X employed
My = Marginal product of factor Y
Y = Number of units of factor Y employed
Q = Quantity of product.

For this equation to be valid, however, one condition must be fulfilled, namely, the production function must be homogeneous and linear. This implies (1) that the quantity of the factors employed may be increased or decreased by small increments, and (2) that when the proportions in which the factors are employed remain constant, a given percentage increase in quantity of factors will lead to a corresponding percentage increase in quantity of product.[2]

An arithmetical illustration of the principle of imputation is presented in Appendix A of this chapter.

Cost of Production

A production manager in search of the least costly organization of production will vary the combination of the factors until their several marginal products are proportional to their prices. This may be illustrated.

Suppose a given productive process requires two factors X and Y, and that the price of X (Px) is \$2 and the price of Y (Py) is \$1. Suppose also that the production manager has combined the two factors in such proportions that the marginal product of X (Mx) is 4 units and the marginal product of Y (My) is 1 unit. In this situation the final unit of X is yielding 4 units of product at a cost of \$2 or 50 cents per unit of product. The final unit of Y, on the other hand, is yielding 1 unit of product at a cost of \$1 or at \$1 per unit of product. Under these conditions it would pay to increase the use of X which would yield additional product at 50 cents per unit and reduce the use of Y which is yielding additional product at a cost of \$1 per unit. As this substitution of X for Y takes place, the marginal product of X would fall and that of Y would increase. The most advantageous combination would be achieved when enough of Y had been replaced by X so that $\dfrac{Mx}{My} = \dfrac{Px}{Py}$, i.e., in this illustration until the ratio between Mx and My was 2 to 1. This might be reached, for example, when $Mx = 3.2$ and $My = 1.6$. At this ratio the product obtained from the final unit of both X and Y would cost $62\frac{1}{2}$ cents, and there would be no gain from further substitution.

---

[2] The production function is in a sense always linear. If the increase in quantity of factors occurs by duplicating the existing productive organization in all respects, the increase in output must necessarily be proportional to the increase in factor inputs. In practice it is sometimes not necessary to increase the input of some factors, especially management, in proportion to the increase of the others. This is due to lack of homogeneity rather than to lack of linearity.

In actual practice, the marginal product is not often consciously used as a criterion for evaluating the productive contributions of the various factors and for determining the proportions in which they are employed. Rather, production managers usually seek that combination which yields the greatest total product per dollar of factors, i.e., the combination which involves the least cost per unit of product. The attention of production managers is on average cost per unit of product rather than upon marginal product. However, the condition of least cost is that the factors shall be so combined that their several marginal products are proportional to their respective prices. See Appendix B of this chapter.

Appendix A—The Principle of Imputation

The principle of imputation may be illustrated by means of a hypothetical example. Assume that two factors, X and Y, are employed in the production of a certain good, and that they may be combined in varying proportions. In order to ascertain the fraction of the product that may be imputed to each of the factors for any given combination, it is necessary to estimate the marginal product of each factor in each combination. This may be approximated by a simple arithmetical method. (This illustration assumes that the production function is homogeneous and linear.)

In Table III, hypothetical data are presented showing the total product (column 4) that would result with different quantities of

TABLE III

Estimated Marginal Product of Factor Y with
Varying Combinations of Factor X and Factor Y

1	2	3	4	5	6	7	8
Combination of the Factors: Ratio of Factor X to Factor Y	Quantity of Factor X	Quantity of Factor Y	Total Product	Increment of Y	Additional Product Resulting from Increment of Y	Additional Product per Unit of Increment of Y (Column 6 ÷ Column 5)	Estimated Marginal Product of Y
4–1	100	25	20	...	..	..	...
3–1	100	33⅓	41	8⅓	21	2.5	2.25
2–1	100	50	74	16⅔	33	2.0	1.70
1–1	100	100	144	50	70	1.4	1.00
1–2	100	200	204	100	60	.6	.35
1–3	100	300	213	100	9	.1	−.05
1–4	100	400	192	100	−21	−.2	...

factor Y when factor X is held constant at 100. From these figures it is possible to compute the amount of additional product (column 6) that would result from the addition of each increment of Y. Since each increment of Y (column 5) consists of several units, the average addition to product per unit of Y added may be determined for each increment of Y by dividing the additional product resulting from the entire increment by the number of units of Y in the increment. This gives the *average* marginal product for the units of Y within the increment (column 7). For purposes of approximation, it may be regarded as the marginal product when the amount of Y is at the mid-point of the increment. When the marginal product at the mid-point of each of the several increments has been estimated in this way, the marginal product at the upper limit of each increment (which is required in this discussion) would be approximately half-way between the marginal product at the mid-point of the increment and the marginal product at the mid-point of the next increment. On this basis, the marginal product at each of various amounts of Y may be estimated as shown in column 8. These figures conform to the original definition of marginal product as the amount by which output would be reduced if one unit of the factor were withdrawn, or, what is precisely the same thing, the portion of the product attributable to one unit of the factor.[3]

The marginal product of Y, as estimated for any given amount of Y, applies not only to that particular amount but also to any other amount so long as the *proportion* between X and Y remains constant. For example, when 50 units of Y are combined with 100 units X (combination 1-2) the marginal product of Y is estimated to be 1.70. This marginal product will be precisely the same, no matter what the absolute amount of Y, so long as X and Y are combined in the proportion of 1 to 2. This can be demonstrated by computing the marginal product of Y, when X is held constant at, let us say, 200 or 300 instead of 100, always provided the *ratios* between the two factors are not altered.

It is also possible to obtain a similar schedule of the marginal product of factor X. This is presented in Table IV. The marginal product of X presented for any given value of X relates to the stated

---

[3] Marginal product may be estimated somewhat more simply by a graphic method. Since the marginal product of a factor is defined as the loss in product due to the withdrawal of one unit of the factor, the marginal product may be ascertained merely by measuring the *slope* of a curve expressing the relation between quantity of variable factor (assuming all other factors constant) and the quantity of product. The marginal product at any point on the curve is estimated simply by reading from the curve the decrease in product associated with a decrease of one unit in the variable factor.

proportion in which X and Y are combined, not to any particular absolute amount of the factor.

TABLE IV

Estimated Marginal Product of Factor X *with Varying Combinations of Factor* X *and Factor* Y

1	2	3	4	5	6	7	8
Combination of the Factors: Ratio of Factor X to Factor Y	Quantity of Factor Y	Quantity of Factor X	Total Product	Increment of X	Additional Product Resulting from Increment of X	Additional Product per Unit of Increment of X (Column 6 ÷ Column 5)	Estimated Marginal Product of X
4–1	100	400	80	100	−43	−.43	....
3–1	100	300	123	100	−25	−.25	−.34
2–1	100	200	148	100	4	.04	−.11
1–1	100	100	144	50	42	.84	.44
1–2	100	50	102	16⅔	31	1.86	1.34
1–3	100	33⅓	71	8⅓	23	2.76	2.29
1–4	100	25	48	...	...	....	....

Given the marginal products both of X and of Y, for various combinations of the two factors, it is then possible to determine the portion of the product that may be imputed to each factor for any particular combination. For example, as shown in Table V, when 100 units of X are combined with 200 units of Y, total product is

TABLE V

Imputation of Total Product to Factor X *and Factor* Y

1	2	3	4	5	6	7	8
Combination of the Factors: Ratio of Factor X to Factor Y	Quantity of Factor X	Quantity of Factor Y	Marginal Product of X (See Table IV)	Marginal Product of Y (See Table III)	Product Imputed to X (Column 2 × Column 4)	Product Imputed to Y (Column 3 × Column 5)	Total Product (Q) (Column 6 + Column 7)
4–1	100	25	....	....	....	....	....
3–1	100	33⅓	−.34	2.25	−34	75	41
2–1	100	50	−.11	1.70	−11	85	74
1–1	100	100	.44	1.00	44	100	144
1–2	100	200	1.34	.35	134	70	204
1–3	100	300	2.29	−.05	229	−15	214
1–4	100	400	....	....	....	....	....

204. Of this product, 134 may be imputed to factor X. This amount is determined by multiplying the marginal product of X (1.34) by the number of units of X employed (100). Similarly, the amount of

product that may be imputed to Y is 70, this amount being determined by multiplying the marginal product of Y (.35) by the number of units of Y employed (200). The amount imputed to X (134) plus the amount imputed to Y (70) equals the total product (204). Thus, the total product, calculated as the sum of the amounts imputed to the two factors (as shown in column 8 of Table V), corresponds to the originally assumed total products from like amounts of the factors (as shown in column 2 of Table II). This is in accord with the imputation principle that the amount of product attributable to each factor is equal to the marginal product of that factor times the number of units employed, and that the sum of the products imputed to each of the several factors is equal to the total product resulting from the entire process.

The importance of this principle of imputation, historically, is that it provides a tenable basis for the marginal productivity theory of distribution. According to this theory, the product of industry under capitalism tends to be distributed to the various factors according to the marginal product of each. The principle of imputation furnished evidence that distribution according to marginal productivity would exactly exhaust the product.[4]

Appendix B

In Table VI hypothetical data are presented for the total product (column 3), and for the marginal products of various combinations of factors X and Y (columns 4 and 5). The ratios of the marginal product of X to the marginal product of Y are shown in column 6.

To determine the cost of production per unit of output (columns 7 and 8), it is necessary to determine (for each combination) the total cost by multiplying the price of each factor by its quantity and adding the results. The total cost is then divided by the quantity of product (column 3) to get cost per unit of product.

In the first illustration (column 7), where $Px = \$4.30$ and $Py = \$5.00$, the least costly combination is 100 units of X employed with 125 units of Y. At this combination the ratio of Mx to My is .86.

---

[4] Some of the more famous discussions of this subject are: P. H. Wicksteed, *Co-ordination of the Laws of Distribution*, reprinted by the London School of Economics, London, 1932; P. H. Wicksteed, *Common Sense of Political Economy*, London, 1910, pp. 550-574; F. A. von Wieser, *Natural Value* (edited by William Smart), London, 1893, pp. 69-113. For an excellent critical discussion of the development of this theory, see George Stigler, *Production and Distribution Theories*, New York, 1941, pp. 320-387.

TABLE VI

Least-Cost Combination of Factors

1	2	3	4	5	6	7	8
NUMBER OF UNITS OF THE FACTORS EMPLOYED		Total Product	Marginal Product of X (See Table IV)	Marginal Product of Y (See Table III)	Ratio of Marginal Products of X and Y	COST PER UNIT OF PRODUCT UNDER VARIOUS FACTOR PRICES	
X	Y					$Px = \$4.30$ $Py = 5.00$	$Px = \$7.29$ $Py = 3.00$
100	50	74	−.11	1.70	......	\$9.21	\$11.88
100	57	89	−.02	1.59	......	8.02	10.08
100	67	108	.10	1.47	.07	7.10	8.64
100	80	124	.25	1.24	.20	6.73	7.85
100	100	144	.44	1.00	.44	6.42	7.10
100	125	165	.67	.78	.86	6.37*	6.70
100	150	184	.95	.59	1.61	6.42	6.40
100	175	196	1.14	.47	2.43	6.64	6.39*
100	200	204	1.34	.35	3.83	7.01	6.51
100	225	208	1.54	.24	6.42	7.46	6.74
100	250	211	1.78	.13	13.69	7.92	6.97
100	275	213	2.02	.04	50.50	8.47	7.30
100	300	213	2.29	−.05	......	9.02	7.63

* Least-cost combination.

This is equal to the ratio of Px to Py which is also .86 (4.30 ÷ 5.00 = .86).

In the next case (column 8), the least costly combination is 100 of X to 175 of Y. The ratio of Mx to My is 2.43 which also is the ratio of Px to Py. The same principle would hold for other price combinations.[5]

These illustrations are intended to show that when a production manager strives to attain the least costly combination of the factors he is in reality adjusting the combination of the factors so that marginal products are proportional to prices. He is after all relying on the marginal principle in determining the use of his factors.

[5] In experimenting with a table of this kind, one will find that the least-cost combination always approximates, but does not always exactly satisfy, the condition of proportionality between marginal products and prices. This is due to the fact that the magnitudes employed are finite. They would have to be infinitesimal if the condition were to be satisfied exactly. In other words, the problem is one which can be solved precisely only by calculus.

Chapter 9

CAPITAL

The several preceding chapters have shown that all production is basically attributable to the primary factors—labor and land use. They have indicated that the physical results obtained from various applications of these factors are determined in accordance with the several laws of production, among these the law of diminishing returns. The theory of production up to this point, however, has been seriously incomplete because the role of *capital* in the productive process has been entirely ignored. This deficiency will now be remedied by discussing in some detail the place of capital in production. In so doing, the nature and role of labor and land use will be further clarified.

Production and Time

Production requires not only labor and land use but also *time*. Even in the direct appropriation of consumable commodities readily available in nature, short intervals of time are required between the beginning of the process and the enjoyment of the goods derived therefrom. However, in the vast majority of productive processes—whether in a primitive or modern society—long periods of time must elapse between the initial preparatory stages and the ultimate completion of products. In many cases the period of time may cover months, years, or even decades.

The fact that production is time-consuming means that at any given moment there exists: (1) a quantity of material things which are the result of past applications of labor and land but which have not yet completely fulfilled their purpose in the achievement of human ends, and (2) a quantity of non-material things—human attributes, skills, or propensities—which have been derived from past productive efforts but which, because embodied in living persons, have not yet completely served their ends. These material and nonmaterial things, existent at any moment of time, are the present manifestation of prior productive efforts which have not yet been brought to fruition. Together, they constitute, for the particular moment, the available supply of intermediate means of production, or as they are commonly called, *capital goods.*

Material Capital Goods

Material capital goods include things at every stage in production from the very earliest to the latest along with all the things used in ancillary processes. For example, a cross-sectional examination of the bread industry at any point of time would reveal a great variety of material capital goods including wheat growing in the fields, wheat in elevators, wheat in transit, wheat in process of milling, flour in storage, flour in transit, bread in process, bread in transit, bread on grocers' shelves, and bread in household kitchens.[1] At each stage there would be machinery, buildings and equipment in use, and stores of supplies such as lubricants, fuel, and stationery. Moreover, in the production of each of these things equipment and goods-in-process would be on hand at all stages in their production. All these things together would make up the stock of material capital goods devoted at any given time to the production of bread in the near or remote future. These material capital goods may conveniently be thought of as "bread-in-process" because each of them, as it is used up in production, contributes toward the provision of the final commodity, bread —in a figurative sense is "converted" into bread. Thus, the material capital goods in existence at any moment of time include those things (1) which are the result of past productive efforts and (2) which have not yet completely served their ends.

A third criterion is necessary, however, in order clearly to distinguish capital goods from land. Land has been defined in

---

1 Strictly, consumer inventories are capital goods. In ordinary usage they are not so regarded.

Chapter 1 to include the "produced" features of the environment that are nondepreciating—such as dams, road cuts, and similar permanent alterations of the terrain. Thus, the term "material capital goods" is reserved for those produced features of the environment that are *subject to depreciation*. The implication of this distinction is that the continuous production of material capital goods is a necessary part of the general process of production; the constant depreciation of these capital goods requires that they be regularly replaced by newly produced capital goods if production is to be continued. This is in sharp contrast to the produced but permanent features of the environment which are not subject to depreciation through use. Once in existence, they become the basic conditions of economic life unless they are subsequently changed by deliberate action, when again they become permanent and basic. The distinguishing feature of capital goods, then, is that they are reproducible and depreciating so that their production constitutes a regular stage in the continuous process of producing economic goods.[2]

Nonmaterial Capital Goods

The nonmaterial capital goods include all those attributes of human beings which have been "produced," through activities called, broadly, education or culture dissemination. Education, as the term is used here, comprises all activity directed toward the end of imparting to human beings skills, attitudes, beliefs, values, tendencies, or other characteristics. It is the process by which the plastic and amorphous creature that we call "biological man" is molded according to the extant social pattern. Education in the broad sense is one of the most important branches of production. Every society devotes to it a substantial share of its factors of production including a part of the labor of parents, teachers, clergymen, factory foremen, and authors, and, in addition, the labor and land required to

---

[2] The distinction between land and capital is not sharp. Nothing is absolutely permanent and it may be that nothing is absolutely nonreproducible. Thus the category of land may be, strictly speaking, empty. However, the rate of depreciation for some things is so slow that it is disregarded in practice.

produce such educational facilities as schools, churches, and books.

Education is oriented toward two main purposes: (1) to produce skills, knowledge, and other attributes in individuals as a means to the production of economic goods, and (2) to produce the attributes in individuals which are considered desirable for their own sake or good in themselves.

Education for the first of these two purposes is a necessary stage in the production of virtually all economic goods. To obtain a steady supply of medical services, for example, it is necessary continuously to train physicians, surgeons, nurses, pharmacists, and orderlies; to maintain a steady supply of hospitals and clinics where these individuals may carry on their work, it is necessary to train bricklayers, carpenters, and architects; to produce a steady flow of needed drugs, workers in pharmaceutical factories must be trained; and to produce the required surgical equipment, appropriate factory workers must be trained. In short, to ensure a regular supply of medical service, or any other economic good, it is necessary continuously to train the thousands of different types of workers required. If this process of training were to cease for any considerable period, the decline, retirement, and death of already trained workers would so deplete the ranks of the available labor supply that production would be drastically curtailed. Thus the education of workers is a regular stage in the production of all commodities, and the maintenance of production at any given rate is dependent upon the recruitment and training of new personnel to replace the workers who drop out.

Education for the second purpose, namely, to produce attributes in individuals which are considered desirable for their own sake, must also go on continuously in order that oncoming generations may participate in the desired benefits.[3]

At any given moment in the history of a society, then, there are in existence human beings with attributes, propensities, and skills which have been produced through past produc-

---

[3] In practice it is difficult to distinguish between educational activities designed to train workers for productive service and those designed to develop individual traits which are considered good in themselves. The training of workers involves much more than the mere teaching of specialized skills and techniques; it includes also many aspects of general education.

tive efforts and which comprise the available nonmaterial capital goods.[4]

The concept of *nonmaterial capital goods* makes possible a somewhat more precise definition of *labor* as a primary factor of production. Labor, in the ordinary sense of work performed by human beings, must be regarded as a blend consisting of the services performed by the basic biological man "as he must have issued from the hands of nature" and by the nonmaterial capital which has been invested in him through prior productive activities (education). Thus labor, in the ordinary sense, cannot be regarded wholly as a primary factor; a distinction must be made between the aspect of it which is primary and that which is the outcome of prior productive efforts. In practice, of course, it is impossible to distinguish between the two elements.

Capital

The following is a classification of the various types of things and human attributes which may comprise the supply of capital goods, material and nonmaterial, at any given moment of time:

I. Material Capital Goods.
　　1. Things employed in the productive process but which do not enter directly or immediately into the attainment of human ends.
　　　　a. Durable things which, though depreciating, render their productive services over a relatively long period of time, e.g., factory buildings, freight cars, machinery, wharves, and governmental buildings.
　　　　b. Nondurable things which are quickly destroyed or dissipated in the productive process, e.g., coal, office supplies, lubricants.
　　2. Stores of commodities in process, e.g., raw materials awaiting fabrication, partly finished commodities in

---

[4] Attributes which have been produced as a means to the production of economic goods may be thought of as analogous to durable material capital goods such as machinery and business buildings; whereas those attributes which have been produced for their own sake may be thought of as analogous to durable "consumer goods" such as automobiles and clothing.

process of manufacture, commodities in transit or in warehouses and stores.[5]

3. Things which are employed directly in the attainment of human ends.

  a. Durable things which render their direct services over a period of time, e.g., clothing, houses, churches, pleasure automobiles, furniture, golf clubs, yachts.

  b. Nondurable things in the hands of ultimate consumers but which have not yet been consumed, e.g., household stocks of groceries, drugs, fuel.

II. Nonmaterial Capital Goods.

1. Attributes of human beings which have been "produced" as a means to the production of economic goods.

2. Cultural attributes of human beings which have been "produced" as an end in themselves.

The items mentioned in this outline represent a cross section of the supply of capital goods at any given moment. They also represent a reasonably faithful picture of the supply of capital goods through a period of time. The actual physical composition of the supply of capital goods would change over a period of time. The depreciation, dissipation, and consumption of things, and the decline or death of persons results in the progressive destruction of the various capital goods that existed at any point in time. The continuity of the production process would result, however, in the replacement of the elements used up, so that the cross section of the supply of capital goods presents a similar pattern through time. Any changes in the pattern would be the result of arranging current productive activities so that the rate at which particular capital goods are being supplied will differ from that at which old ones are being used up. The supply of some capital goods would, of course, diminish if dissipation occurred more rapidly than production, whereas the supply of others would increase if production exceeded dissipation. On the whole, however, the composition of the

---

5 For goods which are produced intermittently because of seasonal or other variable factors (for example, farm crops) part of the process of production is the storage of these goods between production periods. The period of storage is a part of the time involved in the whole process.

total stock of capital goods in a going society ordinarily changes very slowly. Thus it is possible to regard the supply of capital goods figuratively as the embodiment, at a moment of time, of an abstract *fund* which exists through time. The things which comprise the fund are constantly changing form, disintegrating, being consumed, or otherwise undergoing change. The fund continues through time, the specific things of which it is composed being constantly replaced by new things. The fund may be compared to the water in a lake which is continuously being drained by an outlet and continuously replenished by an inlet. The water level will remain constant if the inflow and outflow are equal, will rise if the inflow exceeds the outflow, or fall if the outflow is greater than the inflow. A body of water is always present even though the particular units of water are continuously changing.

The Quantity of Capital as a Function of Time

It has already been pointed out that the existence of capital goods is necessitated by the fact that production takes *time;* that the supply of capital goods in existence at any time within any industry is simply the present manifestation of prior applications of labor and land which have not yet "matured" into final goods; and that the uninterrupted production of any good is possible only through the continuous maintenance of a supply of capital goods (capital) within the industry. Indeed, the amount of capital used in a productive process (where a given amount of labor and land is employed) is *proportional* to the length of the average time interval between the applications of labor and land and the completion of the product. The longer the average time interval, the greater the amount of capital required to maintain continuous production. Or the same idea may be formulated in this way: The amount of capital used in a productive process is equal to the average time interval multiplied by the amount of labor and land employed.[6]

An arithmetic illustration of the relation between capital and time is presented in the appendix to this chapter.

---

[6] In a practical situation, it is not possible to measure directly the amount of time involved in a productive process. However, in view of the proportionality

Appendix

In the production of any commodity, the various steps in the process take place in a time sequence or in a series of stages. The total time required for the entire process may be measured by averaging the time intervals between the several applications of labor and land and the completion of the product. This concept of the time required in a process of production must, of course, be distinguished clearly from another possible concept, namely, the time elapsing between the initiation of the process at the earliest stage and the completion of the product.

Suppose that a given process is carried on in five stages and that these stages are spaced one month apart, the final stage occurring when the finished product passes into consumption. Assume that at each stage a certain percentage of the land use and labor employed in the process is applied. (Quantities of land used and labor are measused in terms of value). The time involved in the process would then be measured by computing the weighted [7] average time between the applications of land and labor and the completion of the product.

TABLE VII

Time Sequence of a Hypothetical Productive Process

Stage in the Productive Process	Time of Application of Labor and Land (Expressed in Months Prior to Completion of Final Product)	Percentage of Total Input of Labor and Land Applied at Each Stage
I	4	5%
II	3	5
III	2	10
IV	1	30
V	0	50
		100%

This is illustrated by means of hypothetical data presented in Table VII. According to these data, the weighted average interval of time involved in the process is .85 months.[8]

---

between time and capital, the amount of time (in months) may be measured simply by dividing the amount of capital required by the amount of labor and land employed per month.

[7] The weights, of course, are the percentages of the total input of land and labor applied at each stage in the process.

[8] $\dfrac{(4 \times 5) + (3 \times 5) + (2 \times 10) + (1 \times 30) + (0 \times 50)}{100} = .85$ months.

The time required for a productive process is, as stated above, proportional to the amount of capital necessary if the process is to be continuously maintained. This may also be illustrated by a hypothetical example. Suppose that a particular commodity can be produced by either of two methods, A or B; and that the time required for method B is greater than that for method A. The time sequences of each of the two processes are shown in Table VIII. Method A is clearly more direct than method B; the time required for method A is .85 months [9] and for method B is 2.15 months.[10]

TABLE VIII

Time Sequences of Two Alternative Methods of Production

Stage in the Productive Process	Time of Application of Labor and Land (Expressed in Months Prior to Completion of Final Product)	Percentage of Total Input of Labor and Land Applied at Each Stage	
		Method A	*Method B*
I	4	5%	15%
II	3	5	20
III	2	10	40
IV	1	30	15
V	0	50	10
		100%	100%

The steady maintenance of production under either method requires that each stage in the process be repeated each month. Thus, if 100 units of land and labor are to be steadily employed under method A, 5 units must be engaged each month at stage I. Since four months elapse between this stage and the completion of the product, 20 units of capital goods (5 x 4) will always be in existence as a result of previous applications of land and labor at this stage and will be necessary to maintain production at the same rate. Similarly, 5 units of land and labor must be engaged each month at stage II which is three months prior to completion of the product. The capital in existence as a result of previous production at this stage will always be 15 units. Moreover, 20 units of capital will be in existence as a result of production at stage III and 30 units

$$[9] \frac{(4 \times 5) + (3 \times 5) + (2 \times 10) + (1 \times 30) + (0 \times 50)}{100} = .85 \text{ months.}$$

$$[10] \frac{(4 \times 15) + (3 \times 20) + (2 \times 40) + (1 \times 15) + (0 \times 10)}{100} = 2.15 \text{ months.}$$

from stage IV. Since stage V takes place at the time the product passes into consumption, no capital results from production at this stage. Thus, if production is carried on steadily month after month, with 100 units of labor and land employed under method A, capital amounting to 85 [11] will be in continuous existence. On the other hand, if 100 units of labor and land are employed under method B, 215 [12] units of capital will be required. The amount of capital needed in the two methods is exactly proportional to the time required. (For method A the time was .85 months; for method B, 2.15 months.)

---

[11] $(4 \times 5) + (3 \times 5) + (2 \times 10) + (1 \times 30) + (0 \times 50) = 85.$

[12] $(4 \times 15) + (3 \times 20) + (2 \times 40) + (1 \times 15) + (0 \times 10) = 215.$

Chapter 10

CAPITAL AS A FACTOR
OF PRODUCTION

For most commodities there are numerous possible alternative methods of production. These vary from one another not only because each involves a unique combination of various types of land and labor, but also because the period of production for each—therefore the amount of capital required—is different. In general, methods of production which are relatively efficient are often relatively time-consuming (capital-requiring). Given quantities of land and labor often yield more product (or the same product may be forthcoming with smaller quantities of land and labor) if the method used is relatively indirect than if it is direct—provided the method in each case is appropriate.

Why Capital Is Productive

The superior efficiency of the relatively lengthy methods of production may be explained, not by any magical power possessed by time per se, but rather by the simple and obvious fact that *relatively* efficient methods are often *relatively* time-consuming. Usually, the more efficient methods are those which make possible (*a*) the application of the mechanical principles of the wheel, lever, inclined plane, etc.; (*b*) the use of non-human sources of power; (*c*) specialization; and (*d*) division of labor. In other words, the more efficient methods are those which require the use of much machinery and equipment (capital goods), and which, therefore, are relatively indirect and lengthy. The advantages of applying mechanical principles, power, specialization, and division of labor are not realizable

94

through the more direct methods; hence, these methods are often of inferior efficiency.[1]

That indirect (capital-requiring) methods of production may be more efficient than direct methods may be illustrated by the example of fishing. There are many possible different methods of "producing" fish. Fish may be caught with unaided bare hands, spears, hooks and lines, nets and traps; the fishing operations may be conducted from shore, by wading, or from boats; the boats may be powered by human labor, wind, or steam. The tackle may be manufactured by hand or by machine methods; etc. It is immediately obvious that in general the more indirect methods are of greater efficiency than the more direct methods. A given quantity of labor and land can produce more fish if used under a method requiring a steam trawler equipped with nets and appropriate equipment than under methods requiring only unaided bare hands or the use of simple gear. In general, the efficiency of the various other methods of producing fish is clearly correlated with the degree of their indirectness. This is also true in the production of the great majority of other goods. Thus, assuming that a given amount of labor and land is employed in the production of a given commodity, the quantity of product will be functionally related to the amount of capital employed, an increase in capital being associated with an increase in product. The immediate problem, then, is to investigate the precise nature of this functional relation.

Capital and the Laws of Production

It is probable that, up to a certain point, the use of capital is subject to increasing returns. The more direct methods are almost always grossly inefficient. Man can do little without at least a minimum of tools and equipment. The increase in product with the adoption even of a slightly indirect method is usually spectacular. For example, the adoption of primitive spears in fishing, involving only a negligible increase in capital, would bring about a manyfold increase in output per man.

---

[1] The discussion in the first section of this chapter assumes zero rate of obsolescence.

With the adoption of methods of greater indirectness, further sharp increases in product would be obtained, but as the amount of capital was increased, the effect on product of further additions to capital would become progressively less until finally the point of diminishing returns would be reached. At this point the adoption of methods requiring still more capital would lead to an increase in product proportional to the increase in capital. Beyond this point increases in capital would be associated with less than proportional increases in product. By this time the chief advantages in relatively lengthy methods would have been attained, and the gain from additions to the capital employed would be much less significant. This would be illustrated by the gain obtained in the fishing industry through the substitution of steam for wind power. Finally, if the quantity of capital is extended sufficiently, a point is reached (constant or decreasing total output) where it is no longer possible to add to product by adopting still more indirect processes. At this point it is likely that the adoption of more lengthy methods would result in a loss in efficiency. For example, in many actual situations where it would be easily possible (from a technical point of view) to replace direct labor by automatic machinery, such replacement would lead to a loss of efficiency because the labor and land required to produce and operate the machines would be greater than that needed to carry on production under the direct method. In the fishing industry, for example, it might be possible to employ more capital by utilizing ships on the style of luxury liners instead of the usual modest fishing craft or even by building bridges to the fishing banks. Indeed, these innovations might well increase the output of fish per man directly employed. But it is obvious that applications of capital would reduce the efficiency of the entire fishing industry, because the cost of such fantastic capital goods would far exceed the gain to be expected from them. Indeed, the fact that capital is subject to decreasing total output places a positive limitation upon the successive adoption of more indirect methods.

If the methods used are sufficiently indirect for producers to be able to take advantage of the principal gains from the use of tools and machinery, nonhuman power, specialization, and division of labor, further increases in capital lead only to relatively small increases in product and finally to no increases. This limitation to the adoption of indirect methods is often ignored by those who predict that someday we shall operate our entire productive mechanism merely by pressing a few buttons connected with a vast complex of automatic machinery. One of the difficulties which prevents the adoption of more automatic machinery (even when capital is superabundant) is that ultimately the complexity of such machinery increases the cost of its production and use in terms of land and labor to the extent that its use actually becomes less efficient than the use of more simple machines. The ultimate consequences of excessively indirect methods was illustrated with beautiful absurdity in the early cartoons of Rube Goldberg where amazingly complicated machines were devised for such momentous tasks as flicking ashes off the end of a cigar.

What has been said of the advantages of indirect methods applies not only where the indirect applications of land and labor are used to produce *material* capital goods, but also where used to produce nonmaterial capital goods. In general, production is more efficient when part of the process includes the training of the workers who take part. Up to a certain limit, the additional training of workers leads to greater efficiency. Beyond this limit further increases in training would lead to no addition in product, and might even result in a reduced output, because the extra land and labor applied to educational work would yield more if applied directly.

The tentative conclusion is reached that capital, like land and labor, is subject to the law of diminishing returns. The statement of this law with special reference to capital is as follows: Assuming that given quantities of labor and land are employed in the production of a given commodity, the amount of product depends on the method employed; the amount of product forthcoming from the various methods depends in part on the length of time or the quantity of capital required; increases in capital will, up to a certain point, result in more than proportional increases in product (increasing returns); beyond that point, in less than proportional increases in product (diminishing returns); until finally, further increases will result either in no further additions to product or even to decreases in product (constant or decreasing total output).

This statement of the law of diminishing returns as applied to capital must be qualified and explained. In its present form it is misleadingly definite.

First, as has been indicated, there is nothing inherently advantageous in the use of capital. It is possible to lengthen productive processes without in any way adding to product. Among the many possible methods of producing a given commodity, it is likely that some of the more lengthy methods will be less efficient than some of the more direct methods. Moreover, among several methods, each requiring substantially the same amount of capital, some may be more efficient than others; a given increase in capital may under one method lead to a reduction in product and under another to an increase. Thus, in discussing the effect of changes in the quantity of capital, it is necessary to specify which of the several possible methods is to be considered. In this regard it is most useful to assume that for each amount of capital the product shall be considered to be that which would be forthcoming from the most efficient known method. This makes possible a definite schedule showing the relation between the quantity of capital and output—assuming given quantities of labor and land.

Second, it must be observed that each change in the quantity of capital represents a more or less fundamental change in method of production. This is in contrast to the law of diminishing returns as applied to labor and land which assumes that variations in the quantities of the factor are accompanied by no significant changes in the "basic" method.[2] The law of diminishing returns as applied to capital is based upon no such assumption, since most significant changes in the quantity of capital are necessarily definite changes in basic method.

Third, the law of diminishing returns as applied to capital refers to quantities of labor and land and quantities of capital measured in terms of *value* units. Thus when it is assumed that the quantity of labor and land is held constant, it is implied that

2 Any variation in land or labor is, of course, associated with at least a minor change in the capital required. This is true because the various types of labor and land are not applied simultaneously; hence any change in the proportions of labor and land will almost certainly affect the average *time* involved in the process and thereby the amount of capital required. Such a decrease or increase in capital could hardly be said to have an independent effect upon product.

only the *value* of the labor and land employed, not the physical units themselves, remains unchanged. It is not assumed that under different methods of production the actual physical units of the labor and land shall be held constant, but only the quantity of these factors measured in terms of value units. Similarly, quantities of capital are measured in terms of value units; in practice, then, a variation in quantity of capital means not only a variation in the physical quantity of the particular kinds of capital goods employed, but also may mean a variation in their types. This is in sharp contrast to the law of diminishing returns from labor and land which is stated solely in terms of physical units of the factors. The use of value units is adopted only because no satisfactory measure of physical units of capital is known.

Fourth, the functional relation between quantity of capital and product is likely to be irregular and discontinuous. This is explained by the fact that changes in the quantity of capital represent significant changes in method of production. An increase in the quantity of capital at one point may make possible a method of much greater efficiency, thus yielding a substantial increase in product; whereas a further equal increase in capital may make possible no improvement in method or may even lead to a loss of efficiency; yet a still further equal increment may make possible the adoption of a method more efficient than either of the other two.[3] Thus the principle that additions to capital lead to increases in product is no more than roughly approximate. A curve representing the relation between these two variables would be anything but smooth and continuous. Nevertheless, with allowance for irregularities, the relation between quantity of capital and output would be roughly in accord with the principle of diminishing returns. The irregularity of this functional relation is in contrast to the usual regularity of the relation between quantities of land or labor and product.

Finally, fifth, the relation between quantity of capital and output is stated solely in terms of given technical knowledge. The discovery of new methods of production would make possible increases in the amount of product that could be pro-

---

[3] In some cases there would be no known method involving particular amounts of capital, so that the product at these amounts would be zero.

duced with certain amounts of capital (assuming given amounts of land and labor), thus changing the form of the relation between capital and output.

These modifications and limitations of the law of diminishing returns as it relates to capital suggest that this law expresses no more than a rough tendency, that it is much less definite and rigorous than when applied to land or labor.

It may be inferred from the law of diminishing returns as related to capital that those methods of production will always be uneconomical in which capital is subject either to decreasing total output or increasing returns, and that only those methods will be economical in which capital is subject to diminishing returns. Those methods in which capital is subject to decreasing total output will be uneconomical because less product is obtainable than could be secured if a method requiring less capital were chosen. On the other hand, it will be uneconomical to use those methods in which capital is subject to increasing returns since it would be possible to increase product by using less land and labor with any given quantity of capital. Hence, the conclusion is reached that in the interests of efficiency capital must always be employed under conditions of diminishing returns. As pointed out above, the functional relation between quantity of capital and amount of product is often irregular or discontinuous; hence, as the quantity of capital is increased there may be successive phases of increasing returns, diminishing returns, and decreasing total output. The principle still holds, nevertheless, that only those methods will be economical in which capital is subject to diminishing returns.

Capital as a Primary Factor of Production

In producing final goods by indirect or roundabout methods, production takes place in a sequence of processes. Labor and land are first used to produce capital goods, which are then combined with additional labor and land to produce capital goods of a higher order; these, in turn, are combined with additional labor and land to produce capital goods of a still higher order, and so on until ultimately a final product emerges. Since the capital goods at each stage are susceptible to depreciation, it is necessary—in order to maintain the output of the final good at a given level—for production to be carried on continuously at each stage so that capital goods can be replaced as they become worn out and are discarded. As a result of carrying on production in this manner, there is always on hand at any given time a stock of capital goods which may conveniently be thought of as goods-in-process. These capital goods are the present embodiment of past applications of labor and land that have not yet matured into final products. To borrow a term from Marx, they are "congealed" labor and land. They are the links that connect labor and land with its final product, or the medium through which labor and land are converted into final goods. In this sense, the production of final goods is basically attributable not to the machines, equipment, buildings, and skills employed, but rather to the primary labor and land used to produce these things. This, however, does not tell the whole story.

The productivity of a given quantity of labor and land depends partly upon the manner in which it is employed. More product is generally obtainable when this labor and land are employed by indirect methods than when employed directly. But in order to utilize the superior indirect methods, a stock of capital goods at various stages in the process is indispensable. Capital, then, is the *sine qua non* of indirect productive methods. The extra product resulting from the indirect applications of labor and land is attributable to capital, and capital may be regarded as a primary factor of production distinct and separate from labor and land. Moreover, it is possible to ascertain the marginal product of capital (and thus to impute a portion of the total product to capital) just as in the case of labor and land.

As already pointed out, the existence of capital is a manifestation of the fact that production takes time. It has also been shown that the amount of capital required for a given productive process is proportional to the average time interval between the various applications of labor and land and the completion of the product. In fact, capital and time (in this sense) represent two different aspects of the same phenomenon. Thus, to the extent that capital is employed in any productive process, labor and land must be applied *prior* to the completion of the final good. This means that a condition to the provision of capital goods is that labor and land which might have been devoted to the attainment of immediate ends must be used instead for the attainment of more distant future ends. Machines must be produced before consumer goods. Thus, the provision of capital involves the sacrifice of more immediate wants in favor of distant satisfactions. That capital may be made available, it is necessary that the group (or some individuals in the group) postpone possible immediate satisfactions to the more or less distant future, that they "wait." Thus, the primary factor of production which we have called capital is reducible ultimately to *waiting*, and the advantage of indirect methods which we ordinarily regard as attributable to capital is thus ultimately dependent upon the willingness to wait, i.e., to postpone satisfactions until the future.

Waiting is the indispensable condition of all indirect production. Sometimes, however, the impression is created that waiting is involved only when the total stock of capital is increased—that when it is held constant no waiting is required. This view ignores the fact that even the replacement of existing capital goods is production directed toward the more or less distant future. It overlooks the fact that the resources used to produce these capital goods might have been used for the attainment of more immediate satisfactions. It can thus be concluded that wherever there is capital, there is also waiting.

In order to classify capital as a primary factor of production, it is necessary to show not only that it has productivity distinct from that attributable to labor and land, but also that it is *scarce*. Capital would be of little or no concern in the study of economics if it were not scarce relative to the amount of it that could be used advantageously. On the other hand, if capital is scarce, it becomes an object of economy. To the degree that it is scarce, the more efficient known methods of production could not be adopted, and in order to economize the available supplies it would be necessary to adopt methods of less than optimum efficiency. Under these conditions any increase in the supply of capital, by making possible the adoption of more efficient methods, would lead to an increase in the social product; and conversely, any reduction in the supply of capital, necessitating the adoption of less efficient methods, would lead to a reduction in the social product. The question arises, then, Is capital scarce, and if so is it likely to be always and inevitably scarce?

Since capital is created through the process of waiting, or deferring consumption, the scarcity of capital, if there be such, must be explained in terms of a reluctance or inability on the part of the social group or its members to wait, i.e., to devote productive energies to the provision of goods for the distant future rather than for the immediate present. Capital becomes scarce only if the reluctance or inability to wait is so great as to prevent the accumulation of capital up to the level of abundance. But before approaching the problem of whether or not capital, or waiting, is scarce, it will be useful to digress briefly in order to formulate a precise statement of what is meant by *scarcity* as applied to capital.

A thing or service is said to be scarce whenever its quantity is so limited that more than the amount available could be employed to advantage. This principle may be used in determining whether or not capital is scarce, but its application to capital is subject to a peculiar modification. Capital goods represent the commitment of labor and land to future purposes. Consequently, the ultimate productivity of capital is always conjectural. The future—for an individual or a society—is shrouded in uncertainty. An expected want may not materialize, technical changes may nullify an investment; disease, death, fire, tornado, earthquake, or invasion may disrupt plans; or a thousand other contingencies may affect the outcome of the investment either (1) in terms of quantity of physical product or (2) in terms of the value of that product. The productivity of capital tends to be offset in part by the fact that future eventualities cannot be predicted with certainty. Consequently, the production of capital goods cannot be said to be productive unless the expected return, *after due allowance for error*, is greater than would be obtained from a similar application of labor and land to present purposes. Thus, whenever the quantity of capital is such that the additional product from further increments of capital is offset by expected losses due to unforeseeable contingencies, capital is no longer scarce. Under these conditions no additional capital could be used to ad-

vantage.[4] Thus the amount of capital that represents abundance
or scarcity depends not only upon the quantity of capital at
hand but also upon the character of the prevailing uncertainties. Some of these uncertainties may be part of the physical
environment and outside human control, whereas others may
be purely man-made, or institutional. Nevertheless, whatever
may be their source, the extent of these uncertainties determines the quantity of capital that can be effectively employed. In short, capital ceases to be scarce long before it
becomes abundant in terms of the amount that could advantageously be employed if there were perfect certainty regarding
the future.

Having indicated the meaning of scarcity as applied to
capital, let us now turn to the problem of whether, in view of
the conditions determining its supply, capital is likely to be
scarce.

Economists have traditionally assumed that capital is always and necessarily scarce. They have supported this assumption, overtly or by implication, by two arguments, both of
which are of questionable validity. First, it has been held that
the supply of capital is restricted by an inherent reluctance on
the part of human beings to wait. This idea has been developed
into a psychological theory of *time preference*, namely, that
people tend to value future goods less than present goods, and
are hence unwilling to produce for the future unless they expect thereby to obtain more goods than could be got by employing similar quantities of labor and land for immediate
purposes. In other words, waiting will take place only if capital
yields a return, and this it cannot do unless it is scarce. Hence,
it is asserted, the phenomenon of time preference ensures that
the supply of capital can never become abundant. Second, it is
argued that historically capital has always been scarce, and

---

[4] In so far as there are differences of opinion as to the extent of the uncertainties prevailing at a given time, there will also be differences of opinion as to the
quantity of capital that can be used to advantage. However, if the system is
viewed in retrospect, rather than in prospect, it will be possible to know what, in
fact, were the uncertainties facing the group at any given point in its history,
and it would be possible to determine whether, after taking loss (errors) into
account, capital was actually scarce (at the given time) in the sense that more of
it could have been used to advantage (at that time).

therefore it may be expected to continue to be scarce in the future. Let us now examine these two arguments.

The theory of time preference may be criticized on the ground that the preference for present over future goods is probably not an inherent quality of human beings. It may be true that persons or groups who are existing at or near the level of subsistence will usually prefer present to future goods in the sense that they will prefer living to dying. But for those who enjoy a comfortable surplus over and above the bare necessities for survival, the relative valuation of present and future goods will depend almost entirely upon cultural factors such as customary standards of consumption, the relative abundance of present goods, attitudes toward thrift and the accumulation of wealth, concern for the interests of children or future generations, the distribution of wealth and income, the degree of security of life and property.[5] For example, Weber and Tawney have shown that the rate of capital accumulation during the early capitalistic era was closely related to the ascetic attitudes of Protestantism.[6] It is easily possible that for given individuals, and even for whole societies, attitudes might be developed such that future goods would actually be preferred to present goods, or such that a higher value would be placed upon provision for future generations than provision for living individuals. Indeed, millions of persons in the United States are saving substantial sums without regard for a return on their capital and even when, risk taken into account, the return is less than zero. Thus, any categorical statement that capital is inevitably scarce because of the existence of an alleged impatience to consume cannot be accepted as universally tenable, though it may be reasonably valid under particular conditions, e.g., the expansionary phase of capitalism during the past two centuries.

The second defense for the view that capital is inevitably scarce is the historical argument that capital has, in fact, always been scarce and can reasonably be expected to remain so in the future. This argument is, however, highly misleading. In the first place, the assertion that capital has in the past always been

---

5 See pp. 229–231 for a more extended discussion of this point.

6 Max Weber, *The Protestant Ethic and the Spirit of Capitalism* (translated by T. Parsons), London, 1930. R. H. Tawney, *Religion and the Rise of Capitalism*, London, 1926.

scarce is by no means unquestionable. The scarcity of an object is always *relative* to the amount of it that can be used to advantage. But the amount of capital that can be used to advantage depends partly upon the extent of the prevailing uncertainties and partly upon the *technology*. Thus, the fact that primitive societies have possessed only small quantities of capital may signify, not necessarily a scarcity of capital, but rather a high degree of uncertainty plus a limited technology. In view of the hazards to which they were subjected and the limitations upon their knowledge of indirect methods and storage, it is possible that if these societies had possessed more capital they would have been unable to put it to good use.[7] This does not deny that capital has often or usually been scarce, but only suggests caution in jumping to the conclusion that it has, in fact, always been scarce. In the second place, the historical argument is faulty because it ignores the fact that the scarcity of capital in the past may at times have been due quite as much to the destructiveness of wars and to idleness during depressions as to any inherent inability or unwillingness to create capital.

Finally, third, the productive power of the present and foreseeable future so unimaginably exceeds that of the past as to make wholly irrelevant any conclusions about capital formation based upon a projection into the future of past conditions. In fact, it is only within the past two or three generations that technical advances have made possible in a few countries a comfortable surplus—over and above pressing creature needs—available for rapid capital formation. At the present time in the United States, the rate of capital formation at full employment is so great that the capital stock of the country could easily be doubled in the short span of twenty or thirty years.[8] It is by no means fantastic to look forward to the possibility of an abundance of capital. Indeed, there are some who argue that the inability of the capitalistic system to maintain full em-

---

[7] On this point it is also possible to take the reverse view that technology is limited by the availability of capital and that an addition to capital will call forth the technical discoveries to make use of it.

[8] According to estimates of Dr. Simon Kuznets (*National Income and Capital Formation*, National Bureau of Economic Research, New York, 1937), the total increase in the capital of the United States during the eleven years 1919 to 1929, at 1929 prices, was $84.3 billion (p. 48). At this rate, the capital stock could be doubled in twenty-eight years (p. 49).

ployment is due to the fact that capital becomes superabundant with a resulting shortage of *profitable* investment outlets for saved funds.

It may be concluded that capital is not invariably and inevitably scarce. Thus, in spite of the fact that capital is productive, it may be regarded as a primary factor of production only when it is, in fact, scarce. Otherwise, it becomes a free element, the use of which need not involve economizing.

Chapter 11

CAPITAL ADJUSTMENT

It has been pointed out that capital is created when labor and land are applied prior to the ultimate satisfactions which they are intended to provide. The origin of capital goods is production—production in advance of consumption. Capital goods are destroyed, on the other hand, through (1) dissipation in the productive process, as when machinery is worn out or supplies are exhausted, (2) consumption, as when pleasure automobiles are worn out or food is eaten, and (3) the mere "ravages" of time, as when individuals lose their faculties and die or buildings decay and disintegrate even though not used. Consequently, both the size and composition of the stock of capital goods varies depending upon the rate at which new capital goods are being produced and that at which existing capital goods are being used up.

The stock of capital goods (which we shall refer to as the *capital stock*) would remain intact and unchanged through time, if current production were organized so that new capital goods of each type were being provided at the same rate as that at which old ones were being used up. Under these conditions, the output of final goods would proceed at a constant rate, and the methods of producing these goods would remain unchanged. A cross section of the production system at any point of time would be exactly like that at another (with allowance for seasonal variations), except that the specific materials included in the capital stock would be continuously turning over as new capital goods were replacing those dissipated. It is obvious, however, that the capital stock need not remain stationary. It is likely to vary from time to time in composition, in magnitude, or in both. The composition of the capital stock varies if there is a change in the relative quantities of the constituent capital goods; the magnitude of the capital stock varies when there is an increase or decrease in the aggregate quantity of capital goods.

Changes in the Composition of the Capital Stock

The composition of the capital stock is subject to change with each variation in (1) the relative outputs of different goods, and (2) methods of production. First, if the output of any one good is expanded while that of another is contracted, a change in the composition of the capital stock is called for. There must be an increase in the quantities of the capital goods used in the expanded industry and a decrease in the quantity of those used in the contracted industry. Second, if a new technical method is adopted for producing any good, a change in the composition of the capital stock is likewise required. The types of capital goods appropriate to the new methods must displace those needed for the old method.

Whether the occasion for a change in the composition of the capital stock is a variation in product or method, the change can be brought about only if the production of some capital goods exceeds depreciation while the depreciation of others exceeds production. For example, if the output of housing is to be decreased while the supply of automotive transportation is to be increased, the production of new houses must occur at a slower rate than the depreciation of existing ones, and the production of new automobiles must proceed at a more rapid rate than the depreciation of old ones. As a result of the two simultaneous processes, the supply of houses will diminish and that of automobiles increase. In this way the composition of the capital stock will change. Similarly, if machine methods are to become more important, relative to hand technique, in the manufacture of shoes, the production of new shoe machines must proceed at a more rapid rate than the depreciation of the old, and the production of hand tools must cease or proceed more slowly than depreciation. As a result, the capital stock will include a relatively more generous amount of shoe machines and a smaller supply of hand tools.

Changes in the Magnitude of the Capital Stock

Similarly, the magnitude of the capital stock is likely to vary with each change (1) in the relative output of different goods or (2) in methods of production. First, an increase in the capital stock becomes necessary if there is an expansion in the output of goods requiring lengthy and roundabout methods (e.g., wine, apples, or housing), accompanied by a corresponding decline in the output of goods which can be efficiently produced by more direct methods (e.g., grape juice, cabbages, or haircuts). Conversely, a relative decrease in the production of goods requiring lengthy methods, other things being equal, tends toward a reduction in the stock of capital. Second, an increase in the quantity of capital becomes necessary as a result of the adoption of more indirect methods of production, for example, the replacement of hand methods by machine processes; and a decrease in the quantity of capital is associated with the adoption of more direct methods. Let us now examine in greater detail the effect of these changes on the magnitude of the capital stock.

Assume that the supply of labor and land for an entire society is given, and that these resources are being employed so that new capital goods are being produced at a rate just sufficient to replace the old being used up, and the stock of capital goods and the output of final goods remains unchanged through time. Let us examine, one at a time, the effects upon the quantity of capital of several hypothetical changes in this static state.

First, suppose that it is decided to increase the production of apples, a commodity which necessarily requires a lengthy productive process, and to decrease that of cabbage, which can be efficiently produced by a much shorter process. Clearly, in order to increase the output of apples, it will be necessary to start orchards the product of which will begin to be realized only after five or ten years, and the entire product of which will be forthcoming only during a period of fifty or a hundred years. In order to plant and cultivate the orchards, it will be necessary to withdraw labor and land from the cultivation of cabbage, the product of which would have been consumed within a single year. But when used to develop orchards, the product of the labor and land will not be dissipated or consumed in the near future. Rather, the new plantings will continue to bear fruit for many years to come. Inasmuch as the production of capital goods will have exceeded the dissipation or consumption of capital goods, the capital of society is increased. However, in order to obtain this capital, i.e., to provide for the production of apples in the remote future, society has sacrificed the possibility of obtaining cabbage in the near future. Moreover, as a result of the shift from the production of cabbage to apples, the time interval or "waiting" between the applications of labor and land and the completion of the products has been extended.

Second, suppose that it is decided to substitute machine methods for hand methods in the manufacture of shoes. In order to produce the new shoe machines it will be necessary to withdraw labor and land from other uses. This labor and land might be drawn from many different sources including shoe production; but for purposes of illustration, let us assume that it is drawn from the rubber-tire industry. This will tend to reduce the output of tires because, unless tire production is maintained continuously at all stages, output cannot be maintained indefinitely.[1] As a result of the withdrawal of land and labor from the tire industry, the quantity of capital goods employed in that industry must be lessened since current replacements will now fall short of current depreciation. The use of this same labor and land for the production of shoe machines, however, will tend to build up the capital in the shoe industry, because the production of new shoe machines will now exceed the depreciation of those already in use.

The total capital stock of society will not be increased by this transfer, however, unless the addition of new shoe machines more than offsets the decline in capital devoted to the tire industry. Such an increase will occur only on the condition that the labor and land transferred to the shoe industry are employed, on the average, at a relatively *earlier* stage in the productive process than if they had been employed in the tire industry. (By "earlier" is meant more in advance of completion of the product.)[2]

---

1 Allowance must be made for the very considerable durability of some types of capital goods. For example, tire production could be maintained for a substantial period without the production of new factory buildings.

2 To illustrate, if the labor and land in question is valued at $100,000, and

Discontinuities in the Growth of Capital

One aspect of the process by which increases in the capital stock are brought about has not been touched upon, namely, the tendency for the increase in capital goods to occur irregularly and in waves. For example, as a result of a decision to produce more apples, as in the above illustration, the planting of new orchards would soon provide an ample stock of apple trees to meet the new requirements. Once the number of trees had been built up to the required amount, further plantings would be needed only at the rate necessary to offset the current destruction of old trees. In other words, during the period of building up the stock of apple trees, plantings would likely be greater than would be necessary in order to maintain the supply at the new permanent level. As a result, there would tend to be a temporary surge of planting during the period of increase with a following decline in plantings to the permanent amount required to offset depreciation. The new permanent level, however, would be greater than the original level because current depreciation would be larger with the greater supply of apple trees. Thus, at the end of the period of growth some of the re-

---

if, on the average, it had been employed in the tire industry three years in advance of completion of the product, the continuous employment of this labor and land in the tire industry would have resulted in capital goods of $300,000. If, on the other hand, the same labor and land are applied continuously to the production of shoe machines, on the average, five years in advance of consumption, the increase of capital in the shoe industry will ultimately be $500,000. Thus, with the transfer from more direct to less direct uses, the total capital of society will have been increased. On the other hand, had the increase in production of shoe machinery been accomplished with resources from industries where they would have been applied, on the average, less directly than in the shoe industry, the total capital stock would have been diminished. It is clear, then, assuming a given supply of labor and land, that the stock of capital can be increased as a result of the adoption of a more lengthy method only if, as a result, labor and land are transferred from more direct to less direct uses, that is to say, if the average interval between application of factors and completion of the product is lengthened. And it is also evident that such a lengthening in the productive process represents a postponement of consumption—an increase in "waiting."

An increase in the capital stock whether occasioned by a change in the relative outputs of different goods or by the adoption of new methods always involves (1) a lengthening of the average time interval between application of labor and land and completion of the product and, therefore, an increase in waiting, and (2) the production of new capital goods in excess of the dissipation of old ones. Without these two conditions, the increase in the capital stock cannot occur.

sources diverted to the production of new apple orchards could be returned to other pursuits, e.g., producing cabbage.[3] The same line of reasoning applies when the increase in the supply of capital goods is occasioned by the adoption of a more lengthy method.

The irregularity in the growth of capital goods tends to be accentuated in the case of very durable capital goods. A considerable period may elapse before any replacement is necessary, and replacements may then be concentrated within a short period. For example, if shoe machines are serviceable, on the average, for ten years, and only two years of production is required to build up the required supply, no further production is needed for about eight years. But at this time the entire supply must be replaced within a period of almost two years. Thus the production of shoe machines would be carried on rapidly for only two years during each decade. In practice, this variability, though significant, is lessened by the fact that not all the machines will have precisely the same life. Some may last only four years and others as long, perhaps, as fifteen years, so that the replacement of the first batch of machines will not be concentrated entirely within a span of two years. Moreover, replacement of the second batch will tend to be even more diffused, and so on, until finally the production of shoe machines would be stabilized, in the absence of intervening changes, at a more or less constant rate per year.

That growth of capital goods tends to occur in waves or spurts appears to be a conclusion of rather general validity. It would be only in unusual circumstances that the growth of capital would occur steadily and at a uniform rate. It might occasionally happen that a shift in demand would occur slowly and at a more or less uniform rate over a very long period, but this is most improbable. And it is even more unlikely that new

---

3 It is, of course, conceivable, if an infinite period of time were allowed, that the supply of capital goods could be increased without necessitating a reduction in the output of the capital good when the supply had reached its ultimate level. This could be accomplished by immediately stabilizing production at an amount that would be just sufficient to offset depreciation when the supply had reached its ultimate level. As long as the supply was less than this amount, the rate of production would exceed current depreciation so that the supply of the capital goods would grow. As the supply increased, however, current depreciation would become greater, so that the *rate* of growth would decline; nevertheless, growth would continue until, at infinity, the goal would be reached.

methods would be introduced gradually over a very long period.

Because of the irregularity in the growth of particular capital goods, it cannot be concluded, however, that the general expansion of all kinds of capital goods necessarily involves similar discontinuity. Many different kinds of capital goods are produced simultaneously. A spurt in the production of one may be offset by a decline in the production of another so that the growth of the capital stock may be more steady than that of any particular capital good. This means that an increase in the supply of any one capital good may be achieved without removing resources bodily from more direct uses, transferring them to less direct uses, and then shifting them back again to more direct uses. Instead, in a growing society a certain portion of the social resources can be regularly and continuously devoted to the building up of capital. These resources can be shunted from the production of one type of capital good to another, and the need for transferring resources from direct to indirect uses and back again can be avoided. Nevertheless, experience shows that capital expansion often occurs in waves. Indeed, a leading characteristic of business cycles is variability in the rate of production of capital goods.

The Growth of Labor and Land in Relation to the Growth of Capital

In Chapter 9 it was shown that the amount of capital required in any one process, assuming that given quantities of labor and land are employed, is proportional to the amount of time involved in the process, i.e., to the average interval between the applications of labor and land and the completion of the product. This relationship holds also for the entire supply of capital employed by society. Assuming a given supply of labor and land, the aggregate amount of capital required by society will be proportional to the average time involved in all the productive processes taken together. An increase in capital can occur only through a lengthening of the average production period—either through a change in relative outputs of different goods or through a change in methods. However, if the supply of labor, land, or both is increasing, it is possible to achieve an increase in capital without any changes in the relative outputs of different goods or in methods. An addition to the supply of labor and land represents an increase in aggregate productive power, making possible the production of more goods. In order to bring about this increase in output of final goods, it is necessary to enlarge the supply of capital goods. Any increase in the output of final goods can be sustained only if there is a corresponding increase in production at the earlier stages.[4] Thus, to give effect to the increased supply of labor and land, it is necessary to bring about a corresponding increase in the supply of capital. Hence, it is necessary for the production of new capital goods to exceed the dissipation of old ones. In a growing society, therefore, a larger proportion of resources must be devoted to the production of capital goods than in a stable society of similar size.

---

[4] In practice, a change in the supply of labor and land would likely cause a change in the available proportions of various types of labor and land which would probably call for changes in method of production.

Chapter 12

PRODUCTION AND CAPITAL: SUMMARY

We now draw together the principal conclusions of Part III (Chapters 6 to 11) on Production and Capital.

The two fundamental laws of production are: (1) Different types of goods require different methods of production involving different types and combinations of the factors; and (2) In the production of any particular good, different combinations of the factors will yield different results in terms of quantity of output.

The second of these principles refers to the functional relation between the quantity of factors and quantity of output. The more precise functional relation is expressed in the principle of diminishing returns: (1) If the *proportions* in which the factors are employed remain unchanged, output will vary directly and proportionally with the quantity of factors employed; and (2) When several factors are combined in a given process, if the amount of any one factor applied in a given way be varied, assuming the other factors to be held constant, (a) an increase in the variable factor will result in a more than proportional increase in the physical product up to a critical point designated the point of diminishing returns, (b) further increases in the variable factor beyond this point will result in a less than proportional increase in physical product, until finally (c) additional increases in the variable factor will add nothing to product or even cause it to diminish.

When two or more factors are employed in a given productive process, that combination where lies the point of diminishing returns for one of the factors will also be at the point of constant or decreasing total output for the others taken together. From this it may be deduced that increasing returns for one factor occur simultaneously with decreasing total output for the others, and therefore that it is economical to employ the factors in such proportions that all are subject to diminishing returns.

By determining the *marginal product* of any factor, it is possible to identify its contribution to the total product. Thus a basis is provided for the rational combination of factors. The portion of total product imputable to any factor is equal to its marginal product multiplied by the number of units employed. The resulting imputed products of the several factors engaged in a given process, when added, are equal to the total product resulting from the particular combination of the factors.

The most advantageous combination of the factors is that in which their several marginal products are proportional to their respective prices. Such proportionality is achieved when the factors are employed in the least costly combination.

Inasmuch as production is a time-consuming process, the uninterrupted continuance of production presupposes the existence of capital goods which are the present manifestation of prior productive efforts that have not yet been brought to fruition. These capital goods are divided into two classes: (1) material and (2) nonmaterial. The material capital goods consist of physical things such as buildings, machines, inventories, etc., and the nonmaterial capital goods consist of human attributes derived from past productive efforts which we call education or culture transmission. Capital goods are distinguished by the fact that they are (1) produced and (2) depreciating; the production of capital goods is thus a regular and ever-recurrent part of the continuous process of production.

The amount of capital required in any productive process (assuming that a given quantity of labor and land is employed) is proportional to the amount of *time* involved (time is defined as the weighted average interval between applications of labor and land and completion of the product). In general, the more efficient methods of production are relatively lengthy; consequently, a condition of the adoption of the more efficient methods is that capital be employed. In this sense, part of the product of relatively indirect methods may be attributed to capital. Empirically, it appears that capital is subject to the same laws of production that apply to labor and land. When combined with fixed quantities of labor and land, successive increases in capital yield more than proportional increases in product up to a certain point; further increases in capital yield less than proportional increases in product; and finally, still further increases add nothing to or may even detract from product. The law of diminishing returns as applied to capital, however, is somewhat less rigorous and definite than when applied to labor and land. Moreover, capital is even less susceptible to precise physical measurement than labor.

The stock of capital goods of a society will remain constant in all respects if the production of each type of capital good keeps pace exactly with the depreciation of that capital good. The stock of capital goods will tend to vary in composition, in magnitude, or both when rates of production and of depreciation are unequal. These changes will likely occur whenever there is a variation in the relative outputs of different goods or in the methods of production. An increase in the magnitude of the capital fund can occur only (1) if there is an increase in the average length of the productive processes, or (2) if there is an increase in the quantity of labor and land.

This completes the discussion of Part III on Production and Capital. The purpose of this and the preceding several chapters has been to state general principles concerning the physical process of production. These principles are part of the ultimate conditions which must be taken into account by all societies in the allocation of resources for the purpose of achieving human ends.

PART IV

Social Economy

Chapter 13

THE CONCEPT OF ECONOMY

We have now completed our preliminary examination of the economic system and of its institutional and physical foundations.

The economic system was defined as the complex of social institutions by which the use of the means of production is controlled and regulated. The specific functions of the economic system were found to be fivefold: (1) to select the personnel who are to administer the means of production, (2) to regulate the supply of the factors of production, (3) to determine what specific goods shall be produced and in what amounts, (4) to control the manner in which the factors of production shall be organized, and (5) to regulate the use of the goods produced.

In the performance of these functions a society is inevitably subject to two basic conditions or limitations of a purely physical nature. The group is limited, first, by the quantity of its primary means of production,[1] and second, by the character of the physical laws of production. These two conditions together determine what is within the realm of possibility for the group—what are its productive potentialities.

Within the bounds set by these physical restrictions, however, the possible ways in which a society may use its resources are almost infinitely diverse. The precise manner in which a given society uses its means of production will depend in large part upon the character of its economic institutions, and this in turn will depend upon the historic experiences of the group from which its institutons have emerged.

The great social significance of the task accomplished through the economic system is to be explained largely by the fact that the means of production are capable of many different

---

1 Assuming population given. See page 4, footnote 5.

uses—thus necessitating some sort of provision for selecting, from among the numerous possibilities, the particular uses to be made of the available means. For example, a given plot of land, which may be capable of employment as a wheat farm, a pasture for cattle, a hunting preserve, a factory site, or for any one of a hundred other purposes, must be allotted to a specific use. Or a given human being, who might conceivably serve in the capacity of plumber, carpenter, lawyer, merchant, musician, or in any one of several thousand occupations, must be assigned to one specific job. The fact that these and other means of production are capable of an almost infinite variety of alternative uses inevitably raises the problem of how these resources ought to be used, i.e., what use of them is *best* or *most desirable* or *most economical*. This problem is of crucial significance in view of the obvious fact that the well-being of the members of the group depends largely upon the manner in which its means of production are employed, in the sense that some uses of them may contribute vastly more than others to the achievement of the ends of the group or to the ends of the component individuals.

The following several chapters will be devoted to the question of what constitutes the *best* or most economical use of resources. The importance of this investigation can hardly be overestimated, because the idea of *social economy* is essential not only to an understanding of the economic system, but also to the intelligent appraisal of programs for modifying the economic system and to the comparative evaluation of different types of systems. The idea of economy is, however, a tenuous one, enshrouded in unanswered—perhaps unanswerable—issues, and based upon precarious assumptions. This very elusiveness, however, enhances the importance of this inquiry, because it is well to understand the limitations of the concept and the dangers associated with its uninformed application.

Social economy may be defined simply as the best or optimum use of the means of production.

The concept of economy, as applied to the affairs of a society, is quite consistent with the everyday usage of the term "economy" as applied to personal or business affairs. We ordinarily think of economy as the avoidance of waste or the careful use of goods and resources. By waste we mean merely the dissipation of useful things without obtaining the satisfactions that could have been derived from them, i.e., the failure to use them in the best or optimum or most economical manner. Similarly, when we refer to the careful or sparing or frugal use of goods or resources, we mean the use of things in such a way as to get the most out of them, i.e., the use of them in the best or optimum or most economical manner.

When the term "economy" is defined as the best use of resources (whether from the individual or social point of view), the concept is disconcertingly indefinite, because "best" is a purely relative term. Any given use of resources can be judged bad, indifferent, good, better, or best only in relation to some definite *end*. From the point of view of an individual, for example, lavish expenditures on the entertainment of friends would represent a bad or uneconomical use of resources *if* the end in view were saving for old age. The same use of resources, however, might be economical *if* the purpose were to gain prestige through "conspicuous waste." Similarly, from the social point of view, the use of the means of production to provide a bath tub for every family would be judged a bad use of means if the all-engrossing end were national defense against a foreign aggressor. This same use of resources might be considered good, however, if the end was the encouragement of personal cleanliness and health. Thus, any judgment of the economy or dis-economy of a given use of resources must always presuppose specific ends. The degree of economy achieved by a society in the use of its resources may be judged, for example, in terms of ends as diverse as military power, enhancement of the prestige and authority of a monarch, gratification of a privileged minority, eternal salvation for the members of the group, artistic creation, the maximum growth of population, or the "general welfare." For each of these ends a different use of means would be most appropriate. Thus there can be no universally valid statement as to precisely what constitutes an economical or uneconomical use of resources. The idea of economy is relative to ends.

In countries where the liberal tradition has flourished, it has become almost axiomatic that the most desirable goal in the use of resources is the attainment of maximum aggregate satisfaction for the individual members of the group. The use of resources is judged chiefly in terms of this particular end.[2] For example, the assertion that a certain policy will lead to the uneconomic use of resources implies that aggregate satisfaction would thereby be diminished; and conversely, the statement that a particular policy is economical implies that an increase of aggregate satisfaction would be forthcoming. This aggregate, it should be emphasized, is regarded as the sum total of the amounts of satisfaction enjoyed by all the members of the group taken together.[3]

In the following discussion of social economy in the use of resources, the assumption throughout is that maximum aggregate satisfaction *is* the end, and the terms "economy" and "maximum aggregate satisfaction" are used interchangeably. It should be emphasized, however, that maximum aggregate satisfaction represents only one possible end, and that a similar discussion might be carried on assuming any one of a number of different ends; for example, world domination by the United States, or propagation of the Buddhist faith.

---

[2] However, maximum aggregate satisfaction from the use of resources (in the narrow sense) may be deliberately sacrificed in the interest of "higher" goals such as the extension of human liberty or the development of the human personality.

[3] The following are two typical statements where economy and maximum aggregate satisfaction are regarded as identical.

". . . by economy is meant the employment of our resources with prudence and discretion, so that we may derive from them the maximum net return of utility." J. N. Keynes, *The Scope and Method of Political Economy*, 4th ed., London, 1930, p. 1.

"It is generally agreed that the aim of a good civilization is to provide the maximum satisfactions from life for the maximum proportion of the whole population." *New Republic*, Dec. 9, 1940, p. 777.

Chapter 14

MEASUREMENT OF SATISFACTIONS

The concept of maximum aggregate satisfaction is essentially quantitative. It refers to the maximization of a quantity of satisfactions to be enjoyed by the people of a society. Consequently, if the concept is to have practical significance—if it is not to be a mere phrase devoid of content—there must be some means whereby quantities of satisfaction can be made susceptible to measurement. Without the possibility of such measurement, there would be no practicable way of determining the degree to which, in any given situation, maximum aggregate satisfaction is approached, or of ascertaining what particular use of resources would, in fact, lead to maximum satisfaction. Thus, the validity of any statement regarding the conditions that are necessary to the attainment of economy is dependent upon the availability of a suitable technique for reducing satisfactions to quantitative terms. The problem of this chapter, then, is to develop a practicable means of *measuring* satisfactions. As will be shown, under certain assumptions *prices* may be used for this purpose.

Social economy (maximum aggregate satisfaction) is possible only under two conditions. First, each individual must use whatever means are at his disposal in the manner that will yield him the greatest amount of satisfaction obtainable from those means. In order to accomplish this, he must arrange his affairs so that he may provide for satisfactions having greater importance or urgency ahead of those having less significance; he must make sure that no lesser satisfaction is provided so long as greater ones are neglected.[1] Second, the means of the entire soci-

---

[1] This first condition is based upon two assumptions regarding human behavior. First, it is assumed that the actions of human beings, at least in the economic sphere, are designed for the attainment of expected ends, that human

ety must be apportioned among its individual members in such a way that aggregate satisfactions will be maximized. That is to say, the means must be distributed so that all of the more important satisfactions for all individuals are provided ahead of the less important satisfactions of any individual; in other words, that no less important satisfaction shall be made available to any individual so long as more important satisfactions of other individuals are denied.

If either of these two conditions is not met, the aggregate of satisfactions will be something less than maximum. Individuals will be either "wasting" or otherwise "misusing" the means at their command so that optimum results are not obtained, or the division of means among the members of the group will permit favored individuals to obtain minor or even trifling satisfactions when other persons are forced to do without significant or even major necessities.

With these two conditions in mind, let us now turn to the problem of measuring satisfactions in terms of price. First we shall tackle the problem of measuring the various satisfactions experienced by *one* individual, and later we shall deal with the more delicate problem of measuring the satisfactions obtained by *different* individuals.

One Individual

Assume a society in which money is in general use, where each individual is given his means in the generalized form of money income, where prices are placed on available goods, and

---

conduct is purposive. This is in agreement with the common-sense view—certainly individuals *believe* that they are pursuing known ends, and generally they behave *as if* they were. Indeed, the fact that most economic decisions are inevitably oriented toward the future—often the very distant future—lends support to the validity of this assumption. If individual conduct were not purposive, the idea of economy or of efficiency would be virtually unthinkable.

Second, it is assumed that the individual is able to compare the desirability of different ends, and the necessary sacrifices in achieving these ends. This implies that the individual must be able (1) to measure the relative importance of various possible satisfactions in the sense of being able to determine which are more and which less urgent and (2) to judge the efficacy of means to the attainment of these satisfactions. This, of course, by no means implies that he actually achieves the result he is seeking. It means only that he *attempts* to manage his activities on the basis of what he conceives his interests to be.

where the individual is allowed formal freedom of choice in the expenditure of his income for various goods. Let it be assumed further that each individual is subject to the principle of diminishing utility, namely, that as he extends his purchases (expressed as a rate per period of time) of any one good, the increment of satisfaction added by each successive unit of the good tends to decline.[2] Finally, assume that each individual distributes the expenditure of his income among different goods in such a way as to obtain as much satisfaction for himself as possible under the established system of prices. Under this elaborate array of assumptions, the individual will first arrange to provide the good which he needs most urgently; having obtained a certain quantity of this good, additional units will yield less satisfaction than could be obtained if the same money were used to buy the good of next urgency; so he will turn to the purchase of this second good; having obtained some of the second good, he will then start acquiring the next in order of urgency; and so on. When he has extended his purchases so that his entire income is exhausted, he will have arranged his expenditures so that the *last penny* devoted to any one purpose adds exactly as much to his total satisfaction as the last penny spent for every other purpose. So long as he has failed to "balance his margins" in this manner, he will have obtained something less than maximum satisfaction. By increasing his expenditures on goods for which the "last penny" yields relatively large satisfactions and decreasing his outlay on goods for which the yield from the last penny spent is relatively small, he will be able to increase his satisfactions until, when the margins are balanced, the maximum amount of satisfaction obtainable with his income will have been achieved, and he will then have no incentive to alter his budgetary scheme.

To illustrate, a starving, naked, homeless individual may regard the appeasement of hunger as the greatest of his needs. But give him enough food to satisfy his immediate hunger and to provide for a few meals in the future, and he will regard the provision of clothing as his most important end. Given raiment, he will turn to the quest of shelter. Given everything to satisfy creature needs, he will seek prestige, social position, friends,

---

2 See pp. 45–46.

education, religion, security, excitement, new experiences, or power. If he uses too much of his income for one purpose, the returns from the surplus of money used in this way will be less than could have been attained if the same money had been used in another way; if too little income is used for a given purpose, the return from money applied in this way will be greater than from similar money used for other purposes. He obtains a maximum of satisfaction only when his income is apportioned among various uses so that the satisfaction obtained from one penny in any one use will be equal to the return obtained from one penny in every other use. Otherwise, he will gain by reallocating his income.

In the actual world, this fine balancing of margins can be only roughly approximated for the reason that many goods are acquired only in large "lumps," so that a nice adjustment of the relative quantities of different goods purchased is not possible. For example, one must buy a whole automobile or none at all; one cannot purchase one half or one tenth of an automobile. Hence, it is unlikely that the last penny spent on automobiles would always give a reward exactly equal to that obtained from the last penny spent on, let us say, furniture or ice skates or butter. This "lumpiness" of goods, however, does not alter the fundamental principle involved, but only provides a technical obstacle to the precise realization of the principle. So far as is possible under actual conditions, each individual (assuming that he seeks maximum satisfaction from the expenditure of his income) will strive persistently toward the attainment of balanced margins. If all goods were infinitely divisible, in the sense that any one could be obtained in any conceivable quantity, then the margins could be exactly balanced. To the extent that goods are not so divisible, such balancing cannot be completely attained.

If this "imperfection" is ignored and perfect homogeneity assumed, an individual, in seeking maximum satisfactions, must arrange his expenditures so that the satisfactions acquired from the last penny spent on each good are equal. From this it follows that the amount of satisfaction obtained from the final unit of each of the various goods acquired will be *proportional to the prices of these goods*.[3] For example, if the price of bread is ten

---

[3] This conclusion applies strictly only if the units of the various goods are infinitesimal.

cents a loaf and of eggs twenty cents a dozen, it may be inferred that an individual will adjust his purchases of the two goods so that the addition of one dozen eggs will add twice as much satisfaction as the addition of one loaf of bread—or that the loss of one dozen eggs will diminish satisfaction twice as much as the loss of one loaf of bread. Thus, on the assumption that an individual attempts to maximize the satisfaction obtained from the expenditure of his income, the prices of the various goods purchased may be regarded as measures of the satisfactions obtained by him from the *marginal units* of the goods. Any changes in the prices will, of course, alter his scheme of expenditures, causing him to reduce his purchases of those goods for which prices have risen and to increase his expenditures for those for which prices have fallen. Also, any change in his tastes will cause him to alter his expenditure pattern. After adjustment to any new set of prices, however, the satisfactions obtained from the marginal units of the various goods will again be proportional to the prices of these goods. Thus the prices paid by an individual, whatever they may be, constitute a measure of the marginal satisfactions to him of the various goods he purchases.

Different Individuals

Let us now turn to the problem of measuring the marginal satisfactions obtained from the various goods by *different* individuals. This immediately raises the troublesome question of whether or not it is possible to compare, meaningfully, the satisfactions or other states of feeling experienced by different individuals. For example, is it possible to know whether Peter would obtain more satisfaction from a new bicycle than Thomas would derive from a new set of carpentry tools? Or whether a rich man will get more pleasure from feeding sirloin steaks to his dog than a hungry poor man would get from eating these steaks? Or which of two boys at a dinner table will get the most satisfaction from eating a single remaining piece of candy? In practice, particularly within families, decisions are made every day involving comparisons of the amounts of satisfaction received by different individuals. The identical problem appears in society at large, whenever the issue is raised as to how incomes ought to be distributed among individuals. Since satisfactions can be experienced only by the person receiving them, there is no strictly objective method of making such interpersonal comparisons. As Thoreau said, "Who shall say what prospect life offers to another? Could a greater miracle take place than for us to look through each others eyes for an instant?" [4]

For a moment, however, let us waive the problem of interpersonal comparisons [5] and assume, tentatively, that incomes are in fact distributed among individuals so that the aggregate of satisfactions obtained with these incomes is maximized. Under such a distribution of income, the amount of satisfaction acquired by any one individual from the last penny of his income would be equal to the amount of satisfaction obtained by every other individual from the last penny spent by him. In other words, the distribution of income which maximizes aggregate satisfaction is such that the marginal satisfaction from income is equal for all persons. Any other distribution of income would yield less than maximum satisfaction, because it would always be possible to increase aggregate satisfactions by taking income away from those whose marginal satisfactions were relatively small and giving it to persons whose marginal satisfactions were relatively large. That which was taken away would be less than that which was added on. [6]

Now, assuming (1) that incomes are distributed so that the final penny of income received by one person yields exactly as much satisfaction as the final penny received by each other person, and (2) that each individual budgets his expenditures so that the final penny spent for one commodity yields exactly as much satisfaction as that derived from the final penny spent for each other commodity, it follows that the satisfaction derived from the final penny expended by any person on any commodity is exactly equal to the satisfaction derived from (a) the final penny spent on any other good by that person, (b) the final penny spent on that good by any other person, and (c) the final penny spent on any other good by any other person. If all the "final pennies" spent by all persons yield equal amounts of satisfaction, it follows (assuming that quantities of goods are meas-

---

4 *Walden*, Riverside Library edition, Houghton Mifflin, New York, 1929, p. 11.
5 See pp. 200–210.
6 As will be shown in Chapter 19, this does not necessarily imply *equal* distribution of incomes.

ured in small units) that the amount of satisfaction obtained by any individual from the final unit of any *good* will be in proportion to the price of that good. Hence, *price becomes a measure of the marginal satisfaction to any person of any good.*[7]

For example, if the price of bread is ten cents a loaf, it may be inferred that each individual will regulate his purchases of bread so that the additional satisfaction obtained from the final loaf purchased (marginal satisfaction) will be exactly equal to that obtained by all other individuals from the final increment purchased by them. And if, at the same time, eggs are twenty cents a dozen, the marginal satisfaction from one dozen eggs for all persons is just twice that from one loaf of bread. It must not be overlooked, however, that this conclusion is valid only on the basis of two important assumptions, neither of which is necessarily conformable to conditions of the actual world: (1) that each individual spend his income in a manner which will yield maximum satisfaction, and (2) that income is distributed so that the final penny received by any one person yields as much satis‹ faction as the final penny received by each other person. The detailed discussion of the significance of these two assumptions is reserved for Chapters 19 and 20.

---

[7] Cf. Alfred Marshall, *Principles of Economics,* 8th ed., London, 1930, p. 15: "The advantage which economics has over other branches of social science appears then to arise from the fact that its special field of work gives rather larger opportunities for exact methods than any other branch. It concerns itself chiefly with those desires, aspirations and other affections of human nature, the outward manifestations of which appear as incentives to action in such a form that the force or quantity of the incentives can be estimated and measured with some approach to accuracy; and which therefore are in some degree amenable to treatment by scientific machinery."

Chapter 15

PRINCIPLES OF PRICING FOR SOCIAL ECONOMY

In the preceding chapter it was shown that, under certain important assumptions, the prices to which consumers are subject provide a measure of their marginal satisfactions. With this principle as a foundation, it is possible to formulate a set of rules which must be followed if a correct system of prices is to be established, i.e., a system of prices which is consistent with the most economical use of goods and of factors.

Pricing Principles for the Short Run

Production is on the whole an unwieldy process subject only to gradual change and adjustment. This is due primarily to the fact that most production is indirect and requires elaborate preparatory activities. At any given time, therefore, the supply of goods is largely determined by prior decisions and is more or less fixed. Thus, in the short run, consumption must be adjusted to already determined production, although in the longer run, to be sure, production must be adjusted to consumption.

In view of the fact that the supply of goods is relatively fixed at any given time, a part of the economic problem is to fix such prices on these goods as will ensure their being used to advantage.

The first rule to be followed is that there must be a uniform price for all the units of any single good. The price of each bushel of potatoes, for example, must be the same as that of every other bushel. If it were not so, some individuals would be charged a higher price for potatoes than others; this would result in violating the principle that greater satisfactions must have precedence over lesser ones. The marginal satisfaction from potatoes on the part of individuals paying a higher price would be relatively great because, in view of the high price, their purchases would be curtailed. On the other hand, the marginal satisfaction from potatoes of individuals paying a lower price would be relatively small. If the price were made uniform, on the other hand, the first group would increase their purchases and the second group would curtail theirs. As a result of these changes, the gain in satisfaction to the first would be greater than the loss of satisfaction to the second. Hence, assuming that price is a valid measure of marginal satisfactions, the placing of uniform prices on all units of each good is a necessary prerequisite to the attainment of economy.[1]

The second principle is that the uniform prices on the various goods must be established at those levels which will equate the amounts of the various goods that people will want to purchase (demand) with the amounts available (supply). The demand of each individual for the several goods will depend, of course, upon the prices of these goods, any change in any of the prices inducing him to reallocate his expenditures. At any given set of prices, however, each individual is able to decide how much of each good he will want to purchase; and the aggregate of these individual demands constitutes the total demand, under this particular set of prices, for each of the various goods. Thus, under the assumption that the supply of each of the goods is fixed, this principle requires the establishment of a system of prices such that demand will be equated with this supply.

This set of prices will be more advantageous than any other; it will lead to the most economical use of the given supply of goods. Suppose, for example, that the price of a good were set so that the amount people would wish to buy was greater than the supply. In this case, certain individuals would be able to obtain a portion of the good at a price lower than other indi-

---

[1] Price discrimination may be justified on the ground that it may compensate for an "unjust" distribution of money income. If lower prices are charged to those whose money income is regarded as deficient and higher prices to those with superfluous incomes, then the *real* income of the first group is increased and that of the second group decreased. This type of discrimination is common in modern society. For example, the lower income groups are sometimes charged a smaller rent, proportionately, for their houses than are other groups; similarly, the poorer classes are given medical care at lower rates than the rich; undernourished children are given free milk; etc.

viduals would be willing to give for that same portion. This would constitute a violation of the principle that lesser satisfactions should be denied until satisfactions of greater importance are provided for. There are likely also to be incidental wastes and disorders involved when prices are set so that demand exceeds supply. The competition of buyers to obtain a portion of the limited supplies is likely to lead to unnecessary hurry in order to reach the source of supply before the entire amount is sold out. This in turn is likely to require queuing up with endless waiting, as in retail shops of Russia during the early thirties or everywhere during the war. In more extreme cases, the shortage of goods might lead to physical combat among rival would-be purchasers—witness the spectacle of women competing for ninety-eight-cent hats around the bargain counter of a department store. Moreover, with prices so low that demand is in excess of supply, the more aggressive and ruthless members of society by "barging in" would be able to get large amounts of the good and hence profiteer at the expense of the more meek and mild individuals.

On the other hand, if prices were set so that supply would exceed the demand, there would be no problem of disorder or of unsatisfied buyers at the prevailing price. Instead, buyers would be unwilling to purchase the entire supply, and the surplus would simply go unused. If the commodity was perishable, it would be destroyed, if nonperishable, it would merely accumulate in the hands of sellers. In any event, the aim of economy would not be achieved since a portion of the good would be used in a manner that would yield no satisfaction, whereas if it had been made available under different terms, it could have satisfied human wants.

To conclude, the attainment of economy requires that prices be set so that the demand for each good is exactly equal to the available supply. Then there will be no unsatisfied buyers and the entire supply of each good will flow into consumption in an orderly manner.[2]

---

2 Disorder has sometimes occurred when the prices of necessities have risen to such heights that they have been practically unattainable, as during a blockade or crop failure. This is usually a demonstration of the people protesting against profiteering or against their inability to compete with the richer members of the group, or perhaps simply against the inescapable consequences of the situa-

To summarize, the economical use of a given supply of goods requires that uniform prices be placed upon them so that the amount of each of the various goods that people will wish to buy (demand) will be exactly equal to the amounts available (supply).

Pricing Principles for the Longer Run

Let us now take a longer view, dropping the assumption that the supply of goods is fixed and postulating instead that the supply of the primary factors of production is fixed.[3] The problem is to establish a system of prices which will lead to the most economical use of these factors. We shall assume throughout this chapter that the factors are divisible so that they can be combined in any desired proportions. Whereas, under the preceding assumption, the solution consisted in placing uniform prices on each good which would equate the demand for it to the available supply, in the present case the solution is, generally, to place uniform prices on each *factor* which will equate the demand for it to the available supply. The solution for the longer run is basically identical to that in the short run except for the fact that the demand for the factors is indirect and complex.

Character of Demand for the Factors

The special character of the demand for the factors is due to several circumstances. (1) The demand for the factors is usually not a direct demand but is generally *derived* from the demand for the products which the factors are instrumental in producing. (2) The demand for any product is a joint demand for the several factors used in producing it. (3) Most factors are used in producing several products so that the demand for any factor is a composite made up of the demands for its use in the production of the several products. Finally, (4) the demand for a given product cannot be regarded as a demand for definite quantities of the several factors used in producing it because the

---

tion. In such cases the price system must generally be supplanted by rationing if a semblance of order is to be maintained.

[3] Chapters 21 and 22 deal with the problem of the supply of the factors.

factors can be combined for any productive purpose in widely varying proportions.

Despite these complications, the demand for any good may be regarded as a demand—though indirect—for the factors used in producing it. Thus, the person or firm or public agency which manages the production of the good is to be regarded as a mere middleman or converter who assembles the factors and sells their combined services in the form of the good. When individuals buy *goods,* they are, actually and basically, buying factors of production, and the satisfactions they receive are derived ultimately from these factors. Thus, the problem of achieving an economical use of a given supply of factors is almost precisely the same as that of achieving an economical disposition of a given supply of goods, as already discussed. It is a matter of placing uniform prices on the *factors* which will measure the amounts of satisfaction derived from them, and at the same time of making these factor prices effective to the consumers of goods.

It is so important to see clearly that a good is really a "combination" or "synthesis" of factors that it may be worth while to press the point further. The production of a good is, in many ways, analogous to the formation of a chemical compound by synthesis of elements. For example, sodium and chlorine are the chemical constituents of common salt. To produce chemically a kilogram of salt requires certain definite quantities of sodium and chlorine. But to produce salt in this way requires something besides sodium and chlorine; it requires the labor of the persons who are to carry on the process, the land, and the capital. Moreover, to produce the sodium and chlorine requires additional labor, land, and capital. To produce the machinery and equipment required in the process calls for still more labor, land, and capital; and so on. In short, salt, viewed as a *chemical compound,* is a synthesis of given quantities of chemical elements; salt, viewed as an economic good, is a combination or synthesis of given quantities of "economic elements" (factors of production), namely, various quantities of labor, land, and capital.[4] For this reason, the demand for a good is reducible to a demand for

---

4 "Factor" is defined in Webster's Dictionary as "One of the elements, circumstances, or influences that contribute to produce a result; a constituent."

the quantities of the factors necessary to produce the number of units of the good demanded. The analogy is, of course, not perfect. From the chemical point of view, the synthetic production of one kilogram of salt requires certain definite quantities of sodium and chlorine. But the production of one kilogram of salt, embodying these definite quantities of sodium and chlorine, can be carried on with many different combinations of the factors of production. The process might be carried on chiefly by labor, with only a few minor tools and pieces of equipment. Or it might be carried on with large and expensive automatic machinery. Moreover, there are ways of obtaining salt other than by a synthetic process; for example, by mining it, or by evaporating sea water. Each different process comes to approximately the same end result, but through entirely different combinations of the factors of production. Nevertheless, whatever the particular combination of factors may be, the ultimate product may be regarded as a synthesis of *these* factors.[5]

Conditions of Economical Allocation of Factors

In order to achieve an economical allocation of the factors, five conditions must be met. First, there must be a uniform price for all units of each factor. Otherwise, in those fields of production where the price charged for the factor was high, the demand would be restricted to only the more important uses (as measured by price) ; and in those fields where the price was low, the demand would be extended to less important uses. If a uniform price were established, however, the use of the factor could be increased in those fields where it had been limited and could be restricted where it had been overextended. The increased satisfactions from the one use would more than counterbalance the curtailed satisfactions in the other use, on the assumption that marginal satisfactions are important in proportion to price.

Second, the price of each factor must be equal to the value of its marginal product. We have seen (under appropriate assumptions) that the price of a good may be regarded as a measure of the satisfaction afforded by it. We have also observed that

[5] Cf. Knut Wicksell, *Lectures on Political Economy,* Vol. 1, London, 1935, pp. 97-100.

a good may be regarded as the synthesis of the several factors used in producing it. It follows, then, that if the price of each factor is set equal to the value of its contribution to product, then the price of that factor may be regarded as a measure of the satisfaction afforded (indirectly) by it. In other words, if the price of each factor is to become a measure of the satisfaction it yields, then its price should be equal to the value of its marginal product.[6]

Third, each factor of production must be allocated so that the value of its marginal product will be equal in all of its various uses.[7] For instance, if a given type of labor yields a marginal product of $1 per hour in producing wheat and 50 cents per hour in producing corn, it will clearly pay to transfer some of this labor from corn to wheat until the marginal products (in terms of value) are equalized. Otherwise, the labor would be used to furnish satisfactions of less importance from corn, as measured by price, when satisfactions of greater importance from wheat were being neglected.

Fourth, the factors must be organized for the production of each product in the least costly manner. The real cost of producing a unit of any one commodity lies in the fact that this production uses up factors which otherwise could be used for other purposes. The cost is in the form of a sacrifice of alternative opportunities for satisfaction; the achievement of minimum cost, then, is dependent upon the discovery of a method for ascertaining which combination of the factors involves the least sacrifice of alternatives. Again, we resort to pricing as a measuring device. A high price on the factor indicates that it is in great demand relative to the amount of it that is available, that each unit of it is very important, and that the use of a unit for any purpose involves a large cost or sacrifice. Conversely, a low price indicates that the importance of any one unit of it is slight. Thus, in using the factors in any given productive process, the real cost of production (i.e., the amount of alternative satisfac-

---

[6] The marginal product of a factor refers to the loss in product that would be sustained if one unit of the factor were withdrawn.

[7] When an industry is composed of a number of plants, the marginal product of a factor could also be defined as the loss in product that would be sustained if one unit of the factor were withdrawn from a *plant*, since, in effect, the withdrawal of a unit from the industry would necessarily come from some plant.

tions sacrificed as a result of the use of the factors) is minimized when the factors are organized so that average cost per unit of product is at a minimum.

The achievement of minimum cost means that in each process of production the factors used are those capable of providing alternative satisfactions of the least importance so that the employment of these factors entails a minimum of sacrifice. The achievement of minimum cost is a necessary prerequisite to the attainment of maximum satisfaction, because, so long as more costly methods are being employed, factors are used to provide lesser satisfactions when they might be employed to yield greater satisfactions.

The question of what particular organization of factors will be least costly, under any given set of factor prices, will be determined by the character of the known physical conditions of production, i.e., the production functions. The achievement of least cost requires that the factors be combined in such proportions that each is subject to diminishing returns, and that the marginal products of the several factors be proportional to the prices of the factors.[8]

The achievement of least cost also requires that the optimum size and geographic location of plants be attained, that transportation systems be laid out appropriately, etc. The many interesting and important questions relating to the spatial organization of the economy are ignored in this discussion.[9]

Fifth, the prices placed upon the various factors of production must be such as to equate the demand for each of them to the available supply (which we have assumed to be fixed). If the price of a given factor is above this level, the demand for the factor will be less than the available supply; if the price is below this level, the demand will exceed the supply. In other words, the demand for a factor varies inversely with its price.

The explanation of this relationship between the price of a factor and its demand is twofold. (1) In accordance with the first

[8] See Chapters 7 and 8. Special additional provisions are needed to cover the case where several products are produced jointly.

[9] See *Alfred Weber's Theory of the Location of Industries* (translated by C. J. Friedrich), Chicago, 1929; F. A. Fetter, "The Economic Law of Market Areas," *Quarterly Journal of Economics*, May, 1924, pp. 520-529; Harold Hotelling, "Stability in Competition," *Economic Journal*, March, 1929, pp. 41-57.

condition above, an increase in the price of the factor entails a corresponding increase in the prices of all the products whose production requires this factor (other things being equal). This increased product price will have the effect of restricting the demand for the product and hence of restricting the demand for the factor. (2) In accordance with the third condition, to be explained below, an increase in the price of the factor means that the factor must be employed more sparingly, in combination with the other factors. That is, it will be economical to substitute other factors for this one. A decrease in the price of the factor will have the reverse effects, tending to bring about an increase in the demand for the factor (1) by lowering the price of the goods in the production of which the factor is used, and (2) by requiring that this factor be used more generously in combination with other factors.[10]

If the price of a factor is such that the demand for it does not equal the available supply, the factors are almost certain to be used uneconomically. If the price is too high, the demand will fall short of the existing supply, some units of the factor will be unemployed, and the potential productivity of these unemployed units will be lost to society. On the other hand, if the price is too low, the demand will exceed the supply, and there will appear to be a shortage of the factor. Under these circumstances, the allocation of the factor among different uses will likely be uneconomic because there would be no way of assuring that the limited supplies would find their way into the more important uses to the exclusion of the less important. At the low price, the factor might be used for purposes in which its contribution to product would be less than in other possible but not realized uses.

The Pricing Principles

The preceding section outlined five conditions that must be met if an economical allocation of factors is to be achieved. These were: (1) A uniform price must be placed upon all units of each factor; (2) The price of each factor must be equal to the value of its marginal product; (3) Each factor must be allocated so that the value of its marginal product will be equal in all of

---

10 See Chapter 8.

its various uses; (4) The factors must be organized in the production of each product in the least costly manner; and (5) The prices placed upon the various factors must be such as to equate the demand for each of them to the available supply.

All five of these conditions will be fulfilled if the following three rules are applied:

1. A uniform price must be placed on all units of each factor.
2. The quantity of the various factors used in producing each good should be adjusted so that the value of the marginal product of each factor will be equal to its price.
3. The price of each factor should be set so that the demand for it is equal to the available supply.[11]

If these rules are followed, the five conditions referred to will be realized: (1) The price of each factor will be uniform. (2) This price will be equal to the value of the marginal product of the factor. (3) Each factor will be allocated so that the value of its marginal product will be equal in all of its uses. If, in each use, the marginal product is made equal to the price, and the price is uniform for all units of the factor, then the marginal product of the factor must be equal in all uses. (4) The factors will be organized in the least costly manner. As pointed out in Chapter 8, the condition of least cost is that the factors be organized within each firm so that their physical marginal products are proportional to their prices. This condition will be met if the value marginal products of the several factors are equal to their respective prices. (To convert physical marginal product to value terms, it is necessary only to multiply the quantities by the price of the product under consideration.) A condition of least cost for the entire industry is that the industry must be organized into firms of appropriate number and size. The rules take care of this also. If any firm is too large or too small to produce at least cost, the marginal-value products of the factors will no longer be equal to their prices, and can be made equal only by a suitable adjustment in scale. (5) The demand for each factor will be equal to its supply.

---

[11] Cf. A. P. Lerner, *The Economics of Control*, especially pp. 57-71, 117-136. Professor Lerner's discussion is exceptionally clear and concise and contains important new analysis.

An Alternative Formulation

The three pricing rules for economically allocating the factors may be criticized on the ground that they are not stated in concepts that are ordinarily used and understood in practical affairs. Businessmen and government officials almost never think in terms of "marginal product." Hence, it may be useful to translate these principles into the language of the real world. This requires that two new rules be substituted for the second rule. The new rules are (*a*) that the price of each product should be equal to its average cost of production, and (*b*) that the production of each product should be organized in the least costly manner.

These two rules correspond, for example, to the actions of private businessmen in competition. They try to make profits by obtaining prices in excess of average cost. To this end they sell for the highest price they can get and produce at the least possible cost. But they are stopped from making profits (in the long run) by competition. On the other hand, if they cannot obtain a price at least equal to average cost, they will suffer losses which will eventually force them out of business. Thus, as a result of tendencies toward elimination of both profits and losses, price tends toward the level of average cost—when production is organized in the least costly manner.

When the factors are allocated in accordance with the two substitute principles, approximately the same results are obtained as when the value of the marginal product of each factor is equated to the price of that factor. But before discussing the relation between the second pricing principle and the two substitute principles, perhaps we should digress briefly to define average cost.

Average cost, in this context, is defined as the total outlay for the factors used in producing the good divided by the number of units of the good produced. For example, in the production of shoes, certain quantities of labor are required at various stages on the part of farmers, railroad men, machine operatives, salesmen, and others. Also required are certain quantities of capital and land. With all the facts regarding the production of shoes, we could draw up a schedule showing the precise amount of each type of labor and land, and the amount of capital required to place a given quantity of shoes of a particular type into the hands of consumers. Then, given the prices of each of these factors of production, we could compute the cost of producing these shoes by multiplying the quantity of each factor used by its price and adding these results. Finally, we could determine average cost by dividing the total cost by the number of shoes produced. Average cost may thus be regarded as the sum of the outlays required to buy the particular quantities of the several factors needed to produce *one* unit of the good.[12]

To return now to our main argument, the problem is to show that the rule "marginal product equal to price of the factor" is the equivalent of the two rules "average cost equal to price of the product" and "production at least cost."

First, we can show that when marginal product is equal to price, price and average cost are automatically equated. This may be demonstrated by referring to the principle of imputation which was discussed in Chapter 8. According to this principle, if the marginal (physical) product of each factor is multiplied by the number of units of it employed, and the several results are added, the sum will be equal to the total output. In equation form, this was written (for two factors, X and Y):

$$1. \qquad M_xX + M_yY = Q$$

This equation refers to money values as well as to physical quantities. In that case, the marginal products and the total product are expressed in value terms instead of physical quantities, the conversion being accomplished merely by multiplying each of these quantities by the price of the product. The expanded equation is (Pg = price of the good or product):

$$2. \qquad PgM_xX + PgM_yY = PgQ$$

If the prices of the factors are equal to their respective marginal-value products, then the price of factor X will be PgM_x and

---

[12] In an industry containing many firms, the costs of all firms would be equalized in the long run. The lower *cost* of any one, due to its use of superior resources, would be offset in the factor market where superior resources would be priced higher than inferior resources. As a result, the average cost of all firms would be the same and would be equal to the average cost for the industry. Average cost refers both to the average cost of a firm within an industry and to the average cost of the entire industry. In this context a firm is defined as one or more plants under unified management. The term is not restricted to the private-enterprise system. See pp. 156–158.

that of factor Y will be $PgMy$. The total amount paid to factor X will be $PgMxX$, and the total amount paid to factor Y will be $PgMyY$. The total cost will be $PgMxX + PgMyY$ which is equal to the amount received from the sale of the product, PgQ. If total cost and total receipts are equal, average cost and price (average receipts) must also be equal. Average cost is total cost divided by number of units of output (Q), and price is total receipts divided by number of units of output (Q). Dividing both sides of equation 2 by Q, we derive a third equation which states that the product price is equal to average cost:

$$3. \qquad \frac{PgMxX + PgMyY}{Q} = Pg$$

As indicated, when the marginal-value products of the factors are equal to their respective prices, price and average cost are equated. But the mere equalization of price and average cost does not ensure that average cost shall be at a minimum. Price could be equal to an average cost far above the minimum. To achieve minimum cost, the physical marginal products of the factors must be proportional to the prices of the factors. But if this condition is achieved, and at the same time price is equated with average cost, then the marginal-value product of each factor will necessarily be equal—as well as proportional—to its price. Hence, the rule "marginal-value product equal to product price" is equivalent to the two rules "average cost equal to product price" and "production at least cost."

To summarize, the alternative formulation of the pricing rules, in which the second and third rules replace the second rule of the earlier formulation, follows:

1. A uniform price must be placed on all units of each factor.
2. The price of each good must be equal to its average cost of production.
3. In the production of each product, the factors must be organized in the least costly manner.
4. The price of each factor should be set so that the demand for it is equal to the available supply.

Although the first alternative formulation is to be preferred for its simplicity and for technical advantages, this second formulation will be used in the remainder of this book because, as pointed out, it corresponds to the language of practical affairs.[13]

Summary

Let us now retrace briefly our progress in this chapter. The problem has been to determine what prices must be established if given supplies of goods and given supplies of the factors are to be used economically. The basic hypotheses were (1) that price is a measure of marginal satisfactions, and (2) that goods or factors are used to greatest advantage when greater marginal satisfactions are provided ahead of lesser marginal satisfactions.

It was concluded that a given supply of goods would be used most economically if a uniform price were placed on all the units of each good so that the amount which people would wish to buy would be equal to the amount available. Prices established according to this rule, however, would only guide the use of goods already produced and would not aid in achieving a correct allocation of the factors of production. To accomplish this purpose, and at the same time to guide the use of goods already produced, four rules were found necessary: (1) A uniform price must be placed on all units of each factor, (2) The price of each good must be equal to its average cost of production, (3) The factors must be organized, for the production of each product, in the least costly manner; and (4) The price of each factor must be set so that the demand for it is equal to the available supply. These four rules boil down to the following statement: Uniform prices must be placed upon the factors so that the demand for the factors, when they are combined in the least costly manner, will be equated with the available supply.

---

13 Cf. A. P. Lerner, *op. cit.,* pp. 128-132. The four pricing rules may also be formulated in terms of marginal cost rather than average cost. In this case the second rule "price of product equal to average cost" is revised to equate the price of each good with marginal cost. When the factors are divisible, so that production in each firm can be carried on at minimum cost, marginal cost and average cost are equal. Under these conditions, the principle that price should equal marginal cost is identical to the principle that price should equal average cost. However, when the factors are indivisible so that the least costly combination of the factors cannot be attained, marginal cost and average cost are not necessarily equal. In this case the correct principle is that price must equal marginal cost. This exception will be discussed in Chapter 17.

The technique of *pricing* is a paramount element in each of the four conditions. The central significance of pricing is explained by the fact that economic calculation requires a technique of measurement whereby it is possible to compare the results from alternative uses of resources. Prices provide a common denominator or common measure of the relative importance of different factors and of different goods in contributing to human satisfactions. With the use of prices, therefore, it is possible to establish rules which, if followed, will lead to the most economical use of resources.

Although these four conditions relate directly to the *pricing* process, yet at the same time they all have to do with the *allocation* of the factors of production among the many possible alternative uses of these factors. The fulfillment of the four conditions means that the factors of production are being used in the most economical manner in relation to the valuations of consumers.

Any change in these valuations would, of course, alter the allocation of the factors necessary to meet the four pricing conditions. For example, assuming economy to begin with, suppose that the demand for shoes is increased, while that for suits is correspondingly decreased. This would mean that some of the factors used in producing shoes would be in greater demand than similar factors used for other purposes, that the price of shoes would rise above cost of production, and that, therefore, the prices paid for the use of the factors employed in the shoe industry would be greater than the prices paid for similar factors elsewhere. To maintain the original allocation of the factors would mean that factors capable of being used in producing shoes would be more urgently demanded for this purpose than for other purposes. At the same time, the demand for some of the factors used in producing suits would be decreased, and the price of suits would fall below cost of production. Therefore, in order to correct the dis-economy, a reallocation of the factors would be required. It would be necessary to transfer factors out of the suit industry; as a result, the supply of suits would be curtailed until the price would rise to a point of equality with cost of production. On the other hand, it would be necessary to transfer factors into the shoe industry, until the output of shoes was increased sufficiently for the price of shoes to fall to the point of equality with cost. These changes in demand would also probably require changes in the prices of the factors. The increase in demand for shoes would be basically an increase in the demand for the particular factors used in producing shoes. A reduction in demand for suits would at the same time be a reduction in demand for the particular factors used to produce these goods. If in shoe production we assume the use of factors totally different from those used for producing suits, then an increase in the price of the "shoe factors" and a decrease in that of the "suit factors" would be required. These changes in prices would affect the costs of producing all goods using either group of factors; this in turn would tend to vary, in all fields, the combinations which would be least costly. To the extent, however, that the same factors were used to produce shoes and suits, the reallocation would be a mere transfer of factors from the fields of decreased demands to those of increased demands without any change in prices of the factors. When, however, the four pricing conditions had been re-established, the available supply of factors would again be employed in the most economical manner.

Chapter 16

PRINCIPLES OF PRICING FOR SOCIAL ECONOMY (*continued*)

Let us assume a society in which the supply of each of the factors of production is given, and then let us attempt to ascertain exactly what disposition of these factors will be most economical. On the basis of the argument in the preceding chapter, we know that economy is achieved when four conditions have been established, namely: (1) that a uniform price is placed on all units of each factor, (2) that the price of each good is equal to its average cost of production, (3) that the factors are organized in the least costly manner, and (4) that the demand for each factor is equal to the available supply. The problem is to formulate a consistent set of equations expressing these conditions.

Before such a set of equations can be constructed, however, two types of relationships must be stated. First, the *production function* for each good must be known, i.e., the relation between the quantity of factor input and the quantity of product. Second, the *demand functions* must be known, i.e., the relation between the prices of the several goods and the quantity of each of them which consumers will choose to purchase. The problem is to determine what amount of each factor will be used to produce each good and what amount of each good will be produced (when the four conditions of economy are satisfied). Incidentally, the price of each factor and of each good will also be determined.[1] For convenience we shall assume that there are two factors and two goods.

---

[1] For an excellent and admirably clear presentation of the economic system by means of simultaneous equations, see E. H. Phelps Brown, *The Framework of the Pricing System*, London, 1936.

The various "given" conditions and unknowns can be summarized as follows:

Givens:

The total supply of factor A, A
The total supply of factor B, B
The production function for good 1, $F(a_1, b_1)$
The production function for good 2, $F(a_2, b_2)$
The demand function for good 1, $F(P_1, P_2)$
The demand function for good 2, $F(P_1, P_2)$

Conditions (corresponding to the four pricing rules):

1. Uniform prices must be placed upon all units of each factor.
2. The price of each good must be equal to its average cost of production.
3. The factors must be employed in least costly combinations.
4. The demand for each factor must be equal to the available supply.

Unknowns:

Amount of factor A used to produce good 1, a_1
Amount of factor A used to produce good 2, a_2
Amount of factor B used to produce good 1, b_1
Amount of factor B used to produce good 2, b_2
Amount produced of good 1, S_1
Amount produced for good 2, S_2
The demand for good 1, D_1
The demand for good 2, D_2
Price of factor A, P_a
Price of factor B, P_b
Price of good 1, P_1
Price of good 2, P_2

There are twelve unknowns; therefore a set of twelve different equations is required to give a determinate system. The first condition (namely, uniform prices) is assumed.

The Equations

We begin by deriving the equations which express the second condition, that the price of each good must be equal to its average cost of production. The total cost of producing the entire supply of a good would be equal to the sum of the outlays for the several factors employed, and the average cost would be equal to the total cost divided by the number of units produced. Thus, the following pair of equations can be written:

$$1. \qquad P_1 = \frac{P_a a_1 + P_b b_1}{S_1}$$

$$2. \qquad P_2 = \frac{P_a a_2 + P_b b_2}{S_2}$$

Next, we derive the equations which express the third condition, that the factors must be employed in the least costly combinations. In the production of any good, the least costly combination of the factors will depend upon the prices of the factors.[2] An increase in the price of any one factor, other things being equal, will cause a shift in the position of least cost so that a relatively smaller amount of that factor will be employed, and vice versa. The least costly combination will be such that the marginal products of the several factors are *proportional* to the prices of these factors.[3]

One of the "givens" in our problem is the production function for each good; in other words, the precise relationship between the quantities of factor inputs and the quantities of product. In our simplified system, these production functions may be expressed as follows:

$$3. \qquad S_1 = F\,(a_1, b_1)$$
$$4. \qquad S_2 = F\,(a_2, b_2)$$

These equations mean that the supply of each good is a function of the quantities of the several factors employed in its produc-

---

2 See Chapter 8.
3 See Chapter 8.

tion. The marginal product of factor A in the production of good 1 (M_{a1}) can, by definition, be computed from the production function by means of differential calculus. It is the derivative of the production function with respect to a_1. Similarly, the marginal product of factor B in the production of good 1 (M_{b1}) is the derivative of this same production function with respect to b_1. Likewise, M_{a2} and M_{b2} are computed as the derivatives respectively of the production function for good 2. In short, given the production functions, it is possible to obtain expressions for the several marginal products.

Given the marginal products of the several factors (M_{a1}, M_{a2}, M_{b1}, M_{b2}), we are ready to formulate another pair of equations in our system, equations expressing the condition that the factors must be employed in the least costly combinations, i.e., according to the principle of proportionality. The first equations state that the marginal products of the two factors must be proportional to the prices of these factors in the production of good 1, and the second states the same thing with reference to good 2.

$$5. \qquad \frac{M_{a1}}{P_a} = \frac{M_{b1}}{P_b}$$

$$6. \qquad \frac{M_{a2}}{P_a} = \frac{M_{b2}}{P_b}$$

Finally, we express the fourth condition, that the demand for each factor must be equal to the given supply of that factor. Since the demand for the factors is derived from the demand for goods and is, therefore, indirect, six equations are necessary. The demand functions, which are assumed to be given, may be stated:

$$7. \qquad D_1 = F(P_1, P_2)$$
$$8. \qquad D_2 = F(P_1, P_2)$$

The equations expressing the condition that the demand for each *good* must be equal to the amount produced are:

$$9. \qquad D_1 = S_1$$
$$10. \qquad D_2 = S_2$$

And the equations expressing the condition that the demand for each factor must be equal to the available supply, i.e., all the units of each factor must be employed, are:

$$11. \qquad a_1 + a_2 = A$$
$$12. \qquad b_1 + b_2 = B$$

We now have twelve equations, and since there are twelve unknowns $(a_1, a_2, b_1, b_2, S_1, S_2, D_1, D_2, P_a, P_b, P_1, P_2)$, the system is complete.

The Problem of Solving the Equations

The solution of the twelve equations would yield values for the various unknown prices and quantities which would satisfy all the conditions necessary for the most economical use of the available resources with the given production functions and demand functions. There are, in general, two methods of solving such a system of equations: first, by means of mathematical techniques, and second, by means of a process of trial and error. Though mathematical techniques are usable so long as the number of unknowns remains relatively small (as in our example), they become unmanageable when the number of unknowns increases, and are wholly useless with a system as complex as would be required if the almost infinite number of variables present in the actual world were included. Therefore, the only practicable solution of the equations is through the method of trial and error.[4] The practicability of this method can easily be demonstrated by means of an arithmetical example. Indeed, this is the method by which the "solution" is achieved in the actual market places of a capitalist society.[5]

The Trial-and-Error Solution

In illustrating the method of solution by means of trial and error, let it be assumed, again, that there are within the system only two factors and two goods. Suppose that there are

---

4 The mathematical solution may become practicable with the new electronic calculators.

5 Cf. Oskar Lange and Fred M. Taylor, *On the Economic Theory of Socialism,* Minneapolis, 1938. See especially p. 52 and pp. 65-98.

available 150 units of factor *A* and 250 units of factor *B*, and that these factors are to be used in the production of good 1 and good 2. Suppose, further, that relations between input of factors and output of goods, the production functions, are as shown in Table IX. This table indicates the amount of good 1 and good 2 that would be produced with varying amounts of the factors. Finally, assume that the relation between the prices of the goods and the amounts consumers would choose to pur-

TABLE IX

Assumed Production Functions

	Good 1			Good 2	
1	2	3	4	5	6
Quantity of Factor *A*	Quantity of Factor *B*	Product	Quantity of Factor *A*	Quantity of Factor *B*	Product
1	.20	.30	1	.20	.40
1	.25	.45	1	.25	.65
1	.33⅓	.50	1	.33⅓	.80
1	.50	.54	1	.50	.87
1	1.00	.64	1	1.00	1.00
1	2.00	.82	1	2.00	1.10
1	3.00	1.00	1	3.00	1.15
1	4.00	1.10	1	4.00	1.14
1	5.00	1.08	1	5.00	1.05

chase, the demand functions, are as shown in Table X. In this table, for each of a number of combinations of prices the demand for each good is shown. For example, in the first row, when the price of good 1 is 3 and the price of good 2 is also 3, it is indicated that consumers will buy 90 units of good 1 and 143 units of good 2. When the price of good 2 is increased to 4 (second row of the table), the demand for good 2 is smaller (100) and the demand for good 1 is greater (100). Were this schedule to be indefinitely expanded, it would show the behavior of consumers under all possible combinations of prices. Incidentally, this schedule is constructed so that the demand for each good varies inversely with the price—when the price of

TABLE X

Assumed Demand Functions

1	2	3	4	5
Price of Good 1	Price of Good 2	Demand for Good 1	Demand for Good 2	Total Expenditure*
3	3	90	143	700
3	4	100	100	700
3	5	83	90	700
3	6	73	80	700
3	7	70	70	700
4	3	85	120	700
4	4	75	100	700
4	5	62	90	700
4	6	55	80	700
4	7	52	70	700
5	3	62	130	700
5	4	60	100	700
5	5	50	90	700
5	6	44	80	700
5	7	42	70	700
6	3	54	125	700
6	4	50	100	700
6	5	42	90	700
6	6	37	80	700
6	7	35	70	700
7	3	49	120	700
7	4	43	100	700
7	5	36	90	700
7	6	31	80	700
7	7	30	70	700

* The total expenditures are equal to the sum of the amounts spent on the two goods. The demand for good 1 (column 3) multiplied by the price of good 1 (column 1) gives the total amount spent for that good. Similarly, the demand for good 2 (column 4) multiplied by its price (column 2) gives the total amount spent for good 2. Since the total expenditures of consumers are assumed to be 700, these two amounts add up in each case to 700. Slight discrepancies are due to the fact that results have been rounded to nearest whole numbers.

the other good remains constant. This is in accord with the principle of diminishing utility and generally agrees with observed experience. In the construction of this table, moreover, it has been assumed that the expenditures of consumers are fixed at 700; therefore, the demands as shown in columns 3 and 4 are such that at each pair of prices the total amount spent on the two goods together is approximately 700.

Given the supply of each of the two factors, the production functions and the demand functions, it is possible to determine the particular allocation of the factors, in fact all of the unknowns in the above equations, by means of a trial-and-error process. The method is as follows: (1) Assume a price for each of the factors. (2) Ascertain which combination of the factors is least costly, *at the assumed prices,* in the production of each good. (3) Compute the unit cost for each good when the least costly combination of the factors is employed. The price of each good may be assumed to be equal to this unit cost, in accordance with the condition that price must equal unit cost. (4) With these prices, compute the demand for each of the goods from the given demand schedules. (5) Referring back to the production functions, determine the quantity of each of the factors required to supply the demand for the two goods when the factors are employed in the least costly combinations. This gives the demand for the factors under the assumed prices. (6) Compare this demand for each of the factors with the given available supply. Unless the "correct" prices of the factors have been assumed from the beginning (the probability of this is very small), the computed demand for each of the factors would differ from the available supply. This would indicate the necessity of correcting the originally assumed factor prices, increasing the price for any factor for which computed demand exceeded supply and decreasing the price for any factor for which the computed demand fell short of the available supply. With the new assumed factor prices, the several steps above can be repeated until, by successive approximation, factor prices are discovered which satisfy the conditions of economy, i.e., production at least cost, price of each good equal to its cost, and demand for factors equal to available supply.

For the particular conditions assumed (supply of factor A 150, supply of factor B 250, production functions as shown in Table IX, and demand functions as shown in Table X), the following values for the several unknowns are found, by the process of trial and error, to satisfy the conditions of economy.

Amount of factor A used to produce good 1 $(a_1) = 50$.
Amount of factor A used to produce good 2 $(a_2) = 100$.
Amount of factor B used to produce good 1 $(b_1) = 150$.

Amount of factor B used to produce good 2 (b_2) = 100.
Amount produced of good 1 (S_1 or D_1) = 50.
Amount produced of good 2 (S_2 or D_2) = 100.
Price of factor A (P_a) = 3.
Price of factor B (P_b) = 1.
Price of good 1 (P_1) = 6.
Price of good 2 (P_2) = 4.

The least-cost combination in the production of good 1 was found to be 1 unit of factor A to 3 units of factor B, and in the production of good 2, 1 unit of factor A to 1 unit of factor B.

Chapter 17

PRODUCTION UNDER
DECREASING COST

In the preceding four chapters, some general principles for the economical allocation of resources have been developed. These general principles, however, even if followed meticulously, would not by themselves solve all the problems encountered by a society in quest of "economy." In this and the following five chapters the general principles will be modified and augmented to take into account some of the more important problems which lie beyond their scope.

In production carried on under conditions of decreasing cost, the factors cannot, by definition, be organized in the least costly manner. Hence the pricing rules for social economy, as outlined in the two preceding chapters, must be modified to take into account this special case. It may be noted that decreasing cost is by no means a rare or unimportant phenomenon. Its occurrence is frequent and widespread. Decreasing cost exists whenever the most efficient scale of output for the plant is large relative to the total demand for its product. For example, the following industries, constituting a very sizable proportion of any modern economy, are probably subject to decreasing cost in varying degrees: electric light and power, illuminating gas, water, sewage disposal, telephone, telegraph, railroad, street transportation, highways, canals, pipe lines, and many others.

Some Definitions

In connection with the discussion of decreasing cost, the terms "firm" and "industry" will be referred to repeatedly. It will be well to begin, therefore, by defining these two terms as they will be used in this context.

A *firm* is here defined as one or more plants operated under unified management. Since our analysis is intended to refer to any type of economic systems—not alone to capitalism—the concept of the firm carries no implications with respect to type of ownership or ultimate control. The *firm*, as we use the term, might refer, for example, to a privately owned enterprise, a cooperative, or a state enterprise.

An *industry*, as here defined, includes all of the firms within the economy which are engaged in producing a given intermediate or final good. The number of firms within any given industry may vary from one to many thousand. In previous chapters [1] we have used the word "industry" to refer to the entire mass of organized productive facilities used, at all stages, in the production of a final good. Under this definition we included in the "bread industry," for example, (1) all the farms, farm machinery factories, flour mills, bakeries, and other such organizations devoted exclusively to one or more stages in the production of bread, and (2) that portion of the railroads, steel mills, retail stores, and other such organizations devoted *in part* to the production of bread. Such a concept of "industry" is not very useful for our present purposes because, for obvious technical reasons, the various stages of a process such as the production of bread are carried on independently in separate physical plants. Only those parts of any productive process are integrated which, for the sake of efficiency, must be carried on together. Thus, instead of using the word "industry" to apply to the entire productive process employed in producing some one final good, we speak of the *railroad industry*, the *coal mining industry*, the *electric power industry*, or the *retail grocery industry*, each of which contributes at one stage or another to the production of many different final goods, or to the *baking industry* or the *shoe manufacturing industry* each of which is concerned with a single stage in the production of a particular final good (or group of closely related goods).

The Nature of Decreasing Cost

An industry is said to be operating under decreasing cost when the average cost of production (per unit of output) varies

---

[1] See pp. 58–61.

inversely with the total amount of product. Under decreasing cost, then, an increase in output is accompanied by a decline in average cost. As will be shown presently, if such an industry is to be operated economically, its entire production must be concentrated within a single firm. Consequently, it is expedient to begin our analysis of decreasing cost by investigating the effect of changes in the output of a firm upon its average cost.

Output and Cost

The fact that average cost for a firm increases or decreases with changes in output is due chiefly to four conditions: (1) Some of the factors of production and some intermediate goods used by a firm are not obtainable in small units, and the efficient use of such "lumpy" facilities requires a relatively large scale of output; (2) As the output expands, the cost of management and supervision tends to increase; (3) In those instances where the firm is an important element in the market for the factors it uses, an increase in output will tend to cause an increase in the prices of these factors; and (4) As the output of a firm increases, the geographic size of its market must become larger, and the cost of transport must therefore increase. Let us take up each of these conditions separately.[2]

First, changes in cost associated with variations of output may be due to the "lumpiness" of the factors or of the intermediate goods used by the firm. In practice, most of these facilities are not infinitely divisible but rather must be obtained in perceptible—and sometimes very large—increments, so that any increase or decrease in the amount employed involves discontinuity. For example, if it is desired to increase the employment of a given type of labor, it is often necessary to add at least one full-time person because it is not always possible or convenient to employ labor on a part-time basis; if manufacturing capacity is to be increased, it must be done by adding a whole machine because one half of a machine is obviously of no use; if a railroad is to be built, a complete roadbed is necessary even though the traffic contemplated would be only half the capacity of the line; in order to sell electric power it is necessary to provide a dis-

---

2 Each is discussed in terms of the long run. The short run will be discussed a little later.

tribution system of wires, poles, transformers, etc., even though the anticipated use of the equipment is only one fourth its capacity; if a grocery store needs a delivery truck, it is necessary to buy an entire truck, because a portion of a truck is of no use, and yet to have a truck for part time may be inconvenient or impossible. One could expand on these illustrations indefinitely. It is not to be inferred that in such cases as these there is *no* adjustability, because in each instance there would be some possibility of partial adaptation of the productive facilities to the requirements of the situation, yet in each case it is likely that perfect adaptation will not be feasible. When some of the productive facilities required by a firm must be obtained in large units or not at all, as is frequently the case, large fixed costs must be incurred if production is to be undertaken. If, under these circumstances, the production of the firm is small, the average cost per unit of output will tend to be high. As production increases, however, the cost connected with the use of these facilities will not increase; consequently, the average cost per unit will fall. For instance, in order for an electric power firm to carry on its production, a distribution system must be provided to serve each of its customers. Let us assume that such a firm is expected to produce 100,000 kilowatt-hours per month, and that the minimum transmission system capable of handling this output would cost, for depreciation and interest, $1,000 per month. The average cost of the distribution system would then be 1 cent per kilowatt-hour. Let us assume, however, that this system would be capable of handling 200,000 kilowatt-hours per month without any additional cost. If, then, the output of the firm was increased to 150,000 kilowatt-hours per month, the average cost for the distribution system would drop to $2/3$ cent per kilowatt-hour; and if the output was increased to its capacity of 200,000 kilowatt-hours, the corresponding average cost would fall to $1/2$ cent. If the production was further increased, it might then be necessary to make additional investment in the distribution system. In this case, the average cost might (but not necessarily) increase.[3] Whenever the practicable level of output that can be

---

[3] The largeness of the units in which some facilities must be obtained may sometimes lead to overutilization. For example, a firm may find that the existing facilities are inadequate, but that it does not anticipate sufficient output to utilize fully the smallest practicable addition to plant. It may then elect to let existing

achieved by such a firm is so small that its most "lumpy" facilities cannot be fully utilized, then any increase in output will tend to bring about a reduction in average cost.

Second, variations in the level of output of a firm may affect the cost of management or supervision and hence influence the average cost per unit of output. When production is on a small scale, the average cost for management may decrease with expanding output, because the cost of given managerial talent can be "spread out" over more units of product. Management is then a "lumpy" factor. As production increases, however, the firm necessarily becomes more complex, and a relative increase in cost of management probably becomes necessary. This may be partially explained by the fact that in a large plant relations between manager and employees become less personal so that relatively more overseers and more devices of control, such as elaborate accounting records and reports, are required. A virtual bureaucracy is created since the responsible executives can no longer keep details at their finger tips. It must be admitted, however, that the nature of the relation between managerial cost and scale of output is not accurately known, so that any conclusions, such as those suggested here, are more or less conjectural. A strong case can be made, for example, for the view that the cost of management per unit of product declines at least until the output becomes very large. What seems to be an increase in cost of management as output increases may actually be only the explicit recognition of managerial functions which in the smaller firm are combined with other functions and called by other names. In a small firm, personnel management may be allocated to labor expense, whereas in the large firm they are charged to "personnel."

Third, the output of a firm may affect the prices of the factors it employs and the intermediate goods it purchases. An increase in output will increase the demand for the facilities required, thus raising the prices of these facilities and so increasing the average cost of production. This effect will be perceptible, however, only in those cases where the firm is an impor-

facilities suffice even though overutilization entails increased cost in the form of accelerated depreciation, more frequent breakdown, additional labor of superintendence, etc.

tant element in the market for the facilities concerned. If the firm occupies a relatively unimportant place in the market for the facilities, then the effect of a change in output on the prices of these things will be negligible.

Fourth, the effect of the output of a firm upon its average cost may be due to changes in the cost of transporting the product to market. To discuss this completely would involve a thorough treatment of the theory of industrial location. It is clear without elaborate analysis, however, that an increase in output must often (but not always) entail an increase in the size of the geographic area served. Moreover, it is reasonable to suppose that such an extension of market area must involve an increase in cost of transport.[4]

From the above discussion it can be seen that the average cost of production for a firm is greatly influenced by variations in the level of its output. For some elements of cost, an increase in output leads to a decline in average cost; for others to an increase. The total effect upon average cost of changes in output is, then, a summation of these separate effects. For firms in most industries, there are important and inescapable fixed costs; therefore, average cost is likely, up to a certain point, to decline with increases in output. Beyond that point, the effect of conditions tending to produce increasing cost begins to counterbalance the gains from the "thinner" spreading of fixed costs, until ultimately further expansions of output are accompanied by rising average cost. The critical point of minimum average cost indicates the level of output at which the factors can be combined most advantageously taking all things into consideration.[5] This output of least cost will be referred to henceforth as the *capacity of the firm.*

---

[4] It should be noted that this argument does not rest upon the assumption that transport costs are "paid" by the firm, i.e., included in its costs. If transport costs are paid by the buyer, and the buyer at the periphery of the market area has the option of purchasing from a closer firm, then in order to attract the peripheral buyer, the first firm will have to make a price concession. This means merely that the increased transport cost is incurred by the firm at the time the sale is made instead of before. The net effect is the same regardless of the manner in which the transaction is handled.

Extension of the market area may not increase cost of transport if the transportation industry is subject to decreasing costs.

[5] The tendency first to decreasing average cost and then to increasing average cost is represented by the customary U-shaped average-cost curve for the *firm.*

Factors Determining Capacity

The particular output at which a firm will achieve capacity will vary enormously from one industry to another, depending largely upon the importance of fixed costs or upon the magnitude of the "lumpy" facilities. Generally, in those industries where large fixed plant is necessary (e.g., steel, automobile) the most efficient combination cannot be achieved except with a very large output. In other fields (e.g., peanut vending, farming), capacity is relatively small.[6]

In order to fulfill the pricing principle that production should be carried on under conditions of least cost, every industry must be organized so that each of its constituent firms is operating at capacity, i.e., at the level of output at which average cost is at a minimum. If the output of some firms is greater than capacity, it will be desirable to reduce the scale of output of these firms and to add new firms organized at the optimum level. On the other hand, if the output of any firms is less than capacity, it will be desirable to reorganize the industry so that the production is carried on by fewer firms each of which is able to achieve the most efficient scale of output. In some cases, however, when the market for the product of the industry is small relative to the capacity of one plant, efficiency may require that the entire output of the industry be produced within a single firm, and even (if the market is small enough) that the output of the firm be restricted to less than capacity. Under these conditions the industry and firm will be identical and the average cost of production for the firm will also be the average cost of the industry. Thus, if such a firm were producing at less than capacity, then the *industry* (or firm) would be one of *decreasing cost,* because any increase in output would be associated with a decline in average cost (until the level of production was reached where average cost would be at a minimum). Thus we reach the conclusion that a decreasing-cost industry is one for which the practicable market is small relative to the capacity of a single

---

[6] It is possible that, in some cases, average cost for a plant would not decrease regularly to a minimum and then increase. Irregularities are clearly possible, though it is probable that there would be only one minimum.

firm, and in which, therefore, production can be carried on most efficiently by a single firm.[7]

The extent of the market available to an industry, i.e., the amount of product it can sell at any relevant price, is determined basically by the demands of consumers (direct or indirect).[8] If the demand remains relatively small (e.g., hatpins or tandem bicycles), the market cannot under any conditions become very great. On the other hand, the capacity of a firm will depend upon the size of the "lumpy" facilities it employs. If they are large and important as elements in cost, the firm must attain a high level of output before average cost will be minimized. On the other hand, if all facilities can be obtained in small increments, the capacity will likely be small. Whether an industry is subject to decreasing cost, then, depends upon the *relation* between the extent of its market and the capacity of the firm or firms of which it is composed. If this relation is such that total output in the industry is less than the capacity of one firm, efficiency requires that production be concentrated in a single firm and the industry becomes one of decreasing cost.[9]

---

[7] In some industries the achievement of the most efficient organization will mean that the permitted number of firms would be more than one, but small. Under these conditions it would seldom be possible to organize the industry so that all firms were producing at least cost. An increase in the demand for the product might not be large enough to warrant the addition of a new firm, but, if provided for by existing firms, might necessitate their producing at a level beyond the point of minimum average cost.

[8] In some cases the market available to the industry must be divided into small segments due to difficulties of transportation. For instance, the total demand for electric power is enormous; yet, due to the high cost of transmission, electricity must be produced near its market. Thus, the market available to any one plant is relatively small.

[9] It is sometimes held that an industry can be subject to decreasing cost even when the extent of the market is far in excess of the capacity of a single firm, so that production can be efficiently carried on in many firms. In such cases, the decline in cost that is associated with increases in the output of the industry is attributed to "external economies." These "external economies" are said to result from the improved organization of the industry following the expansion of its output. This argument, though true in a sense, is somewhat misleading because the so-called "external economies" can be resolved into decreasing costs within some *other* industry. For instance, if the shoe manufacturing industry were subject to "external economies," it would simply mean that one or more industries at an earlier stage in shoe production (e.g., cattle production, tanning, or transportation) were operating under decreasing cost. Thus, an increase in output of shoes would expand the market for one of these other industries, enabling the latter to have decreased cost. Compare, F. H. Knight, *Ethics of Competition*, New York, 1935, pp. 228-230.

Long-Run and Short-Run Decreasing Cost

To clarify the significance of decreasing cost, it is necessary to distinguish between its application in the long run and in the short run. The long run is here defined as a period of time sufficient to bring about any desired variation in the supply of productive facilities, and the short run is defined as a period of time so short that the supply of these facilities is irrevocably fixed.

Decreasing cost, from the point of view of the long run, exists when average cost varies inversely with output, assuming that for each contemplated level of output the kinds and quantities of factors and intermediate goods employed could be adjusted in the manner most appropriate to *that* output. The average cost for each separate output, in other words, is assumed to be the smallest average cost at which that output could be produced if all necessary adjustments in productive facilities were made. Thus, if an industry is operating at a scale of output such that increases in output would be accompanied by reductions in cost *in the long run,* the industry may be regarded as one of long-run decreasing cost. Decreasing cost from the point of view of the short run, on the other hand, exists when average cost varies inversely with output, assuming that the supply of specialized facilities employed in the industry is given. Short-run decreasing cost occurs whenever the more intensive use of existing facilities, which are the result of past and irrevocable investment decisions, would reduce average cost through spreading the cost of these facilities over a larger number of units of output.[10] From these definitions of long-run and short-run decreasing cost, an industry may be subject simultaneously to both short-run and long-run decreasing cost or to short-run but not long-run decreasing cost.

The following discussion relates only to the long run.

Economical Output for Industries Subject to Long-Run Decreasing Cost

When a decreasing-cost industry is operated for profit by capitalist private enterprise, the price must be at least equal to

---

10 In cases where the possibility of adjustment is slight even in the long run, short-run and long-run decreasing costs merge.

average cost (in accordance with the first pricing rule above). Otherwise the firm cannot hope to survive, since its total cost will exceed its total revenue. For this reason it is commonly (I think erroneously) concluded (a) that it is uneconomical for such an industry to be carried on unless, *at some output,* price can be equal to or greater than average cost, and (b) that it is economical for output to be as large as is consistent with the condition that price be equal to average cost.[11] These conclusions have, of course, been criticized by Marshall,[12] Pigou,[13] and many other writers of whom Hotelling is the outstanding recent example.[14] It has been held by these writers that it would be socially desirable to extend production in decreasing-cost industries *beyond* that output which would make possible an equality between price and cost. It is the purpose of this section to discuss this possibility.

For the moment let us assume that the criteria for deciding when it is desirable to establish a decreasing-cost industry are settled, and that the only immediate problem is: What should be the output of such an industry?

Let us assume, for example, that it has been decided to construct a highway connecting two cities, and that the cost of such a project is absolutely fixed and bears no relation whatsoever to the amount of traffic using the road. Thus, the total cost will be the same whether one vehicle or a million pass over the road. Under these assumptions, it is clearly evident that the price of the use of the road ought, in the interests of economy, to be zero, i.e., the use of the road ought to be made free. If, instead, a price is charged, the use of the road will then be restricted since only those persons will travel that way who receive enough satisfaction to make it worth the price. On many occasions, however, individuals will refrain from using the highway—even though they desire to do so—because the satisfaction obtained is not

11 Gustav Cassel, *Theory of Social Economy,* rev. ed., New York, 1932, pp. 104-106.

12 Alfred Marshall, *Principles of Economics,* 8th ed., London, 1930, pp. 472-473.

13 A. C. Pigou, *Economics of Welfare,* 2nd ed., p. 197.

14 Harold Hotelling, "The General Welfare in Relation to Problems of Taxation and of Railway and Utility Rates," *Econometrica,* July, 1938, pp. 242-269. See also, Emery Troxel, *Economics of Public Utilities,* New York, 1947, pp. 441-463.

sufficient to justify the necessary outlay. The charging of a price for the use of the road will thus prevent the achievement of a part of the satisfactions which the road is capable of yielding, yet there is no reason for limiting the use of the road since, by hypothesis, the extra use involves no additional cost.

But, it may be inquired, if the use of such a road is to become free, how will the project be "financed"? The cost of the road must obviously be recovered in some way and yet the charging of a price is ruled out. The answer is that the necessary "finances" must be raised through some form of payment that will not, like a price, be made a condition of using the highway. This, in practice, means *taxation*—taxation sufficient to cover all costs of the industry. This method of finance is, however, subject to one difficulty, namely, that it is likely to bring about a more or less arbitrary redistribution of real income. Those persons who are frequent users of the road stand to gain at the expense of those who would be required to pay taxes but yet would travel little on the road. These redistributive consequences can be minimized if the tax is levied more or less according to "benefit" [15] but in practice could probably not be wholly eliminated. Consequently, over and against any social gain from finance through taxation must be set the possible redistribution of income which would be undesirable, assuming a "correct" distribution of income to begin with.

Let us now make the more realistic assumption that the *total* cost of providing the highway increases as the amount of traffic to be accommodated becomes larger, but that the increase in total cost is less than proportional to the increase in planned output. This means that the industry is subject to decreasing average cost, but that there are marginal costs associated with each increase in traffic. This is illustrated in Table XI, showing the total cost, average cost, and marginal cost of providing a road suitable for different amounts of traffic. The cost schedule is based on the assumption that, for each different volume of traffic, the highway to be provided would be the least costly one that would accommodate that amount of traffic. It is, in other

---

[15] A possible method of taxation would be to classify persons on the basis of their potential or probable use of the road, and to tax the individuals in each group in a manner that would levy upon them their "fair" share of the cost.

words, a long-run cost schedule.[16] Also in the table (column 5) is a hypothetical demand schedule showing the price or toll which would limit traffic to each of the various possible amounts.

Referring to Table XI, average cost would be covered by any toll over 25 cents; therefore, the highway would be a paying proposition if provision were made for any number of vehicles

TABLE XI

Hypothetical Cost Schedules for a Highway

1	2	3	4	5
Amount of Traffic to Be Provided for: Number of Vehicles per Year	Total Cost per Year	Average Cost per Vehicle	Approximate Marginal Cost	Price or Toll Which Would Limit Traffic to Amount Shown in Column 1
50,000	$30,000	60c.	...	70c.
100,000	40,000	40	19c.	56
150,000	49,000	33	17	45
200,000	57,000	29	15	35
250,000	63,000	25	13	25
300,000	70,000	23	11	18
350,000	75,000	21	9	11
400,000	79,000	20	7	5
450,000	82,000	18	5	0
500,000	84,000	17	...	...

between 50,000 and 250,000. It would be clearly in the social interest, however, to provide *at least* for 250,000 vehicles at a toll of 25 cents, because at any amount less than 250,000 the importance of the wants satisfied, as measured by price, would clearly be greater than cost. So far, there can be no disagreement. Moreover, and this is the crucial point, it is also in the social interest to provide for more than the greatest output which would make possible an equivalence between price and average cost—in this case, 250,000—and to charge a price lower, even, than 25 cents. The reason for this is that the extra cost of providing the addi-

---

16 Part of the cost of the use of a highway, it should be noted, may be borne by the owner or possessors of the vehicles in the form of wear and tear on vehicles, danger of accident, loss of time, physical discomfort, etc. In our cost schedule it is assumed that these costs will be equal regardless of the amount of traffic to be provided for. In actual practice, of course, the provision for more traffic is often accompanied by a speeding up of the highway and a reduction in wear and tear on vehicles and passengers.

tional capacity, once it is decided to build the highway, would be small relative to the extra satisfaction that would be obtained through the additional use of the road. For example, if 250,000 vehicles were using the road, the marginal cost of providing for additional vehicles would be only 13 cents. This means that only "13 cents' worth" of resources would need be used in order to provide additional satisfactions valued at 25 cents. Thus, so long as price exceeded marginal cost, there would be a possibility of obtaining net gains in satisfaction by extending the use of the highway, and economy would be realized only when the use of the road was increased to that point where price and *marginal cost* were equal. In other words, it would pay to increase the use of the highway so long as the *additional* satisfactions (as measured by the price paid for them) were sufficient to warrant the *extra* cost. In our example, this implies that the highway should be planned to accommodate approximately 375,000 vehicles, and in order that this number of vehicles might actually use the highway, that the toll be set at about 8 cents per vehicle.

Application of the principle that price should be equal to marginal cost for a decreasing-cost industry means that total revenues will fall short of total cost, and that the firm will not be self-supporting. Therefore it is required that the deficit be made up out of taxation of a kind which will not restrict the use of the road. This taxation, of course, may possibly involve an uneconomical redistribution of income.

The general conclusion is reached that it is economical to adjust output in a decreasing-cost industry so that the price is equal to marginal cost, and to finance the deficit through taxation of a type which will not affect the rate of consumption of the product. In this way the output of the industry is increased so that the fixed costs can be spread out more thinly and average cost reduced. The resulting transfer of resources to the decreasing-cost industry, in order to meet additional variable costs, can be justified because the value of the marginal product of these resources is equal to their price.[17] Or, in other words,

---

[17] The rule that output should be adjusted in a decreasing-cost industry so that price is equal to marginal cost is actually included within the general rule that the marginal product of each factor should be equal to its price. This rule, however, does not adequately cover the fixed factors for which the concept of marginal product does not apply.

the satisfactions obtained are more important (in terms of price) than those which would have been achieved if the same resources were applied at the margin to increasing-cost industries. These conclusions are valid, however, only providing the taxes required to make up the deficit do not have redistributive effects so undesirable as to offset the gain from fuller utilization of fixed plant.[18]

Criteria for Determining Whether a Decreasing-Cost Industry Should Be Established

So far in our discussion of decreasing cost, we have assumed that it has already been decided to start the industry and that the only problem is to find the most economical output. We now must attempt to discover criteria for deciding whether or not it is economical to establish such an industry.

In order to pose the problem clearly, it will be well first to go as far as possible within the area of general agreement. It is always economical to establish an industry, whether under increasing or decreasing cost, if there is some level of output at which price will be at least equal to average cost (i.e., if the demand curve crosses or lies above the average-cost curve). Also, in an *increasing*-cost industry, it is uneconomical to start production unless a level of output can be found where price is at least equal to cost, because under no circumstances will it then be possible for the satisfaction from any single unit (as measured by price) to be equal to cost. With this, we reach the end of the area of agreement. The question that is left is this: Is it ever economical to establish a decreasing-cost industry even if there is no output at which price is at least equal to average cost?

---

18 A minor problem in the achievement of economy arises from the fact that pricing is itself costly. It involves the setting of the price, the marking of the goods, and the setting up of machinery for collecting the money. Thus, whenever a price is very small and the cost of administering high, there may be serious doubt as to whether it is worth collecting at all. For example, if the most economical toll for a bridge should turn out to be 2 cents per vehicle, it would be doubtful whether it would be wise to establish the machinery for collecting the toll and to cause motorists the annoyance and loss of time involved in a toll stop. Such a toll could be justified only if it were necessary to prevent use of the bridge beyond its capacity.

The traditional and most common answer to this question is in the negative. However, the contrary view is gaining ground that under certain circumstances, to establish a decreasing-cost industry is economical even when there is no possibility of finding an output at which price will cover cost. It is held that the industry should be established so long as the *total benefit* from its operation exceeds the total cost involved; and this may be possible even though price and average cost cannot be equated. For example, in Figure 1, the demand curve (*DD'*) lies, at all

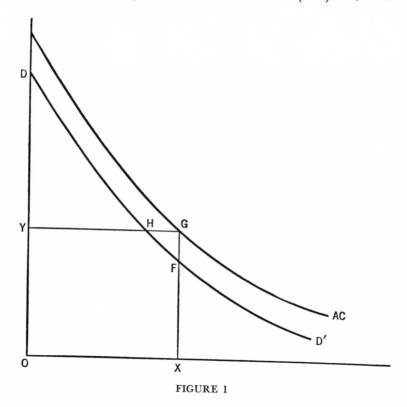

FIGURE 1

points, below the average-cost curve (*AC*). The total benefit from the industry when the output is *OX* may be measured approximately [19] as the entire area under the demand curve

    [19] See Hotelling, *op. cit.*, pp. 246-256 for mathematical discussion of this point.

ODFX. The total cost of this output is *OYGX*, which is clearly smaller than the benefit as measured by the area *ODFX*. (The triangle *FGH* is smaller than the triangle *DYH*.) Therefore, to establish the industry would be economical. To generalize these results, whenever an output can be found at which total benefits exceed total cost, it will be in the social interest for production to be undertaken.

It may be objected that this principle could be applied as well to increasing- or constant-cost industries. This is, however, not possible. If the demand curve for an increasing- or constant-cost industry fails to intersect with the average-cost curve, total benefits cannot possibly exceed total cost.

The conclusion that a decreasing-cost industry should be established whenever total benefit exceeds total cost is misleadingly definite. The impression might easily be conveyed that here we have a completely objective criterion for deciding upon the establishment of a decreasing-cost industry. The difficulty, of course, is that we seldom have the facts regarding demand upon which the estimates of total benefit would be based. The area under the demand curve is usually somewhat conjectural. This, however, is not a totally new problem. Even private entrepreneurs, when considering the establishment of such an industry, must attempt to ascertain the likely demand before investing their money. In other words, the criterion of total benefit does not raise new problems.

Conclusions

The discussion of decreasing cost has yielded two conclusions: (1) That the most economical output for an industry subject to long-run decreasing cost is that which can be sold at a price equal to long-run marginal cost, providing the gain from fuller utilization of fixed plant is not offset by the effects of undesirable taxes; (2) That a decreasing-cost industry should be established whenever, at some output, the total satisfactions to be derived from the product are in excess of the total cost of production. Each of these conclusions represents an extension or modification of the pricing rules in order to take into account the special circumstances of industries subject to decreasing cost.

Chapter 18

COLLECTIVE CHOICE [1]

In the preceding chapter it was shown that the general pricing rules must be modified when applied to industries of decreasing cost. In the present chapter it will be shown that the pricing rules must be further amended if they are to be useful in determining outputs of a special class of goods which we shall refer to as *social goods*.

Social Goods

The very cornerstone of the pricing rules is that resources are to be allocated in response to the choices of *individuals* as reflected in their expenditures of income. It is assumed that no individual will receive any good unless he has paid the established price for it. Under this assumption, price becomes an effective barrier between the individual and available goods; it is a barrier which he must surmount if he is to obtain any good and which excludes him from securing goods for which he is unwilling to pay the price. In actual practice, however, there is a large class of goods for which price exclusion is not practicable. In regulating the production of these goods, therefore, it is not possible to rely upon the guidance of individual demand in the manner presupposed by the pricing theory.

The goods for which price exclusion is impracticable are characterized by the fact that they cannot be divided up into

---

[1] Large portions of this chapter appeared as an article, "The Interpretation of Voting in the Allocation of Economic Resources," *Quarterly Journal of Economics,* November, 1943, pp. 27-48. I am indebted to the editors of the *Quarterly Journal of Economics* for permission to reproduce substantial portions of this article.

units of which any single individual can be given exclusive possession. They are, in this sense, *indivisible*. Such goods have the characteristic that they become part of the general environment—available to all individuals who live within that environment. They are, in that sense, social rather than strictly individual goods. The nature of these social goods may be clarified by illustrations.

Suppose that a malarial swamp is to be drained. All individuals in the vicinity will share in the benefit from this productive service; no one individual will be the sole recipient of the satisfaction, and no person in the area can be excluded from participating in the satisfaction. The resulting freedom from malaria will "permeate" the environment of the entire vicinity, and all who live there will benefit. It is true that the drainage might be carried out in response to the demand of some one individual who would bear the entire cost, but in view of the fact that many individuals will derive benefit from the project, it would be eminently more fair if the cost were to be borne by the entire group of beneficiaries. Consequently, collective action would ordinarily be resorted to in demanding the resources required. The individuals likely to benefit might, for example, form a voluntary association, and divide the cost among them on some mutually agreeable basis. It would frequently happen, however, that some individuals would fail to cooperate because, even without contributing, they could still enjoy the benefits. Under these circumstances, the cooperating group would probably seek a method of coercing the "slackers." This, in practice, would probably mean that the project would be turned over to a governmental body with the power to meet the costs by means of compulsory levies known as taxes. In this way, all persons presumed to derive satisfaction from the improvement would be required to pay a portion of its cost.[2]

Similarly, if military protection is required to ward off threatened invasion, all individuals in the group are likely to benefit from the activities of the armed forces. It would be difficult to exclude any individuals from the benefit and thus to make the receipt of benefit conditional upon payment of a

---

[2] This is not to be interpreted as implying that the taxation would necessarily be based upon the "benefit" theory.

price. Consequently, the provision of this service in response to individual demands would be impracticable since many of the beneficiaries would fail to pay their "share" of the cost. To ensure the success of the military operation, the collective exercise of demand (with taxation) would be necessary. Only in this way would all those who benefit contribute toward the cost.

Like considerations would apply to many of the traditional services of government, including preventive health services, maintenance of law and order, education, fire protection, beautification of the landscape, flood control, and many others.[3] The benefits from all of these goods are more or less "indivisible" and "social." Consequently, the provision of these goods must usually be carried on in response to *collective* rather than individual choice.[4]

Collective choice implies that a single decision is made for a *group* of persons, the decision being reached by political processes. If there are differences of taste among the members of the group, such decisions can hardly be expected to result in equal marginal satisfactions for all persons—as would be required for perfect economy. The problem, nevertheless, is to reach that decision which approaches most closely to the ideal of maximum aggregate satisfaction.

---

[3] Another very special instance of the provision of indivisible goods occurs in connection with that "production" which is designed to add to the body of knowledge, e.g., research, invention, and perhaps the creation of new literature and music. This type of production yields a product which immediately becomes part of the common heritage unless deliberate efforts are made to prevent this from happening. Thus, the production of new ideas must respond to collective rather than individual choice unless, perhaps, a system of patents and copyrights limits the right of individuals freely to use or benefit from the new discoveries. See pp. 5–6, 61.

[4] The fact of collective choice does not imply that the production, to give effect to that choice, must be organized and carried on collectively. For instance, in the draining of the malarial swamp, the actual work could be organized by the state or by a private firm, the decision depending largely upon matters of expediency. The significant fact is that demand is exercised collectively—not that production is organized under the aegis of the group. In fact, the question of whether the state or private enterprise shall perform the entrepreneurial function of organizing and superintending the productive factors is totally unrelated to the character of the demand. Even when demand originates from individual choice, production may be carried on by the state (e.g., postal service or generation of electric power).

Quantitative Measurement of Social Goods

In discussing the ideal output of social goods, it is necessary at the outset to establish meaningful units in which quantities of social goods may be measured. This raises certain difficulties, because most of the things ordinarily regarded as social goods are highly complex. Each comprises whole congeries of particular goods which can be provided in many different ways and in different combinations. For example, an increase in the "quantity" of education available in a given community may take the form of additional buildings, changes in curricula, inclusion of a greater number of students, addition of new educational units such as kindergartens or junior colleges, raising of minimum teacher requirements, etc. Thus, quantities of "education" cannot be measured in simple physical units of volume, time, or weight. There are, however, other practicable quantitative measures of education and other such similar complex social goods.

One approach is to treat separately each component element of the complex social good. Thus, instead of dealing with quantities of "education" taken as a whole, attention would be centered on buildings, equipment, number of teachers, training and grade of teachers, hours devoted to particular subjects, number of students participating, hours of instruction per day, days of instruction per year, etc. Reasonably satisfactory quantitative measures could be assigned to each of these components. This solution is essentially similar to that which is ordinarily applied in measuring quantities of individual goods. Here the good is defined, not in terms of complexes such as food, but in terms of particular components such as cane sugar or No. 2 red wheat. Another possible approach is to measure the quantity of complex social goods simply in terms of their money cost. This solution is based on the principle that any decision to change the quantity of a complex social good may be resolved into two distinguishable parts: (1) a decision as to the relative priorities of various particular component services, and (2) a decision as to the amount of the over-all increase or decrease. If the scale of priorities is established so that it is known what particular services are to be added with increasing expenditure and what services are to be dropped with decreasing expenditure, then the quantity of the complex social good can be usefully measured in terms of the amount of money expended.

Each of the two approaches is useful and each is applicable to certain practical situations. Whenever the scale of priorities is not definitely established or agreed upon, the separate treatment of each component in terms of physical units would be preferred. On the other hand, whenever the scale of priorities is clearly established or whenever the determination of the scale is to be referred to experts or representatives, the second approach of measuring quantities in terms of cost would be preferred.

The following analysis is arranged so that either of the two measures may be employed alternatively. If physical units are used, increasing, constant, or decreasing cost may apply, whereas if cost units are used, only constant cost may apply. It should be emphasized that the quantity of a social good, whatever measure is used, refers to the quantity available in the community as a whole, not necessarily to the amount available to any particular person or consumption unit.

Ideal Output of Social Goods

Suppose that the citizens of a given community are faced with the task of deciding how much public education should be made available. It is inevitable that the citizens will differ regarding this question. Some, perhaps, will wish to have no education under any circumstances, some will want no more than the three R's, and others will desire a highly developed system of schools. Assuming a "correct" distribution of income, each person's taste can be expressed by a curve indicating the amount of money he would be willing to give up in order to have successive additional quantities made available in the community. Such a curve would be analogous to an individual demand curve. It would express, for different possible quantities of education, the individual's marginal rate of substitution between education and other goods (money). A series of such curves of individual marginal substitution is shown in Figure 2 for a community which is assumed to contain three persons (MS_a, MS_b, MS_c). The marginal rates of substitution of the three individuals, for each quantity of education, can be added to give the total marginal rate of substitution of the entire population. In this way a "curve of total marginal substitution" (*TMS* in Figure 2) can be constructed, expressing the amount of money the members of the group collectively would be willing to give up in order to obtain successive units of education. This curve

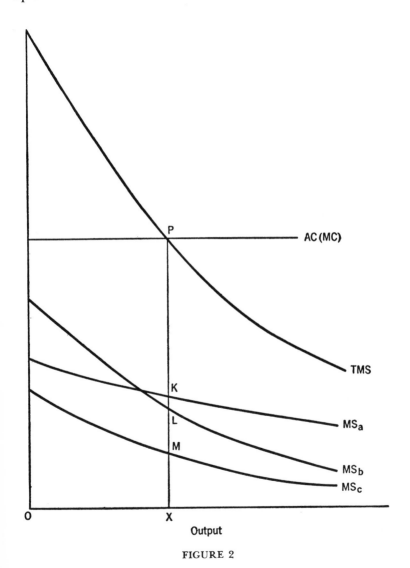

FIGURE 2

corresponds, as closely as is possible under the conditions, to the familiar curve of total demand.[5]

One of the cardinal principles in determining the output of an individual good is that price should equal average cost or marginal cost, whichever is relevant. This implies that the ideal output is indicated by the point of intersection between the demand curve and the appropriate cost curve. Through the use of the curve of total marginal substitution, this principle can be adapted to the problem of determining the ideal output of a social good. Thus, to continue with our illustration, the ideal output of education is indicated by the point of intersection between the curve of total marginal substitution and the appropriate cost curve—which one depending upon whether increasing or decreasing cost prevails at relevant outputs. This is shown in Figure 2 (assuming constant cost) by the point of intersection (P) between the curve of total marginal substitution (TMS) and the curve of average cost (AC). OX is the ideal output.[6]

Ideal output can also be indicated in another way, which will prove more useful for subsequent analysis. For this, three new curves are required: (1) a curve expressing the average marginal rate of substitution per person (TMS/N), (2) a curve expressing average cost per person (AC/N), and (3) a curve expressing marginal cost per person (MC/N). These curves are derived by dividing the total marginal rate of substitution, average cost, and marginal cost, respectively, by the number of people (N). Ideal output, originally defined as the output at which the total marginal rate of substitution is equal to average (or marginal) cost, can also be designated as the output at which the average marginal rate of substitution is equal to average cost per person (or marginal cost per person). This follows since, at the output

---

[5] It must be noted that this curve differs from the familiar curve of total demand, which denotes the amount of a good that individuals are willing to buy at each of several prices. The demand curve is obtained by adding the number of units of the good that would be purchased by the various individuals at each possible price (horizontal addition); whereas the curve of total marginal substitution is obtained by adding the marginal rates of substitution (expressed in money) of the various individuals at each possible quantity of the social good (vertical addition).

[6] If there were no point of intersection between the two curves, i.e., if average cost were at all outputs greater than total marginal substitution, the service should not be offered at all.

where AC (or MC) equals TMS, AC/N (or MC/N) must equal TMS/N. See Figure 3.

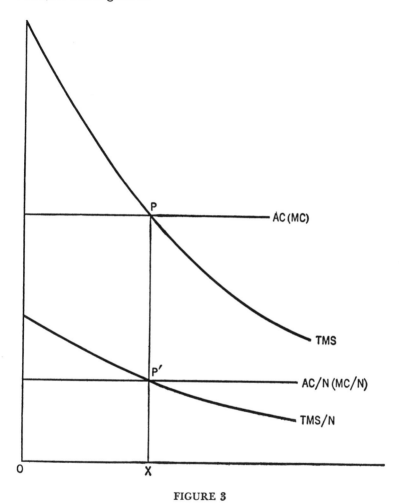

FIGURE 3

Individual Voting on Outputs

It has been shown that the optimum output of social goods is indicated by the intersection of the curve of average marginal substitution (TMS/N) and the appropriate curve of cost per person (AC/N or MC/N). If this formulation is to be practically useful, something must be known—directly or by inference—about marginal rates of substitution and costs. It is, of course, no more difficult to obtain information on the cost of producing social goods than to get similar data on individual goods; but to estimate marginal rates of substitution presents serious problems, since it requires the measurement of the preferences for goods which, by their very nature, cannot be subjected to individual consumer choice.

The closest substitute for consumer choice is *voting*. Consequently, it may be worth while to explore the possible use of voting as a means of measuring or inferring marginal rates of substitution and hence of determining ideal output. Suppose that our community, faced with the problem of determining the precise quantity of education to provide, allows each individual to indicate, by means of voting, the amount of education that he prefers. Each individual's preference will depend upon two factors: (1) the relative amount of satisfaction *he* expects to derive from different amounts of education—as indicated by his curve of marginal substitution, and (2) the cost *to him* of different amounts of education. The latter will depend partly on the total cost to the community of different amounts and partly on the contemplated distribution of that cost among different individuals. Each individual will, of course, vote for that quantity at which *his* marginal rate of substitution is equal to *his* marginal cost. This would be indicated by the point of intersection between his curve of marginal substitution and his curve of marginal cost.

At this point it is necessary to digress briefly in order to introduce four assumptions:

First, it is assumed that all individuals in the community actually vote and that each expresses a preference which is appropriate to his individual interests.

Second, it is assumed that the cost to the community of providing various possible quantities of education is known. Curves AC, AC/N, MC and MC/N can then be constructed.

Third, it is assumed that the cost of whatever amount of education is to be "produced" will be divided equally among all the citizens. Thus the curve of average cost for each citizen will be equal to AC/N and the curve of marginal cost for each citizen equal to MC/N. The implications of this assumption will be analyzed in a later section on the distribution of the cost of social goods.

Fourth, it is assumed that the several curves of individual marginal substitution are distributed according to the normal law of error. This implies that there is a large number of such curves—one for each person—and that these curves are arranged so that at *each quantity of education* the marginal rates of substitution of the several persons are distributed symmetrically about a mode (see Figure 4). Thus, if a vertical line, cutting the several curves, is erected at any point Z along the horizontal axis, the points of intersection (a, b, c, d, e, f, g) between this line and

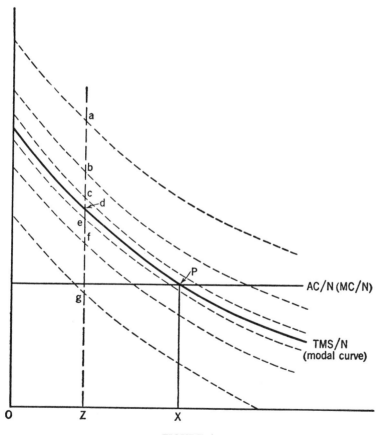

FIGURE 4

the several curves of marginal substitution will tend to be distributed along the line according to the normal law of error. Most of the intersections will occur near the mode (d), but some will occur at varying distances above and below the mode. Indeed, a modal curve can be drawn indicating the position of the mode at each quantity of output, and this modal curve will, still assuming a symmetrical distribution of the curves, coincide with the curve of average marginal substitution (TMS/N).[7]

This assumption can conform to the facts of individual preference only if two conditions are met. (a) The tastes or desires of individuals must actually be distributed according to the normal law of error. Whether this condition is realized in practice is not known definitely, but available information suggests that it is not an unreasonable hypothesis. For example, the data in the Consumer Purchases Study of the United States Department of Agriculture indicate that consumer tastes for individual goods are distributed normally. Three series from this study, selected from hundreds of similar series, are shown in Table XII.[8] (b) All individuals must be potentially in an equal position to benefit from the social good. This condition is not always realized in practice. For example, childless persons may be less interested in education than families with children. Thus, even though the curves of marginal substitution of either class of persons might be arranged symmetrically, the distribution of the curves for the two classes together might be significantly skewed or multi-modal. However, most social goods are or can be made available on relatively equal terms to all persons, e.g., health services, protection from foreign enemies, maintenance of law and order, etc. For the moment, therefore, we shall postulate that all individuals are equally able to benefit from the social good under consideration. In this way, we

---

[7] In a symmetrical distribution the mode and the arithmetic mean are identical. It is to be noted, however, that the symmetry of a frequency distribution may be disturbed by the fact that zero is the lower limit of the data. In terms of the present problem, zero represents the lowest possible marginal rate of substitution (except in cases where the commodity is so abundant as to be a nuisance). At relatively large outputs, therefore, the marginal rate of substitution of some individuals would be zero, and the modal marginal rate of substitution would be less than the average per capita.

[8] For data on the symmetry of the distribution of physical characteristics of human beings, see U. S. Public Health Service, *A Health Study of 10,000 Male Industrial Workers*, Public Health Bulletin No. 162, pp. 31-79.

may continue with the assumption that individual marginal substitutions are distributed according to the normal law of error. Later we shall take up the problem of social goods which are not equally available to all.

TABLE XII

Percentage Distribution of Families by Expenditures for Various Purposes: White, Nonrelief, Native-Born Families, 1935–36[a]

Annual Expenditures for Food: Farm Families with Three or More Children, and with Incomes from $1,000 to $1,499 Per Year, Middle Atlantic and North Central States[b]		Annual Expenditures for Clothing: Village Families with Two Young Children and with Incomes from $1,500 to $1,999, Pennsylvania and Ohio[c]		Total Annual Expenditure for Family Living: Small City Families with Incomes from $2,000 to $2,249, North Central States[d]	
Expenditure	Percentage of Families	Expenditure	Percentage of Families	Expenditure	Percentage of Families
$50–$99	4%	Under $50	4%	$750–$999	2%
100–149	16			1,000–1,249	8
150–199	25	$50–$99	15	1,250–1,499	13
200–249	17	100–149	28	1,500–1,749	21
250–299	19	150–199	33	1,750–1,999	29
300–349	9	200–249	16	2,000–2,249	17
350–399	5	250–299	4	2,250–2,499	5
400–449	3			2,500–2,999	4
450 or over	2			3,000–3,499	1
Total	100%	Total	100%	Total	100%

[a] Data based on Consumer Purchases Study made by the United States Department of Agriculture in cooperation with the Work Projects Administration.
[b] U. S. D. A., Miscellaneous Publication, No. 405, 1941, p. 14.
[c] U. S. D. A., Miscellaneous Publication, No. 422, 1941, p. 17.
[d] U. S. D. A., Miscellaneous Publication, No. 396, 1940, p. 33.

Under the conditions assumed, if the citizens are allowed to vote on the quantity of education to be provided, each person will vote for the quantity indicated by the intersection between his individual curve of marginal substitution and his curve of marginal cost (MC/N). Since the various individuals will presumably be interested in education to varying degrees, as indicated by the dispersion of the individual curves of marginal substitution, a wide variety of preferences will be indicated. Referring to Figure 4, those whose curves of marginal substitution lie in the lower left part of the diagram will favor a relatively small amount; those whose curves of marginal substitution lie in the upper right will favor a relatively large amount. But, assuming that the curves of marginal substitution are distributed according to the normal law of error, one intermediate amount (OX) will be voted for by more individuals than any other single amount. The individuals voting for this quantity are those whose marginal rates of substitution are modal, and the amount voted for by this modal group may be presumed to indicate the point of intersection (P) between the curve of marginal cost per person (MC/N) and the modal or average curve of marginal substitution (TMS/N). Thus voting makes possible the location of one point (P) on the curve of average marginal substitution (TMS/N), namely, the point at which the curve of individual marginal cost (MC/N) intersects with (TMS/N).[9] See Figure 4.

If education is "produced" under conditions of constant cost, as shown in Figure 4, marginal and average cost will be identical. Hence the modal vote will indicate not only the point of intersection between TMS/N and MC/N but also the point of intersection between TMS/N and AC/N. This latter point, as stated above, occurs at the optimum output. Hence the modal vote provides direct information as to the most economical amount of education to provide.

If education is "produced" under decreasing cost, the modal vote will also give the desired information directly. In this case the marginal cost curve (MC/N) lies below the average cost curve (AC/N). However, the most economical output is that at which the marginal rate of substitution and marginal (rather than average) cost are equal. Thus the modal vote directly indicates the most economical output.

If, however, education is produced under conditions of increasing cost, the modal vote cannot directly denote optimum output. It can indicate only the point of intersection between MC/N and TMS/N, not the point of intersection between AC/N and TMS/N which is required. A further elaboration of our technique is therefore necessary.

This case requires a different procedure of taxation. The cost must be raised by means of a tax levied upon each individual in the form of a "price" per unit of the social good, it being

---

[9] In order to designate this point of intersection, it is not necessary that the majority of *all* the voters should prefer this amount. It is only necessary that more persons vote for this amount than for any other.

understood (1) that the price is to remain constant regardless of output, and (2) that the price is to be uniform for all individuals. From the point of view of any one individual, this "price" represents his marginal cost. His marginal cost curve would appear, therefore, as a horizontal line, the height of which would be determined by the "price." Moreover, since the same "price" would be charged all individuals, the marginal-cost curve would be the same for all. This curve is shown in Figure 5 as *IMC* (individual marginal cost).

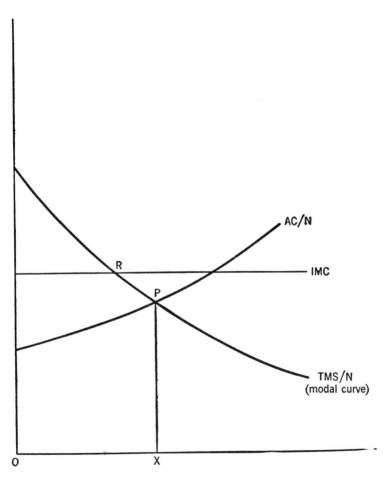

FIGURE 5

Let us now suppose that the "price" of education is set, and that the citizens are asked to vote on the quantity of education they prefer. Each person will, of course, vote for the quantity indicated by the intersection between his curve of marginal substitution and the curve of marginal cost (IMC), and the modal vote will locate the point of intersection (R) between TMS/N and IMC. The optimum output, however, is determined by the intersection of TMS/N and AC/N; the modal vote does not locate this point. From the position of point R relative to curve AC/N, it can be ascertained, however, whether the intersection of TMS/N and AC/N lies to the right or to the left of point R.

If R is above curve AC/N, then the point of intersection lies to the right of R,[10] and output should be increased beyond the amount voted for by the modal group. And if R lies below curve AC/N, the point of intersection is to the left of R and output should be reduced to less than the amount voted for by the modal group. This relationship is to be explained by the fact that if R lies above curve AC/N, the price announced to the voters is so high that (at this price) the modal group prefer less than the optimum amount of the good; and if R is below curve AC/N, the price is so low that the modal group prefer more than the optimum amount. Only when R lies on curve AC/N (i.e., when curves AC/N, IMC, and TMS/N all intersect at the same time) will the vote of the modal group indicate the optimum output.

The result of the voting depends entirely on the price announced. The question arises, then, whether there is any rule by which the correct price could be ascertained in advance of the voting. The answer is in the negative. However, as a result of successive trials and errors over a period of time the correct price could be closely approached, especially since (1) the direction of the error is known after each trial, and (2) more than one point on the TMS/N curve would be known after several trials.[11] It is conceivable, moreover, that the voters might be asked to indicate their preferences at each of several possible prices, so that the position of TMS/N could be ascertained along several points

---

10 Assuming that curve TMS/N slopes negatively.

11 This raises a problem similar to that of deducing a demand curve from a time series.

and the intersection of TMS/N and AC/N could be located immediately.[12]

Individual Voting on Increments
to Existing Outputs

Let us now assume that the individuals of a community are permitted to vote, not on how much of the good they prefer, but rather on whether or not they wish a given increment or decrement to the quantity already provided. This situation is illustrated by school elections, common in the United States, in which citizens are asked to vote "yes" or "no" on a proposed bond issue for the purpose of constructing a new school building.

Suppose the community is composed of seven persons whose marginal substitution curves are distributed symmetrically, as shown in Figure 6, and that the cost of education (or any increment in the quantity) is to be divided equally among them. Assume that quantity OX_1 (Figure 6) is actually being provided and that the people are asked to vote on the question whether or not they wish a small increase in the quantity up to OX_2. All those persons whose marginal rates of substitution at quantity OX_2 are greater than the marginal cost (MC/N) at that quantity will vote "yes," and those whose marginal rates of substitution are less than marginal cost will vote "no." In this case, as shown in Figure 6, the vote will be six in favor of the increment and one against. Suppose, then, that the citizens are asked to vote on another increment which will raise the quantity to OX_3, the point at which MC/N and TMS/N are equal. On this question, one half the citizens will vote "yes" and one half "no." Finally, suppose the citizens are asked to vote on still another increment

---

[12] It is tempting to assume that the average of the amounts voted for by the several individuals represents the optimum output. In fact, it does not. The average amount voted for will be greater or less than the optimum output, depending upon the slope, shape, and position of the individual curves of marginal substitution. Similarly, the assumption that the curves of marginal substitution are distributed according to the normal law of error in no way implies that the results of the *voting* will also be distributed in the same way. The distribution of the vote may be skewed in either direction—depending on the shape of the curves—without violating the assumption that the curves are distributed according to the normal law of error.

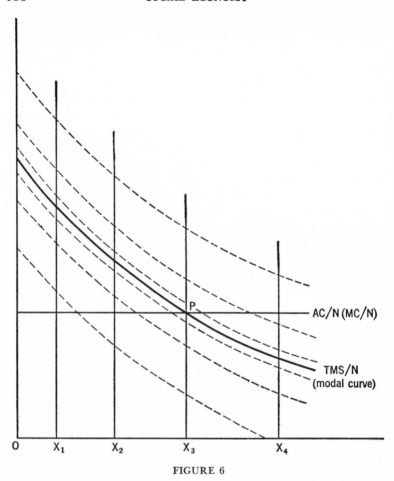

FIGURE 6

which will increase the quantity to OX_4. This time, six persons will vote against and one will be in favor.

From these illustrations it may be seen that as the quantity of education is increased, bit by bit, a majority of the voters will favor each additional increment until a quantity is reached such that the average marginal rate of substitution (TMS/N) is equal to marginal cost (MC/N). At this point the vote is equally divided. Beyond this point, the majority of the voters are opposed to additional increments. Thus it is possible to locate the point of intersection between curves TMS/N and MC/N by finding an increment (or decrement), through trial and error, which is favored by one half of the voters and opposed by the other half.

This procedure makes possible the direct determination of optimum output for "industries" subject to constant cost and decreasing cost. In these cases, the intersection of TMS/N and MC/N determines the most economical quantity of the social good. This procedure does not, however, directly give the answer for "industries" of increasing cost. For them, it is the point of intersection between curves TMS/N and AC/N (not between TMS/N and MC/N) which must be located. This can be done, but only by a procedure so awkward as to be virtually useless.[13]

On the whole, the procedure of voting on increments does not lend itself well to the determination of optimum output. For constant and decreasing cost "industries" it is somewhat more complicated than the method of asking voters to indicate the quantities they prefer, and for increasing cost "industries" it is hopeless.

Alternatives to Voting

In a society which has outgrown the town-meeting stage, it is seldom practicable to decide on the output of specific social goods by means of popular voting. More commonly, public officials (legislators, elected or appointed administrators, dictators, etc.) are endowed with the power to make such decisions and are expected to act in the "general interest." This means that such officials, if they are to carry out their duties, must have methods of finding out what the people want, i.e., how much of each social good should be produced.

The people can be consulted by letting them vote on par-

---

[13] Several separate trial and error procedures would be involved. First an arbitrary fixed "price" per unit of education would be set, so that the curve of marginal cost for the individuals (IMC) would be a horizontal line. Then each individual would be asked to vote "yes" or "no" on successive increments or decrements, until the point of intersection between IMC and TMS/N could be determined. It would be located at the increment for which one half the voters are in favor and one half opposed. After that, in order to find the intersection of AC/N and TMS/N, it would be necessary to adjust the price and again ask voters to express preferences on increments (or decrements), so that other points on the curve TMS/N could be located. By a wearisome process, it might ultimately be possible to find enough points on curve TMS/N so that the intersection between that curve and AC/N could be located.

ticular questions, or perhaps letting them vote for candidates who identify themselves with particular policies. In this case, if the issues are clearly understood, the results of the election can be interpreted as suggested in the preceding sections. In practice, however, the issues are seldom clear-cut. The result of an election can seldom be regarded as an unequivocal indication of public desires. Hence there is a real need for other techniques of gauging public opinion, i.e., finding the points of intersection between the curves of total marginal substitution and average (or marginal) cost. It is for this reason that a number of writers have recently suggested the possibility of using polls, questionnaires, interviews, budget investigations, and other devices involving samples, to study the desires of the individuals who compose the public. Indeed, with the increasing emphasis upon economic planning, it is imperative that these and other techniques for discovering individual tastes and preferences be developed and employed.[14]

If a poll is based on a representative sample of the population, and if the questions are put in the same way as if the entire citizenry were voting, the results can of course be interpreted in exactly the same way. For such a poll to be as reliable as the results of actual voting, however, several conditions would have to be met.[15] First, it would be necessary that the issue had been discussed sufficiently to enable the pollees to become informed. Second, in order to be sure that the individual pollees would use thought and discretion in reaching their decisions, it would be necessary for them to have a sense of responsibility, i.e., to feel that their choices would actually influence policy.

It is conceivable that techniques involving polls and questionnaires would yield information in greater detail than could be obtained through large-scale voting. It might be possible in this way to carry on minute studies of individual preferences, so

---

14 See Maurice Dobb, *Review of Economic Studies*, February, 1935, pp. 137-148; and Barbara Wootton, *Lament for Economics*, London, 1938, Chapters 5 and 6, especially pp. 289-291.

15 The polling of a "scientifically" selected sample might produce more accurate results than general voting, unless arrangements were made to ensure that every person would actually vote. If voting is voluntary, it is possible that the results may represent the preference of a biased sample of the population, including a relatively large proportion of, perhaps, the "politically minded," the well-to-do, or the better educated.

that actual curves showing marginal rates of substitution, instead of merely a few isolated points on curves, could be obtained.[16]

Distributing the Cost of Social Goods

In the discussion of voting it has been consistently assumed that the cost of providing social goods is to be divided equally among all individuals. This assumption requires further examination. If income were distributed "correctly," so that apportionment of the cost of social goods would not be designed for the purpose of redistributing income, the benefit principle would provide the ideal basis for assessing the costs of social goods. Each person would contribute according to the benefit received by him, and the distribution of real income would be unaffected. In applying the benefit principle, each individual would be charged *as if* he were paying a price per unit for the social good, the price being equal to his marginal rate of substitution at the particular amount of the good being produced. Thus, instead of applying a uniform price to all individuals and allowing each to adjust his consumption according to that price, as with individual goods, a uniform amount of the social good would be provided, and the "price" charged individuals would vary according to their marginal rates of substitution. Referring to Figure 2, if quantity OX were being provided, Individual A would pay a "price" equal to XK, and his contribution would be equal to this price multiplied by the number of units of the good provided (OX). The "price" charged Individual A under this arrangement would be such that, if free individual consumer choice were possible, he would choose the particular quantity of the social good that is actually available.[17] In this way his marginal contribution to the cost of the social good would correspond to his marginal rate of substitution, and his real income would remain unchanged. Any other arrangement would result in his

---

[16] The work of Professor L. L. Thurstone in deriving the indifference schedules of actual individuals is suggestive. See his article "The Indifference Function," *Journal of Social Psychology,* 1931, pp. 139-167. The difficulty with this approach is that individuals must be asked what they would do under various hypothetical conditions. There is always the possibility that verbal preferences would differ significantly from actual choices in a real situation.

[17] If the social good were financed in this way, all individuals would vote for the same output, namely, the most economical quantity.

being made worse or better off. Similarly, the "price" charged Individual B would be XL, and the "price" charged Individual C would be XM (Figure 2). Thus the total amount paid by the three individuals would be equal to the total cost of the service.[18]

The application of the benefit principle is difficult, however, because of problems involved in the measurement of benefit. To determine the cost that should be assessed against an individual, if the benefit principle is to apply, requires that something be known about his marginal rates of substitution. At first thought it might be supposed that this information could be obtained from his vote (or other expression of preference). But the individual could not vote intelligently, unless he knew *in advance* the cost to him of various amounts of the social good, and in any case the results of the voting would be unreliable if the individual suspected that his expression of preference would influence the amount of cost to be assessed against him. Moreover, the practical administrative problem of making nice adjustments between individual benefit and cost would be insuperable.

On the whole, the possibility of distributing costs according to benefit is not very promising. It seems clear that some more or less arbitrary alternative method must be adopted. The problem is to find that arbitrary method which will involve the least error and the fewest practical problems. With an initially "correct" distribution of income, an *equal* distribution of cost seems most practicable. This means, of course, that the provision of social goods may involve the redistribution of income. Those individuals who are forced to pay more in taxes than they get back in benefits will find their real incomes diminished, whereas those who pay out less than they receive in return will enjoy an addition to their real incomes. The seriousness of this redistribution is greatly lessened, however, by the fact that many social goods are ordinarily produced simultaneously. Thus the gain to any

---

18 An exception to this solution for the problem of distributing the burden of costs must be made in the case of a social good provided under conditions of decreasing cost. Here economy requires that output be increased to the point where total marginal substitution is equal to marginal cost. At this output, however, if each individual beneficiary were to contribute an amount equal to his marginal rate of substitution times the number of units of the good produced, total revenue would be insufficient to defray total cost. In this case, therefore, it would be necessary to devise an alternative method that would raise sufficient revenue and yet leave the distribution of incomes unaffected.

one individual from the provision of a particular social good may be counterbalanced by a loss to him resulting from the provision of another social good, and on balance the redistribution of income may be slight.

The great advantage of the equal distribution of cost is that it involves only random errors, whereas any other arbitrary distribution introduces a constant bias in favor of some particular group or class. It also has the advantage that it helps to clarify the desires of the public regarding the distribution of social goods. If costs are not distributed equally, variations in amounts voted for by different individuals would depend quite as much upon differences in individual marginal costs as upon differences in individual marginal rates of substitution, and the modal vote would not necessarily indicate the point of intersection between the curve of marginal (or average) cost per capita and the curve of average marginal substitution. Indeed, if the output of social goods is to be determined by the preferences of individuals, it must be possible to obtain expressions of individual preferences unalloyed by differences in individual marginal costs. In other words, a necessary condition to the use of individual preferences in determining the ideal output of social goods is that the cost of social goods be distributed equally. Since equal distribution of cost is desirable on other grounds, as pointed out, this condition does not necessarily render the technique of voting impracticable or objectionable.

It must also be recognized that the condition of equal distribution of cost does not in any way preclude the use of taxation for purposes of redistributing income. It is required only that redistributive taxes be levied independently of taxes for the purpose of financing the production of social goods. This is, of course, at variance with present practice. Commonly the functions of redistributing income and of providing funds for public services are merged into a single tax system. Under these conditions, any expressions of preference on the part of individual citizens are ambiguous in that they reflect not only marginal rates of substitution but also (different) marginal costs.

Neither does the condition of equal distribution of cost require that incomes be distributed equally. The only assumption is that the distribution of income is "correct" in the sense that it is socially accepted. Thus, if some individuals have more income than others, they may well vote for more of a particular social good than others, with less income—if the cost of the social good is uniformly distributed. This corresponds exactly to the fact that the individuals with larger incomes buy more individual goods than persons with smaller incomes. The fact that such differences in income are socially sanctioned implies that the preferences of richer persons ought to count for more than that of the poorer persons in determining the allocation of the society's resources.

Social Goods Not Equally Available to All Voters

Up to this point it has been assumed that any social good voted upon is accessible to all voters upon equal terms, and that differences in individual preferences are to be accounted for solely by differences in taste. This postulate, however, does not always conform to practical reality. When it does not, recourse to the benefit principle becomes more necessary and at the same time more practicable. It would then be desirable to classify the voters according to the amount of potential benefit that they would be expected to derive from the social good, and to tabulate the voting separately for each class. The intersection of the modal curve of marginal substitution and the curve of marginal cost per person (MC/N) could then be located for each class. For example, in Figure 7, the curves of marginal substitution for a group of citizens (Class I) who are in a position to benefit greatly from a social good are shown in solid lines, and the curves of marginal substitution for those able to benefit to a much smaller degree (Class II) are shown in dotted lines. The modal vote of the first group is indicated by P and of the second group by P'. In such a situation, application of the benefit principle would require that the cost assessed against citizens of Class I should be increased and that levied against citizens of Class II decreased, until two conditions are satisfied: (1) the modal output voted for by persons of Class I (indicated by point R) is equal to that voted for by persons of Class II (point R'), and (2) the entire cost of providing the social good is covered. The difficulty with this solution is that if the citizens realize that their voting affects the amount of cost they will be expected to bear, individually or as a class, the results of the voting will tend to be unreliable. Hence the cost to be levied on the several groups must be determined (apparently or in fact) without reference to the voting. Hence other methods of estimating potential benefit—drawing heavily

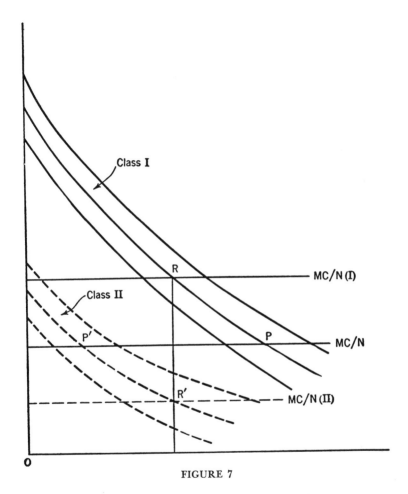

FIGURE 7

upon common sense—are undoubtedly necessary. Such techniques are illustrated by the methods used in many American cities of distributing special assessments for street improvements. By such methods only very rough adjustments, for obvious and clear-cut differences in potential benefit, can be made.

Social Goods Produced in Conjunction with Individual Goods

Social goods are frequently produced, as a sort of by-product, in connection with the provision of individual goods. In such cases the production of individual goods yields, in addition to the ordinary benefits accruing to the individual purchasers of these goods, social goods in which all or many persons in the group—whether consumers of the individual good or not—may participate.

A few illustrations will serve to show that this joint production of individual and social goods is not only possible but relatively common. For example, the practice of afforestation, leading to an increased supply of lumber, may result at the same time in the beautification of the landscape, the improvement of the climate, or the control of floods. A magnificent bridge or a towering skyscraper may not only yield benefits in the forms of transport or housing, but also may result in the creation of a sense of achievement and civic pride for all persons living in the vicinity or may give rise to aesthetic enjoyment to anyone who chances to view these modern wonders. (Incidentally, the San Francisco bridges and the New York skyscrapers are important tourist attractions.) The presence of a physician in an isolated community not only yields benefit to those individuals who become sick and actually use his services, but also confers benefit, in the form of increased security against emergencies, upon all members of the group. A hydroelectric project may result not only in increased electric power but also in improved recreation facilities. The existence of a highly developed merchant marine or railroad system may not only produce transport services but also enhance the national security.

In such cases as these, where individual and social goods are produced jointly, it is clearly necessary to consider the value of the social good when deciding upon the scale of output for the industry. In general, production should be extended beyond the level which would be considered most economical if only the value of individual goods were being considered. The actual increase in output would be determined through collective choice which could be made effective by subsidizing the industry out of funds raised from taxation.

Some forms of individual consumption also yield *social goods*. For example, if private consumers choose to live in houses that are architecturally beautiful or to surround their homes with lovely lawns and gardens, aesthetic enjoyment is provided for all who pass by and the value of surrounding property is enhanced. Similarly, if people clothe and adorn themselves "tastefully," the world may be made more pleasing. Or if people consume large quantities of the "protective foods," such as dairy products and fruits, the social end of widespread good health may be furthered. In the interest of social economy, such consumption ought to be encouraged through reduced prices, and even in some cases enforced. Again, the decision regarding the value of such social goods must be made collectively.[19]

Social Costs

Cost in the usual sense involves the employment of factors which are capable of valued alternative uses. The cost of using a factor is the most valuable alternate satisfaction that is sacrificed because of the fact that the resource is allocated to a particular purpose. In a price system, this cost is expressed as a price charged for the factor, the price being made effective to the ultimate consumer by setting the price of the product equal to its cost of production. There are certain other costs, however, which are not easily brought within the price system. These costs, which we shall call *social costs*, result in the deterioration of the general environment within which people live rather than in the use of specific factors which can be priced.

Social costs may occur in connection with production. For example, smoke nuisances, contamination of rivers, impairment of the beauty of the landscape, excessive noises, unpleasant odors, dust, risk of explosion, etc. Social costs may also arise in connection with individual consumption. For example, smoking may inconvenience nonsmokers or endanger property; excessive playing of radios or saxophones may disturb the peace and tran-

---

19 It may be argued that the enforcement of those consumer choices which are desirable from this point of view is merely a part of the general problem of inducing individuals to choose the "right" things. It is, however, more than that, because individuals may make choices which are thoroughly intelligent and "right" from their point of view but which nevertheless conflict with the social interest.

quillity of others; dogs or cats may make undue noises, destroy vegetation, or endanger small children; the construction of ugly houses may impair the beauty of a neighborhood; drunken driving may endanger the lives of others; failure to send one's children to school may defeat the social end of universal education; the playing of juke boxes may disturb the conversation of others; etc.

Social costs must be taken into account in deciding upon the outputs of industries where production involves such costs. Economy would require that output be such that the product can be sold at a price sufficient to cover all costs including social costs.[20] Otherwise, production would result in a greater dissipation of resources than would be warranted by the importance, measured in terms of price, of the net satisfactions achieved. Thus the most economical output, when social costs are incurred, would generally be smaller, other things being equal, than when social costs are absent.[21] There are two techniques by which social costs might be recognized. First, the industry could be required to provide for abatement of the nuisance, any expense involved to be included in the price of the product. This would clearly be the desirable course when the cost of abatement would be less than the estimated amount of damage done. Second, a tax could be levied against the industry, the amount of the tax to cover the estimated social cost involved. The tax would then become a part of the cost of production for the industry and would be included in the price of the product.[22]

Social costs in connection with consumption must also be taken into account in deciding upon the outputs and prices of goods. The attainment of economy may require that certain kinds of consumption be reduced through taxation or even be prohibited. Whatever action is taken is a matter that must be decided through collective choice.

---

[20] Average or marginal, whichever is relevant.

[21] If, however, the amount of social cost were independent of the scale of output—as might be the case—the existence of the social cost would affect only the decision as to whether the industry should be established and not the decision as to the scale of output.

[22] In case the amount of social cost borne by some persons were greater than that by others, the proceeds of the tax might be used to compensate the persons affected for the damages each has suffered. This would be the reverse of the benefit principle.

Chapter 19

THE DISTRIBUTION OF INCOME

The principles of pricing for social economy rest upon two fundamental conditions: (1) that the distribution of income is "correct," and (2) that consumers (or voters) make the "right" choices. Unless these two conditions are realized, there is no guarantee that the mere fulfillment of the pricing rules will lead to maximum aggregate satisfaction.[1] This and the following chapter, therefore, are devoted to an investigation of the significance and implications of these two assumptions. In this chapter we take up the problem of the distribution of income.

The Principle of Equal Marginal Satisfactions

Assuming that each individual spends his income so that he obtains equal marginal satisfactions from all the goods he buys, it follows that the marginal satisfaction obtained from any one good will measure the marginal satisfaction he derives from the expenditures of his income generally. This may be termed the *marginal satisfaction from income.* The most economical distribution of income would be attained only if income were distributed among individuals so that the marginal satisfaction from income would be equal for all persons. Under this distribution,

---

[1] "It is possible if not probable, first, that some alternative distribution of income would yield a greater sum total of satisfaction; and, second, that whatever the postulated distribution of physical income, some modification of the noneconomic cultural medium in which the S inhabitants live would augment the sum total of satisfaction derived by them from their economic resources. If this reasoning be valid, it follows that maximum satisfaction, in the sense conceived by economists, is a function not only of purely economic variables but also of essentially noneconomic cultural variables." Joseph J. Spengler, "Sociological Presuppositions in Economic Theory," *Southern Economic Journal,* October, 1940, p. 145.

the marginal expenditure by any one person would add to his satisfaction an amount equal to that obtained from the marginal outlay by any other person. A distribution of income different from this would mean that some individuals would be able to obtain greater satisfaction than others from the marginal unit of income expended; greater aggregate satisfaction could then be secured if income were taken from those getting a low marginal return in satisfaction and given to those getting a high marginal yield until the marginal returns were equalized all around.

To illustrate, let us assume that there are three individuals, A, B, and C, and that their incomes are $100, $1,000, and $10,000 respectively. With the $100, A is scarcely able to buy enough food and clothing to keep himself alive, to say nothing of securing the comforts and amenities of life. B, with $1,000, is able to have ample food, clothing, and shelter, but little else. C is able to enjoy all the creature comfort and such luxuries as servants, travel, and expensive recreations. The question involved in determining the most economical distribution of income among the three persons is this: Is the total satisfaction of the three at a maximum under the present apportionment, or could satisfactions be enhanced if, for example, the total income of $11,100 were divided equally among them, giving each $3,700, or if some other distribution were made? According to the principle of equal marginal satisfactions, the most advantageous arrangement could be decided upon as soon as the schedules of diminishing marginal satisfactions from income were known for each of the three individuals. The most economical allocation would require that the "sensitive" individuals with high capacity for enjoying the things that money can buy would be allowed a greater income than the "dullards" or the less highly geared "pleasure machines."

The Problem of Interpersonal Comparisons of Marginal Satisfactions

Application of the principle of equal marginal satisfactions depends upon the existence of methods for measuring, in comparable units, the marginal satisfactions of different individuals. Here we face squarely the fact that satisfaction is a purely personal and subjective phenomenon which does not lend itself to strictly objective measurements, in terms that would make possible the comparison of satisfactions obtained, by *different* individuals. Just as one person's experience of "redness" or "sweetness" cannot be shared by another, so the satisfaction of one individual is inscrutable to another.[2]

The lack of strictly objective measures does not, however, eliminate the social problem of distributing income. A society which wishes to attain economy in the use of its resources must, and does as a practical matter, judge the distribution of income in terms of the satisfactions of the members of the group. Are there, then, criteria of individual satisfactions that are meaningful from the point of view of scientific methodology and at the same time socially comprehensible?

Ideal Distribution of Income Assuming that Meaningful Interpersonal Comparisons Are Impossible

One group of writers has attempted to answer—perhaps dodge—the question on the basis of certain apriori hypotheses.[3] First, it is conceded that meaningful interpersonal comparisons of marginal satisfactions are not feasible, and that therefore any alleged solution to the problem of distribution of income which rests upon the principle of equal marginal satisfactions must be arbitrary. At the same time, however, it is assumed that the "capacities" of individuals to enjoy income are distributed according to the normal law of error.[4] Just as individual differences in height, weight, or "intelligence" may be expressed in terms of a frequency distribution with a great majority of the cases lying near the mode, so (it is assumed) differences in capacity to enjoy income are similarly distributed about the mode of

---

2 Cf. also Lionel Robbins, "Interpersonal Comparisons of Utility: a Comment," *Economic Journal*, December, 1938, pp. 635–641.

3 See Oskar Lange and F. M. Taylor, *On the Economic Theory of Socialism*, edited by B. Lippincott, Minneapolis, 1938, pp. 100-103; also Oskar Lange, "The Foundation of Welfare Economics," mimeographed paper delivered before the Sixth International Congress for the Unity of Science.

4 See pp. 181–182.

a frequency distribution.[5] This may be illustrated graphically
(Figure 8). Let quantities of income be shown on the horizontal
axis and marginal satisfactions from income on the vertical axis.
A curve can then be drawn, for each individual, indicating his

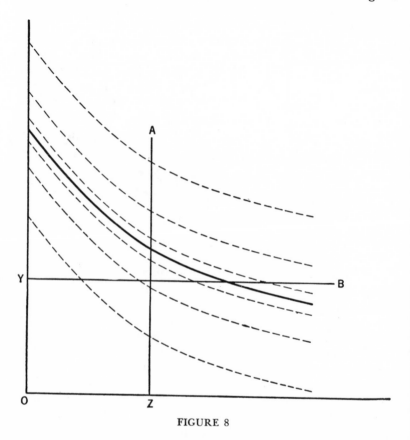

FIGURE 8

marginal satisfaction from income for each amount of income.
Then if a vertical line is erected at any point Z on the horizontal
axis, the points of intersection between the line and the several

---

[5] It is sometimes held that the capacity to enjoy income does not conform to
the normal law of error, but is significantly asymmetrical. The well-to-do, educated to the uses to which income can be put, undoubtedly have considerably
higher curves of marginal satisfaction than the poor who have had no opportunity to acquire refined tastes. This is evidenced by the vulgar consumption of the

curves will be distributed along the line in the manner of a normal frequency distribution—a high proportion of the intersections occurring near the mode.

If the position of the individual curves were known, it would be possible to distribute income so that marginal satisfactions for all individuals would be equal. Thus, if a horizontal line *YB* were drawn cutting the curve of marginal satisfaction for each of the several individuals, the economical amount of income for each person would be indicated by the intersection of *YB* with that individual's curve of marginal satisfactions. The height of *YB* would, of course, be adjusted to conform to the total amount of income to be distributed. Unfortunately, however, assuming that we can have no precise information on the position of the individual curves of marginal satisfaction from income,[6] the distribution must be arbitrary. But, still assuming that marginal satisfactions are distributed according to the normal law of error, that arbitrary solution which involves the least error is an *equal distribution*. Such a distribution will leave only random errors, whereas any other will involve a constant bias in favor of some groups or classes.[7]

The same conclusion can also be reached in another way.[8] Suppose that it is desired to distribute a given amount of income between two persons as illustrated in Figure 9. The total amount of income to be distributed is indicated by the distance O_aO_b. The curve of marginal satisfactions from income for Individual A is represented by curve *A* with income measured along the

---

nouveaux riches or the inability of relief "clients" to make good use of the dole. Thus the mode of the frequency distribution must be representative of a relatively low capacity to enjoy income since most persons have never been educated to the "higher things." This argument is, however, irrelevant because these differences in capacity to enjoy income are cultural in origin—the outcome of a given distribution of income rather than a logical or ethical basis for that distribution. If incomes were to be distributed differently over a long period, it may be supposed that the distribution of individual differences in capacity to enjoy income would also vary, and, to the extent that incomes were distributed less unequally, the skewness in the distribution of individual differences would be greatly reduced.

[6] Voting is not helpful in this case. It would scarcely be practicable to ask people to express preferences on the amount of income they would like to have. They would all want to be millionaires.

[7] Oskar Lange and F. M. Taylor, *On the Economic Theory of Socialism, op. cit.*, p. 103.

[8] I am indebted to Dr. A. P. Lerner for this analysis.

horizontal axis from left to right. Similarly, curve *B* represents marginal satisfactions from income for Individual B with income measured along the horizontal axis in the reverse direction from right to left. The most economical distribution, of course, is that which makes possible equal marginal satisfactions. This is indicated by the intersection of the two curves of marginal satis-

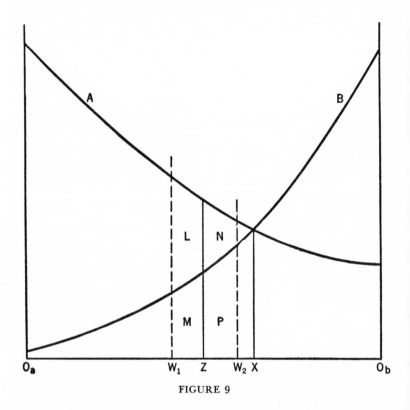

FIGURE 9

faction. Thus the most economical distribution would give Individual A income O_aX, and Individual B income O_bX.

If, as is assumed, we have no knowledge of the two curves of marginal satisfactions, then the distribution must be made arbitrarily, and the problem is to find the solution involving the least probable error. This, it can be shown, is an *equal* distribution. Individual A should have O_aZ of income and Individual B should have O_bZ.

If the distribution is not equal, there is as much likelihood that Individual B will be given more income than Individual A as there is that Individual A will be given more than Individual B. For example, there is as great a probability that the division will be made at any point W_1 to the left of Z, as that it will be made at any point W_2 to the right of and equally distant from Z. If the distribution is made at W_1, the loss in satisfaction to Individual A is measured by the area L plus the area M, and the gain to Individual B by the area M. Thus, the *net* loss from this arrangement is measured by the area L. On the other hand, if the distribution is made at W_2, the gain to Individual A is measured by the area N plus the area P. The net gain is measured by area N. The possible net loss, L, from the distribution at W_1 is greater than the possible net gain, N, from the distribution at W_2. Thus, any possible gain to be achieved by departing from equality is offset by an equally probable, and greater loss. Hence, the probabilities are that an equal distribution is most economical unless data on individual marginal satisfactions are known.

Ideal Distribution of Income Assuming the Possibility of Meaningful Interpersonal Comparisons

The conclusion that an equal distribution of income is the most economical (or least uneconomical) of all practicable arrangements is as much as can be said on the subject so long as it is assumed that interpersonal comparisons of satisfaction are impracticable. There are many who hold, however, that such comparisons can be made—admitting that there are difficulties. It is held that in everyday life we do make these comparisons, and that, although strict accuracy in measurement is not possible, useful approximations can be achieved.

To begin with, by observing an individual's behavior it is possible to get at least a common-sense estimate of the relative degrees of *his* satisfaction at various times. Behavior, in this sense, would include one or more of the following (the more the better): (1) the verbal reports of the individual, (2) his expressions of emotion, (3) what he is (or has been) willing to give up in personal sacrifice to obtain the satisfactions, and (4) physiological reactions. For instance, it requires no great stretch of the imagination to know whether an individual secures more enjoyment from his new car than he obtains from his radio. Moreover, from data of this kind, it is possible to compare in a rough-and-ready manner the satisfactions of *different* individuals. For example, no reasonable person would seriously doubt that a child who is eating a meal eagerly and zestfully is getting more pleasure from his food than a dyspeptic old man without appetite. Neither would there be any difficulty in comparing the happiness of a bride with that of an aged widow who had just learned that her beloved son has been killed in battle. Nor would there be much disagreement as to whether a starving man would get more satisfaction from an assured living than a rich man from a seventh automobile. It is true that we cannot penetrate the consciousness of these individuals in order to measure these satisfactions, yet from the behavior of the individuals (including what they can tell us) we can infer, in a way that satisfies us for most practical purposes, the relative amounts of satisfaction enjoyed by them.

Such "common-sense" interpersonal comparisons are based, however, upon a tacit assumption, namely, that the experiences of different individuals, and their reactions to these experiences, are more or less alike. Thus, when the behavior of two individuals is similar (with allowance for differences in cultural background), it is inferred that they are getting approximately the same amounts of satisfaction. For example, if two individuals are accustomed to make equal amounts of personal sacrifice for a given good, if their various emotional expressions are of similar intensity, their verbal reports indicate more or less equal satisfactions, etc., it may reasonably be inferred, *assuming that the two individuals are essentially similar,* that the satisfactions received by the two are, as a matter of fact, equal. On the other hand, if the one is willing to suffer great privation to get the good, whereas the other is scarcely willing to lift a finger; if one shows great eagerness to get the good and great joy from its consumption, whereas the other has a bored or careless attitude; if one says emphatically that he is obtaining great enjoyment, whereas the other says he is indifferent; it would seem, *assuming that the two individuals are of similar psychophysical character and of similar cultural background,* that the first individual would be obtaining much greater satisfaction than the second.

In interpreting these data, it is also possible for the observer to use himself as a common denominator for measuring the satisfactions of others. He knows how he himself behaves when he is getting different amounts of satisfaction, and so he can use his own experience as a means of comprehending the nature and amounts of satisfaction being enjoyed by others. Moreover, different individuals can often agree in appraising the amount of satisfaction which other individuals are obtaining. This, however, still assumes the essential similarity of the persons whose satisfactions are being compared (including the observers themselves).

There is, of course, no logical proof for the proposition that individuals are similar—in the sense that they react in similar ways or that they see the world similarly—yet this is an assumption that most persons are willing to accept. Indeed, it is only with this assumption that it is ever possible to draw inferences (as we all do every day) regarding the experiences and reactions of others by means of an introspective analysis of our own experiences and reactions. As Barbara Wootton says, in discussing the relative amounts of satisfaction derived from a shilling by a poor man and a rich man,

> I would myself boldly assume that the verdict of common sense is plain enough—in favour of the higher satisfaction-giving power of the poor man's shilling; though admittedly the thing cannot be proved in a logically or philosophically satisfactory way, and there is no way of showing those who find such an assumption unacceptable are wrong.[9]

Similarly, Joan Robinson has stated:

> To a strictly logical mind any discussion of utility to more than one individual is repugnant. It is not really justifiable to talk about maximum satisfaction to a whole population. But common sense protests that if we treat all individuals as being exactly alike it is then permissible to sum their satisfactions, and that human beings, in their economic needs, are sufficiently alike to make the discussion of aggregate satisfaction interesting. Upon this basis we may say that if any two individuals have the same real income they derive the same satisfaction from it. We may further say that if one individual

---

[9] *Lament for Economics*, London, 1938, pp. 192-193.

has a larger real income than another the marginal utility of income to him is less.[10]

If one is willing to accept the view that interpersonal comparisons of satisfactions are possible at least in principle, then the proposition becomes significant that incomes ought to be distributed according to the rule of equal marginal satisfactions. At the present state of knowledge, however, it would be impossible to make *accurate* measurements of the relative marginal satisfactions obtained by different individuals, especially where small differences were involved or where differences had been culturally induced. It would be possible to distinguish clearly in those cases where the differences were extreme (the starving poor man vs. the wealthy tycoon). But even if fine distinctions among individuals should prove impracticable, it would perhaps be possible to divide the population into certain clear-cut classes, using capacity to enjoy income as a criterion, and to adjust the amount of income allotted to individuals in the various classes accordingly. Thus, following the principle of equal marginal satisfaction, it might be concluded that the most economical amount of income for children would be less than that for adults; the amount for a childless married couple less than that for a man and a woman living singly; the amount for a chronic invalid greater than that for an able-bodied person; or the amount for an elderly person less than that for a middle-aged adult.[11]

Within each class of the population the individual differences in marginal satisfactions would presumably be so small that they could not be clearly perceived. Hence there would be strong tendency to treat alike all the persons within each class, i.e., distribute income equally.[12]

---

[10] *Economics of Imperfect Competition,* London, 1933, p. 318.

[11] In adjusting the amount of income to be received by different classes, there is great danger that the observer would let his own preconceptions intrude into his analysis of the capacity of others to enjoy income. For example, it is commonly held that children do not "need" as much income as adults. This conclusion may, however, be a mere expression of an accepted custom which places children in an inferior position, rather than the result of an actual analysis of their relative capacity to enjoy income.

[12] This conclusion follows also from the analysis of the problem of income distribution when the possibility of interpersonal comparisons was ruled out—on the assumption that the capacity to enjoy income is distributed according to the normal law of error.

Qualifications

The discussion of the distribution of income up to this point may be summarized. (1) If interpersonal comparison of satisfactions is ruled out, an equal distribution of income will involve a smaller "error" or less dis-economy than any other arbitrary arrangement. (2) If the possibility of interpersonal comparisons is admitted, the population can be classified on the basis of differences in capacity to enjoy income, and income distributed according to the principle of equal marginal satisfactions, individuals within each class being treated alike. There are, however, at least two additional considerations.

First, because of the fact that people could no longer look forward to the prospect of increasing their income through their own efforts, it is possible that aggregate satisfaction would be less than maximum in a system where income was distributed according to these principles.[13] This qualification would, of course, become insignificant if for "getting ahead" the society could provide other ways than increasing individual incomes. It does, however, remind us that without such a substitute, the distribution of incomes equally or according to the principle of equal marginal satisfactions might remove part of the zest from life.

Second, it is possible that the distribution of incomes along these lines would tend to reduce aggregate satisfaction because, since income would no longer be utilized as the reward for productive efficiency, the quantity of social product would be lessened.[14] In other words, it may be questioned whether people would work industriously or strive to be efficient when the amount of their incomes was no longer correlated with their

---

13 N. Kaldor, "Welfare Propositions of Economics and Interpersonal Comparisons of Utility," *Economic Journal*, September, 1939, p. 551.

14 "What is known of human motivation and the distribution of human abilities suggests very definitely that per capita output will be lower in an economy in which complete equality prevails than in one marked by some inequality." J. J. Spengler, "Sociological Presuppositions in Economic Theory," *Southern Economic Journal*, October, 1940, p. 142. Professor J. M. Clark has suggested, however, that inequality in reward (income) need not carry with it inequality in purchasing power in all departments of consumption. The advantages of the rich may be confined to certain luxuries and pleasures which are nonessential. "Economics and Modern Psychology," *Journal of Political Economy*, February, 1918, p. 146.

productivity. Thus there is a possibility that a larger social dividend made on the productivity principle would yield greater satisfaction than a smaller social dividend made on the principle of equal marginal satisfactions. If income provides the only effective incentive to productive efficiency, it is unquestionable that any possible advantages of equi-marginal distribution would be more than offset by the loss in social product. If, however, other equally effective incentives could be found, then this consideration would lose its relevance.[15] Nevertheless, it must always be held in mind that the equi-marginal distribution of income would almost certainly be uneconomical unless incentives to productive efficiency, other than income, could be devised. Indeed, in the endless debate over the practicability of socialism the major issue concerns the question of whether a socialist society can offer adequate *incentives* without negating its egalitarian premises.[16]

Conclusions

In concluding the whole discussion of the distribution of income, we can say almost nothing definite as to what particular distribution would be most economical. There are strong arguments, at the common-sense level, for equality, with adjustment among classes for clearly distinguishable differences in capacity to enjoy income; and it is likely that the differences among the classes would be much less than might at first be supposed. On the other hand, any distribution based upon this ideal might have to be tempered by the necessity of providing people with significant ways of "getting ahead," and with incentives to productive efficiency. The degree to which this tempering would be necessary would depend upon the historic

---

[15] At this point it is necessary to be clear on the fact that economy is defined in terms of maximum aggregate *satisfaction* and not maximum aggregate *physical product*. Thus the group might prefer a smaller social dividend divided equitably to a larger social dividend divided inequitably, providing the loss in dividend did not more than counterbalance the gain in distribution.

[16] It is, of course, possible to argue that income incentives would be desirable at one stage of cultural development (e.g., in the nineteenth century during which great technological changes were taking place), whereas, at another time, other incentives might be more advantageous.

conditioning of the group and could be ascertained only through a process of trial and error.

These conclusions, vague as they are, rest upon tenuous a priori assumptions regarding either (1) the distribution of individual capacities to enjoy income or (2) the interpersonal comparability of satisfactions. Thus it must be recognized that we have not yet reached a thoroughly satisfactory and definite answer to the question of what is the most economical distribution of income. The type of analysis in which we have indulged has the merit that it recognizes the existence of problems and perhaps makes some small progress toward tentative solutions. However, before the principle of equal marginal satisfactions can be applied as a practical basis for deciding upon the distribution of income, much additional knowledge will be required. At present, we must recognize, there are no magic formulas or strictly objective rules (comparable to the pricing rules) for determining what particular distribution of income would make for maximum aggregate satisfaction—all things considered.

Chapter 20

CONSUMER CHOICE

The second basic assumption underlying the principles of pricing for social economy is that individuals arrange the expenditures of their incomes, in light of prevailing prices, so as to obtain maximum satisfaction. On the strength of this assumption and the assumptions of a "correct" distribution of income, it is concluded that if resources are allocated in response to consumer demand, maximum satisfaction will result. In this chapter we shall examine problems relating to consumer choice.

If individuals are to obtain maximum satisfaction from the expenditure of their incomes, it is necessary (1) that they behave rationally, (2) that they possess adequate knowledge of the alternatives open to them, and (3) that they choose within an appropriate cultural setting. Unless these three conditions are satisfied, free consumer choice cannot be depended upon to make for maximum satisfaction. Yet, as will be shown, there is considerable doubt as to whether any one of these conditions is always attained in practice.

Rational Behavior

It is rather generally agreed that all individuals cannot be expected on all occasions to behave rationally, i.e., to adapt their actions to definite ends. Consequently, it can hardly be supposed that they are uniformly rational in the expenditure of income, that in spending their money they carefully weigh the relative advantages of alternative goods. It is almost certain that impulse, habit, and shortsightedness occasionally, perhaps often, militate against the attainment of maximum satisfactions. Yet it is probable that most persons do adjust their outlays, through a persistent process of trial and error, so that their purchases are reasonably correlated with their ends. Certainly, on the whole, individuals fare at least as well under "free consumer choice" as they would under a system of rationing or dictated consumption.

It is perhaps not too preposterous to assume that the individual, if left free to expend his income as he likes, will attain something approaching rationality. This, of course, does not necessarily mean that the consumer usually spends his income in a manner that would be considered rational by an *observer,* but only that he approaches rationality in terms of *his* ends, whatever they may be. Moreover, the institution of free consumer choice has the great advantage that it makes possible apportionment of goods among individuals according to their particular requirements without recourse to the elaborate administrative machinery and the irritating compulsion that would be required in a system of rationing. Nevertheless, to the extent that the consumer fails to behave rationally, maximum satisfaction is unattained.[1]

Adequate Knowledge

A second condition prerequisite to maximum satisfaction under free consumer choice is that each individual possess or have ready access to dependable information so that he will be intelligently aware of all possible alternatives open to him. Without such knowledge, he will inevitably make choices resulting in less than maximum satisfaction. Yet the possibility of his obtaining this knowledge is remote indeed. Even if the individual is well aware of the various possible ends, nevertheless he finds himself faced with the disturbing necessity of choosing from among thousands of different means (goods), no one of which can be competently judged as to quality or suitability except by specialized technicians. Thus, in attempting to make intelligent choices, the individual is bound to be defeated by the sheer complexity of his task, with the result that he achieves less than maximum satisfaction. In

---

[1] It must not be ruled out, however, that irresponsible and random behavior may itself sometimes be rational in that it may lead to the end of new experience or adventure.

other words, the institution of free consumer choice concentrates an enormous range of decision making in the single individual—thus precluding, in the field of consumer purchasing, the type of functional specialization and division of labor that has contributed so outstandingly to efficiency in production.[2]

There are two partial remedies for the inadequacy of consumer knowledge. The first is the establishment of agencies for the education of consumers. This, however, is costly since it requires the substantial use of economic resources—schools, teachers, books, and the time and energy of the "pupils." Hence such educational activities must be subjected to the principle of economy: they must be performed in the least costly manner and must be carried on only to the extent that the gain through improved consumer choices would compensate for the cost. The second partial remedy would be the employment of disinterested experts to assist consumers in the selection of goods— the use of specialized knowledge as a supplementary aid in choice making. In our own society, for example, there are a number of types of professional experts whose services consist, at least in part, of giving disinterested advice on consumption. Among these are physicians, dietitians, beauticians, architects, interior decorators, consulting engineers, shopping services, and consumer organizations.[3] In every branch of business, salesmen, in spite of their obvious lack of disinterestedness, are looked to for assistance in the perplexing task of consumer selection. Since the services of the expert, whether interested or disinterested, are obtained only at a cost, economy requires that experts be relied upon only to the extent that the resulting improvement in consumer performance compensates for that cost. The reliance upon experts does, however, constitute a partial abdication by the individual consumer of his role as choice maker. In some cases the expert may be merely a source of knowledge; in others he may merely influence the choice; but in some instances he is, for all practical purposes, the choice maker. The latter is true especially in such fields as medicine

---

[2] This point has been developed admirably by Professor W. C. Mitchell in *The Backward Art of Spending Money*, New York, 1937, pp. 3-19.

[3] In a democracy, individual choices regarding social goods are often delegated to representatives who assume the role of expert.

and architecture, where the layman is almost completely without technical qualification. Thus, in a sense, the employment of experts represents an important modification in the content of individual freedom of choice. The essential freedom still exists, however, so long as the individual is free to choose the expert and to reject the advice given. Only when the individual is forced to accept the verdict of the experts is the essence of free consumer choice destroyed.

Appropriate Cultural Setting

A third condition necessary to the achievement of maximum satisfaction under free consumer choice is that the cultural setting is such that consumers *want* the "right" goods. The mere allocation of resources in response to free consumer choice, even assuming rationality and adequate knowledge on the part of consumers, can scarcely be depended upon to give maximum satisfaction unless consumers want—and choose— those goods which, as a matter of fact, will give maximum satisfaction. Traditionally, it has been assumed almost without question that the consumer will select the "right" goods, and that there is no appeal from the valuations of individual consumers. From this assumption has come the rather general belief, popular especially among economists, that it is economical to use social resources to produce anything for which people are willing to pay a price—a somewhat exaggerated version of *de gustibus non est disputandum* or "the customer is always right." This argument is palpably unsound because it completely misrepresents the position of the individual consumer as a free agent exercising independent choices. We know that so-called "freedom" of consumer choice is largely a formal freedom, and that what are called individual choices are for the most part determined through custom, convention, religion, law, education, propaganda, and other social influences. They are manifestations of the culture. The achievement of economy depends, therefore, not alone upon the allocation of resources in response to the free choices of rational and informed consumers, but also upon the existence of a social situation within which individuals will "want" and "choose" the goods that will, in fact, yield maximum satisfaction. Thus, provided consumers act as intelligently with reference to the new as they did toward the original set of wants, a variation in the social situation which will induce a variation in consumer wants may lead to an increase in aggregate satisfaction. This point is so important and so often neglected that further elaboration may be useful.[4]

The wants of human beings arise from certain fundamental interests which, so far as we know, are a part of human nature and, therefore, applicable regardless of time, place, or mode of social organization. Among these interests are perhaps food, sex, bodily comfort, activity, response, recognition, security, and new experience.[5] Any of these interests may be satisfied in numerous possible ways. Each society, as part of its culture, develops and transmits to its members certain socially accepted ways of satisfying these interests. The free choices of consumers, where permitted, are the direct outcome of these group-

---

[4] The view presented here is completely contrary to the traditional and widely accepted idea that the individual consumer is the only adequate judge of his needs and that whatever goods he chooses, merely by virtue of the fact that he has chosen them, will yield maximum satisfaction. The traditional idea is generally based upon one or more of three assumptions, each of which is of doubtful validity. First, it may be based upon a naïve and totally false belief that the behavior of each individual is independent of the culture. Second, it may derive from the more plausible but equally specious and shortsighted assumption that the existing culture, whatever it may be, will produce optimum consumer choices. According to this position, no appreciable increase in human welfare could be brought about through cultural change; hence, cultural change would have no significance in this connection since the amount of satisfaction achieved would be independent of the kind of consumer choices made—provided only these choices conformed to extant social standards. Finally, third, the traditional view may be based upon the assumption that there is a tendency for the culture to become modified through a process of "trial and error" or "natural selection," so that those parts of the culture which tend to inhibit satisfaction are superseded by variants offering scope for greater satisfaction. Thus, admitting that consumer choices are culturally determined, it is still possible to assume that the regulation of production in response to free consumer choice will make for maximum satisfaction. Whether cultural change does proceed along the lines of "natural selection" is one of the moot questions of social theory. The author tends to favor the affirmative answer to the question. However, the process of "natural selection," if existent, is so complex, ponderous, and sluggish, and so many of the "trials" result in "errors," that the adaptation of the culture to new situations is much less than perfect. Thus, even recognizing the selective principle in culture modification, there is wide latitude for maladaptation over considerable periods of time.

[5] Opinion is divided as to just what are the basic human interests and as to how they ought to be classified. For present purposes, the question of the precise character of these interests is unimportant. See pp. 23–28.

sanctioned modes of satisfying interests. This is what is meant by the fact that consumer wants are institutionally or culturally determined. In making his "free" choices, the individual is guided in detail by the accepted usages of his group.

The many possible ways of satisfying any one of the basic interests may differ in power to satisfy and in cost. Thus, if a society is to achieve maximum satisfaction, those methods of achieving interests must become socially acceptable which will provide the greatest aggregate of satisfaction attainable within the limits of the available resources and techniques. This means that if there are two alternate ways of satisfying an interest, each of equal cost, the more satisfying of the two must be selected; if there are two alternatives, each of equal satisfying power, the least costly must be selected; and the satisfaction of any interest must not be carried so far that resources devoted to it would provide greater return if transferred to another relatively neglected interest. Thus the "good society" (assuming that maximum aggregate satisfaction is the end) is one in which the socially accepted ways of satisfying interests are such that there is a proper balance or harmony in the distribution of resources among the several different interests so that maximum satisfaction can be attained. To the extent that this is not true, total satisfactions could be increased by a change in the conventional modes of consumption. For example, a modification of the conventional diet, involving a reduction in cost of food at only a small loss in satisfaction, combined with the social acceptance of an improved but more costly type of shelter might add materially to total satisfaction.

Comparison of Different Societies

The principle that the extent of aggregate satisfaction is partly dependent upon the types of socially accepted modes of satisfying interests raises the difficult question of whether two societies can be successfully compared with respect to the degree of satisfaction which they afford. This, of course, reduces to the problem of whether it is possible to develop a meaningful definition of "aggregate satisfaction" which will lend itself to measurement. (In this context it is not possible to fall back on price as a measure of satisfaction; that technique is feasible only when values are determined by the choices of individual consumers.) In principle, at least, such a definition can be formulated. Satisfaction consists merely in the attainment of basic interests. Failure to attain the basic interests on the part of any one individual leads to tensions, unrest, frustration, neuroses, psychoses, and physical illness. Failure to attain the basic interests on the part of many individuals leads to mass unrest, as evidenced by collective manifestations such as reform movements, rioting, and revolts. Thus the degree of satisfaction in any society is indicated by the extent of the dissatisfaction to be found there, which may be measured by a whole congeries of indexes such as the number of psychotic and neurotic persons, the morbidity rate, the death rate, the birth rate, the suicide rate, the crime rate, the number and character of reform movements, the extent of illicit sex behavior, mass violence, etc. Additional evidence regarding the degree of dissatisfaction may be obtained not only by examining the overt behavior of the members of the group but also by analyzing their utterances. The overt behavior of the individuals and groups is not the sole source of information regarding the degree of dissatisfaction within the society. It is also possible to obtain additional evidence by examining the utterances of members of the society, i.e., the informal remarks and writings of various classes, the literature, the art, the answers to questionnaires, case histories, etc.

The process of determining the degree of satisfaction in a society is in every respect analogous to medical diagnosis. The concept of "good health" or "wellness" as applied to the physical condition of an individual is similar to "maximum aggregate satisfaction" or "general welfare" as applied to a society, and individual "illness" is comparable to social "dissatisfaction." In medicine, the individual is described as "well" when he feels good, and "ill" when he feels bad. The physician, however, is hardly able to determine directly how the patient feels, because only the patient can do the feeling. However, the physician has two sources of information. First he can record a number of facts about the patient, such as temperature, pulse, lesions, malignant growths, and bacteria, which are known to be reliable indexes of the patient's state of health. Second, the physician can obtain reports from the patient as to how the latter "feels." Piecing all the evidence together, the physician can declare that the patient is well or ill, and can even measure degrees of illness in the sense that he can know when a patient is getting better or worse and can know which of two patients is the more seriously ill. Correspondingly, in determining the well-being of a society, the observer can record facts about the society (psychoses, neuroses, morbidity, reform movements, etc.), and can obtain reports from members of the society (incidental conversations and writings, interviews, literature, etc.). Poets and novelists are particularly sensitive reporters. Putting these facts together, he is able to form judgments, not entirely precise, to be sure, as to the degree of satisfaction or well-being in a society, and to compare different societies in terms of the extent of satisfactions afforded. Thus a comparison of the extent of satisfaction in, let us say, Russia and the United States as of the year 1913 is by no means an impossibility.[6]

Recognizing that it is possible, at least in principle, to measure differences in the degree of satisfaction afforded by different societies or by any one society at different times, we return to the problem of consumer choice. Ordinarily, a change in the socially accepted pattern of consumption within a society would be so gradual and on so small a scale that it would be practically impossible to note any significant variation in the extent of satisfaction. Suppose, for example, that through a modification of the accepted diet it would be possible to eliminate the common cold. Provided the new diet were as nourishing, as palatable, and as inexpensive as the original diet (after the completion of all necessary adaptations and adjustments), the social acceptance of the new diet would clearly result in an increase in total satisfaction. Suppose, however, that the new diet is more costly than the old. In that case its adoption would require that resources previously used for other purposes be transferred to the production of food. Improved health would then be obtained at the sacrifice of other interests, perhaps shelter, or new experience, so that the adoption of the new diet would lead to increased satisfaction only if the im-

---

[6] Identification of *satisfaction* with *social well-being* derives from the assumption, implicit throughout this discussion, that the primary social end is maximum aggregate satisfaction. Similarly, the identification of "good health" and individual welfare is possible on the assumption that good health is a primary end.

provement in health would more than compensate for the loss of other satisfactions. In practice it would be extremely difficult to decide whether the adoption of the new diet would, on the whole, enhance total satisfaction. The net change in total satisfaction, if any, would probably not be sufficient for the difference to be measured by means of the crude techniques available. Nevertheless, there is a real problem here, one which continually faces society and which cannot be evaded merely because of its difficulty. A society in quest of maximum satisfaction must, on a common-sense basis, and with whatever inadequate criteria may be available, face the possibility that an increase in total satisfaction might be achieved through a modification of its socially accepted pattern of consumption, and when such a modification involves the sacrifice of one interest to another, the society must be prepared to choose. The act of choice takes the form of a variation in the socially accepted system of values. From these social values are derived the individual values which determine individual "wants" and from which individual consumer choices are derived.

Conclusions

It has been shown that a system operated in response to the free choices of individual consumers will not necessarily achieve economy because (1) consumers are not always rational, (2) consumers lack adequate knowledge, and (3) the cultural setting may prevent consumers from choosing the "right" goods. This is not to be regarded, however, as a condemnation of free consumer choice. As pointed out, the institution of free consumer choice is a marvelous device for registering the individual needs of the many consumers. Moreover, it makes possible a genuine freedom of the individual (i.e., absence from arbitrary authority) in one of the most important areas of human conduct. Thus, the conclusion to be drawn from this section is not that free consumer choice is incompatible with economy, but rather that its operation as an instrument for the achievement of economy is dependent upon rationality, knowledge, and an appropriate social situation, and that without these the mere fulfillment of the four pricing conditions will not necessarily lead to maximum aggregate satisfaction.

Chapter 21

THE SUPPLY OF LABOR

U P to this point in our discussion of *social economy*, we have assumed that the supply of the factors of production is fixed once and for all. Accordingly, the problem of economy has been restricted to the question of what is the best disposition of the *given* factors. This, however, does not solve all the problems. The supplies of labor and capital are subject either to increase or decrease as a result of decisions or actions of members of the society. Therefore, a complete theory of economy must deal not only with the optimum use of given factors but also with the question, What is the most advantageous or most economical supply of these factors? It is the purpose of this and the following chapter to discuss the issues raised by this question.

We shall assume that the supplies of primary *means of production* are given—that there is a certain definite supply of land available to the group and that the numbers, age and sex composition, and basic biological qualities of the population are fixed.[1] The problem will be to determine what supply of

---

[1] The assumption of a given population may be open to criticism on the ground that, since the size and character of the population is one of the determinants of the labor supply, any discussion of economy with reference to the supply of labor must include a discussion of "optimum population." We shall, nevertheless, deliberately ignore this important and interesting question. It may be noted that the effect of changes in population upon aggregate satisfaction is twofold. On the one hand, an increase in numbers represents a potential increase in the supply of labor, subject perhaps to diminishing returns, but on the other hand it represents an increase in the number of consumers or "satisfaction recipients." The effect of changes in the number of people upon aggregate satisfaction, then, becomes highly uncertain. It is possible, for example, that the sum of human satisfactions would be enhanced by a mere increase in the number of consumers even if this growth in population resulted in a diminution of average satisfaction per person. Professor Cannan has suggested that the philosophy of the eighteenth century replaced "the old Christian idea of the desirability of large numbers of persons to praise God by the proposition that a larger number of persons are at

labor and capital is most desirable from the point of view of reaching maximum aggregate satisfaction.

On the assumption that the numbers and basic characteristics of the population are given, the supply of labor is determined primarily by (1) the amount of time which the members of the group devote to labor, and (2) the intensity with which the labor is carried on. Therefore, the problem of determining what is the most economical supply of labor may be reduced to two questions: (1) How much leisure ought people to have? and (2) How hard should people work? It is the purpose of this chapter to discuss these two questions.

Leisure vs. Labor

The distinction between leisure and labor is not a sharp one. The two uses of human time merge at many points. Yet it is possible to develop concepts of labor and of leisure which make possible the classification of most human activities into one or the other category.

Labor may be defined as the use of human time in the production of economic goods, i.e., goods which are transferable or salable in the sense that they could conceivably be enjoyed by persons other than the laborer. Leisure, on the other hand, would include all other uses of human time including such activity (or inactivity) as sleeping, eating, and recreation. Almost (but not quite) the same idea is conveyed when labor is defined as activity carried on for the sake of ulterior ends, and leisure as activity engaged in for its own sake.[2] Whatever definition of these two terms may be decided upon, the supply of labor is partly dependent upon the manner in which the

---

any rate likely to have a bigger aggregate of happiness than a smaller number." (*A Review of Economic Theory*, London, 1930, p. 64.) Hobson brought this idea up to the modern age when he said that "the very essence" of the population question is the evaluation of "life *per se*." (*Economics and Ethics*, New York, 1929, p. xxvi.) For a discussion of optimum population from the point of view of productivity per capita, see Howard R. Bowen, "Capital in Relation to Optimum Population," *Social Forces*, March, 1937, pp. 346-350.

2 Any attempt to distinguish sharply between labor and leisure is certain to exclude the many borderline cases where activity which is pleasurable in and of itself results in the creation of economic goods, and the equally numerous cases where activity that is primarily recreational is indirectly productive because of its effect upon the health or strength or efficiency of the individual concerned.

members of the group divide their time between labor and leisure, and one of the conditions necessary to the attainment of economy is that human time be "correctly" apportioned between the two uses.

It must be recognized at the outset that leisure may be regarded as one of the *goods* which individuals wish to obtain.[3] Moreover, it is evident that leisure, like many other goods, can be secured only at a cost. Just as the cost of producing housing, food, or clothing consists in the sacrificed satisfactions which could have been obtained if productive resources had been used for alternative purposes, so the cost of leisure often consists of the sacrificed satisfactions which could have been available had labor been substituted for leisure. There is, however, one condition under which leisure is not costly, namely, when the amount of it enjoyed by the individual or the group is so restricted that an increase in time for sleeping, eating, and relaxation would actually enhance the production of goods other than leisure. It has been repeatedly demonstrated, for example, that the productivity of workers (at least in the long run) may be increased up to a certain point by reducing the hours of labor (increasing the hours of leisure).

In view of these considerations, it is possible to lay down two general rules for the apportionment of human time between labor and leisure. First, the amount of leisure provided for each worker should be not less than that necessary to make possible the maximum production of goods (other than leisure) by that worker during his entire lifetime.[4] If the amount of leisure were less than this, it would be clearly possible to add to the social product both of leisure and of other goods by shortening the hours of labor.[5] Even a slave master would follow this rule in regulating the working hours of his charges. Additions to leisure beyond the amount required for maximum

---

[3] Pigou refers to leisure as a "quasi-commodity."

[4] If one wishes to introduce the possibility that the product of the future may be discounted in the present, then this rule should be revised so that the present value of the worker's future product be maximized.

[5] A conceivable exception to this principle is that, under certain conditions, the worker may derive such great satisfactions from the labor itself that he prefers to work beyond the point of maximum productivity. In this case, the satisfaction from the labor must be regarded as one of the goods or "products" of that labor, and this product must be taken into consideration in deciding what is the most economical division between leisure and labor.

productivity could, however, be obtained only at the sacrifice
of other goods. As each individual's leisure was increased (his
working time diminished), his productivity of other goods
would steadily decline. The second rule may be stated then:
The amount of leisure for each individual should be increased
up to that point where the marginal unit of leisure would yield
an amount of satisfaction equal to that obtained from the
marginal unit of that individual's labor. This adjustment
would be the most economical one because any deviation from
it would result in a less desirable situation. For example, any
increase in leisure would lead to satisfactions less important
than those sacrificed as a result of the corresponding diminution
of labor; or any decrease in leisure would lead to the sacrifice
of satisfactions more important than those gained by the extra
labor.

The implementation of this second rule would require a
technique for deciding in the case of each individual upon the
most advantageous apportionment of his time. Since this would
involve a measurement of the satisfaction obtained by the
individual from increments of leisure, it would probably be
necessary to utilize the price system. Let us suppose, then,
(1) that each individual is completely free to decide for himself regarding the division of his time between leisure and
labor; (2) that the distribution of income is "correct"; and
(3) that the government or some other central agency places a
price on leisure, and allows each individual to spend as much
of his income as he wishes for this good. Under this arrangement, the more leisure the individual would choose to enjoy,
the less income he would have left over for other goods.[6] In
order to comply with the second rule, it would clearly be
necessary for the price charged each individual for leisure to be
equal to the cost of that leisure—cost measured in terms of
the value of the additional goods which the individual could
have produced if he had worked instead of enjoying leisure.
With the price of leisure set in this manner, each individual
would apportion his time between the two uses so that the

---

[6] For instance, each individual might be permitted, without charge, the
amount of leisure necessary for maximum productivity, but might be required to
pay a price for each additional hour—or what amounts to the same thing, to have
his income reduced for each additional increment of leisure.

satisfaction derived by him from the marginal unit of leisure would be just equal to the value of the goods he might have produced had he devoted this marginal unit of time to labor. The resulting apportionment of time would conform to the second rule.

The pricing of leisure according to cost, as is required in the application of the rule, is unfortunately incompatible with the general principle of economy that each good should be available to all persons at a uniform price. Clearly the cost of an hour's leisure, in terms of sacrificed alternative goods, would vary among different individuals. For the highly talented and productive persons the cost of leisure would be large, whereas for the relatively unproductive the cost would be trifling. Different classes of individuals would thus be subject to different prices for the same good. Superficially this might seem to be an argument against the application of the cost principle on the ground that the satisfaction derived from a marginal unit of leisure would not be equal for all persons. Yet, if maximum aggregate satisfaction is to be held rigorously as the objective of the economic process, these differences in the price charged different persons for leisure would be necessary so long as there were individual differences in productive power. In other words, economy would require a working day for highly productive persons longer than that for persons of less productivity. The limiting case at one extreme would be a person who is so productive (e.g., the President of the United States) that he could not be permitted (or could not afford) a moment of leisure beyond that necessary for achieving maximum productivity; and at the other extreme the person who has no productive power at all and who would therefore be freed from all responsibility.[7]

Intensity of Labor

Having indicated some of the considerations relating to the economical division of human time between leisure and labor,

---

[7] It is possible, of course, that the more productive persons who might be presumed to have more education and broader interests would value leisure more highly than the less productive persons and so would be willing to obtain a considerable amount even at a high price.

a basis has been laid for dealing with the problem of what is the most advantageous intensity of labor.

Clearly the intensity with which a person works will affect not only his productivity, but also the amount of "disutility" (or utility) that he obtains from his work. Thus the decision regarding the most advantageous labor intensity, as in the case of leisure, must be based upon a comparison of variations in productivity with variations in satisfaction or dissatisfaction derived by the worker from his job. It is possible, then, to set forth two rules, similar to those applying to leisure, to guide judgments concerning the most economical intensity of labor. First, the intensity of labor for any individual should not exceed that which is necessary in order to make possible the maximum production of goods by that worker during his entire lifetime. If he works more intensely than this, the reduction in his future productivity through excessive fatigue, ill-health, or shortened life would more than offset any addition to current production. The excessive intensity would reduce output and at the same time (save for very exceptional cases) increase the disutility from the work. Any reduction in intensity below the point of maximum production would, however, be obtained only at the cost of a reduced output of goods. The second rule is, then: The intensity of labor for each individual should be decreased (from the point of maximum output) until the marginal decrements of disutility to the individual are equal to the marginal decrements of product. This adjustment would be most desirable, from the standpoint of maximum satisfaction, since any sacrifice in satisfaction due to curtailment of output would be just counterbalanced by a decline in disutility due to the reduction in labor intensity.

Practically, to find an objective basis for evaluating the relative gains in satisfactions from more goods and lessened labor intensity is not easy. It might be possible to arrange for each individual to be charged a price for the privilege of working at an intensity less than that required for maximum productivity (e.g., a piece-rate system), so that the price charged each individual would be equal to the cost of the reduction in labor intensity. If each individual were then free to choose regarding his own labor intensity, the conditions of the second rule would be satisfied. Each individual would adjust the degree of his effort so that the marginal decrement of labor intensity would yield an increase in satisfaction just equal to the reduction in satisfaction from goods due to that marginal decrement.[8] As in the case of leisure, the cost, and therefore the price, of reduced labor intensity would differ among individuals according to their potential productivity. For the highly productive the price would be high, and for the less productive the price would be low.

The Supply of Labor a Social Problem

The preceding discussion, though suggestive of certain general principles, lacks in realism since it is founded upon the postulate that each individual is free to decide on the amount of time he shall devote to leisure and to labor and on the intensity of his labor. In a society which utilizes complex and highly specialized productive techniques, this freedom of the individual is largely impracticable. Advanced methods of production require, above all else, the utmost in cooperation and coordination among the many individuals engaged. The factory operative, the retail clerk, the bank messenger, the railroad conductor, the schoolteacher, the lawyer, the traveling salesman, must each adapt his hours and the intensity of his labor to the convenience of his fellow workers, his employers, or the consumers who depend upon his services. The efficiency of the productive mechanism would be greatly impaired if the wishes and decisions of each individual in these matters were seriously considered. These decisions are and in most cases must be made on a group basis—perhaps as a result of the decisions of entrepreneurs or officials, but more likely through law and custom.[9] The history of the "eight-hour day," the "forty-hour week," the "legal holiday," and the "vacation with pay" is illustrative of the procedure by which the length of the working period is determined.[10] Similarly, group choices with respect

---

[8] In practice the decision of the individual regarding labor intensity would be related to his decision regarding hours of labor. He might, for example, choose reduced intensity and long hours instead of high intensity and short hours.

[9] Provision may be made for part-time work, and there are some occupations, e.g., free-lance writing, where significant individual choices are possible.

[10] The powerful social drive toward shorter working hours is suggestive that with rising incomes the marginal satisfaction from leisure has become greater than the marginal satisfaction from other goods.

to labor intensity are usual. Throughout industry the tendency is toward the standardization of productive tasks and the development of teamwork among cooperating workers (e.g., on an assembly line). Even where the worker is employed individually so that the speed of his operations does not directly affect other workers, efficiency requires each individual to work with a certain intensity in order to justify his occupying factory space and using machinery. Moreover, in occupations where these considerations do not apply, there are *customary* standards as to what constitutes a "reasonable" day's work and each worker is expected to conform more or less to this standard.

On the whole, leisure and reduced labor intensity are social goods the amount of which must be determined through collective choice.[11] The problems of determining "output" are similar to those encountered in connection with any other social good. It is possible that voting and similar techniques may be useful in giving effect to such collective choice.[12] However, when possible, the amount of leisure or the labor intensity of different individuals should be adjusted according to their preferences and abilities, provided increased complexity of organization does not involve compensating costs.

Summary

The argument of this section may be summarized as follows: (1) Assuming that the size and basic character of the population are given, the labor supply depends upon the manner in which human time is divided between labor and leisure, and upon the intensity of labor during the working period; (2) In a modern economic system characterized by a high degree of specialization and division of labor, only in relatively exceptional cases should the division of time between labor and leisure and the intensity of labor be determined through group decisions or customs that permit latitude for individual choices.

---

[11] To implement this collective action, some system of incentives or penalties must be provided in order to ensure that each individual works the desired number of hours and with the desired intensity. Usually, the provision of incentives for this purpose is connected with the distribution of income, though doubtless other incentives are, or might be, effective.

[12] See Chapter 18.

Chapter 22

THE SUPPLY OF CAPITAL

It is advantageous for a society to have as much capital, including material things and human skills, as can be used productively with the given technology and the available supply of labor and natural resources. So long as the amount of capital is less than this, the productive power of the group will fall short of the possible maximum. Thus any society having a deficiency of capital will do well, in terms of aggregate satisfaction, to build up its capital stock. In order to accomplish this, however, it will be necessary to devote labor and land, which might have been used in producing goods for the more immediate future, to the production of goods for the relatively distant future. In other words, the cost of adding to the stock of capital goods is the postponement of the satisfactions which are to be achieved through the use of current labor and land. Thus the building up of the supply of capital goods involves the sacrifice of satisfactions more or less immediate in favor of *greater* satisfactions (not necessarily to the same persons) in the more distant future.

The problem concerning the supply of capital has to do with the *rate* or *speed* at which the supply of capital should be increased. How rapidly should a society having a capital deficiency build up its stock? Or, what amounts to the same thing, to what extent should consumption in the near future be sacrificed for consumption in the relatively distant future?

The Supply of Capital as a Social Problem

At first glance it might be supposed that the problem of capital supply could be solved in terms of the interests of presently living individuals. Then the most economical rate of capital accumulation would be such that the last dollar saved by each individual would yield a product equal to the sacrifice involved in saving that last dollar. In this case the product would derive from use of the increased capital, and the sacrifice would result from the supposed preference of individuals for present goods as compared with future goods.

Unfortunately, the problem of capital supply concerns not alone the individuals living at the time capital accumulation occurs. Because there is constant turnover in the population, the sacrifice of living individuals in providing additional capital almost always redounds to the benefit of persons yet unborn.[1] Thus, in large measure, the problem of capital supply is one of comparing the interests of different generations—of deciding how much the present living generation should give up in order to provide increased satisfactions for future generations.[2]

The only definite rules for economy in the supply of capital are: (1) That a society should not continue to accumulate capital beyond the amount which could be used to advantage in connection with the given supply of land use and labor and the given technology; (2) That so long as a capital deficiency exists, the society should accumulate capital at least as rapidly as would be indicated by the interests of presently living individuals.

Beyond these general rules, economic theory offers little help in determining the rapidity with which a society ought to accumulate capital. The problem is one which must of necessity be decided by the group in terms of broad objectives. It involves, on the one hand, a comparison of present and future satisfactions for living individuals, and on the other hand, a comparison of the interests of one generation with those of another. Any decision reached would probably take into account not only the desires of living individuals regarding the time shape of their flow of consumption, but also their interest in the survival and progress of their own society or of the human race.

Soviet Russia, for example, has been impelled deliberately to hold an entire generation near the subsistence level in order

---

[1] Conversely, the dissipation of capital already accumulated redounds to the disadvantage of future generations.

[2] Provision for one's own offspring may, of course, provide immediate satisfactions.

to build up the industrial plant which has been deemed necessary to the survival and future progress of the nation. As a result of this policy, new generations may come into possession of a rich heritage based upon the sacrifices of an earlier generation. Whether or not such extreme sacrifices are justified in terms of the end of maximum aggregate satisfaction can be determined only on the basis of a general judgment and not in terms of marginal economic calculus.

Even in a capitalist society where the rate of saving is ostensibly left to individual choice, the motives for saving clearly take into account the social interest in rapid capital accumulation. This is indicated by a mere recital of some of these motives. First, wealth is desired not alone for the ulterior satisfactions it can yield but also for the power it gives, for its symbolic significance, and for the satisfaction to be acquired from the game of accumulation. Second, the family system—combined with the institution of inheritance—provides a strong interest in the welfare of future generations and an incentive to the accumulation of capital up to the very end of a lifetime. Third, the fact that each individual is responsible to provide for himself during the "rainy days" strongly impels saving. Fourth, saving is morally sanctioned and improvidence condemned. Fifth, it is possible to retire from work before old age if one can accumulate sufficient wealth. Sixth, the distribution of income is such that saving is extremely easy for a minority of individuals who have incomes in excess of comfortable living requirements. For all these reasons, the rate of saving under capitalism, even with free individual choice, is much more rapid than would be the case if individuals saved only for the purpose of increasing their own subsequent satisfactions. Indeed, one of the most important public issues in modern capitalist society is whether or not the motives to save are too powerful—whether or not capitalist society is not literally saving itself out of existence.[3]

Investment in Material Capital Goods

Once the supply of capital in general is determined, the problem remains of deciding what is the most economical sup-

3 See pp. 297–304.

ply of each particular capital good. In other words, it is necessary to determine what should be the composition of the given total stock of capital goods—including both material and non-material capital goods.

One fairly simple rule may be laid down: In order to attain economy in the use of resources, investment must be distributed among different industries and different types of capital goods so that the aggregate return from the given total supply of capital, expressed in terms of value of product, will be at a maximum. In order to achieve this, it is required that at each successive instant of time marginal returns from all different forms of investment shall be equal. Otherwise, it would be desirable to alter the composition of the capital stock by increasing and decreasing the supply of those capital goods for which the marginal return is relatively high and low respectively.

The marginal return from an investment may be defined in this context as the *value* of the additional product, per period of time, resulting from the final dollar's worth of labor and land invested in the capital good. The value of the additional product refers to the *actual* product, viewed retrospectively, and not merely to the *expected* product. On this point it may be well to elaborate.

In any society employing lengthy methods of production (using capital), the decisions as to what shall be produced and the commitment of labor and land to the purpose must *precede* the completion of the product. This means that in view of the inability of human beings to make accurate forecasts of the future, it can never be known at any given moment of time whether the composition of the stock of capital goods *at that time* is economical. Most of the capital goods then in existence are designed not only for current but also for *future* production. Therefore, even if the supplies of the various capital goods were perfectly adjusted to present circumstances, or indeed to whatever future conditions might reasonably be expected, one could never be certain that some unexpected changes in the near future might not quickly render this capital adjustment completely inappropriate. In a dynamic and uncertain world, then, it is not possible to judge with acuracy the relative desirability of the supplies of capital goods in existence at any moment in time except in retrospect—and then only after a sufficient number of decades have elapsed for all the capital goods existent at the moment in question to have been used up.

These considerations imply that an economical composition of the stock of capital goods, indeed, an economical use of land and labor, cannot be achieved unless the individuals in charge of production, the decision makers, are able to predict the future accurately. If they are unable to foresee changes (1) in consumer tastes, (2) in the availability of factors, (3) in other conditions affecting production (technology, weather, "acts of God"), their decisions, when viewed in retrospect, are likely to result in the misallocation of the factors. In the period intervening between decisions and the outcome of these decisions, important unforeseen changes may render inappropriate the original course of action. Moreover, any subsequent attempt to correct the resulting misallocation may also end in error because the correction itself may be founded upon what will turn out to be mistaken predictions. Thus, economy is attainable only if the decision makers are able to foresee the future perfectly. To the extent that their predictions are inaccurate, resources are almost certain to be used uneconomically—with overexpansion in some directions and underdevelopment in others.

Up to the present, at least, the ability of human beings to foretell future changes leaves much to be desired. In a dynamic world the task of predicting changes is enormously difficult, and the "probable error" assignable to any particular forecast is almost always high. The redeeming feature of the situation, however, is that the world is in most respects and at most times essentially stable—though it frequently seems otherwise to us— so that fairly reliable forecasts of the future are usually possible on the simple hypothesis that the conditions of the future will roughly resemble those of the present. This is not to imply that change does not occur, or that it can safely be ignored, but only that it usually occurs gradually, that the present is linked with the future by evolutionary sequences rather than by discontinuities. Thus, excepting periods of social or natural cataclysm, the basic conditions of life and of economic activity remain fairly constant over considerable periods and are, in this sense, fairly predictable. Were it otherwise, assuming the art of prediction to remain in its present low state, there would be little prospect of attaining anything that would remotely resemble an economical allocation of resources, and the pursuit of economy would become largely futile. Not only would the allocation of resources be carried on in terms of inadequate and mistaken forecasts, but the rate of change in events and conditions would probably far exceed any possible rate of adjustment in capital supplies.

The relative stability of the basic conditions within which economic decisions are made can be explained by the fact that these conditions are part of the firmly established culture pattern of the group. To a considerable degree this is true for each of three basic determinants of the allocation of resources, namely, (1) the tastes of consumers, (2) the supply of the factors, and (3) the physical and legal conditions under which production must be carried on.

We ordinarily assume, for example, that consumer taste is a peculiarly dynamic and unpredictable element in the economic scene. Yet, a moment's reflection reveals that the stability in consumer tastes far outweighs the instability. The pattern of consumption is a persistent element of the culture, the main features of this pattern being rooted in the habits, customs, and mores of the people and almost always free from violent change. The pattern of consumer tastes at any given time is almost always a good index of consumer tastes in the future. It is not difficult to estimate, for example, the loaves of bread, gallons of gasoline, pairs of shoes, or number of hats that people will want to consume (with given prices and incomes) during the next five years in the United States. Such sudden shifts in consumer tastes as do occur are associated chiefly with the phenomenon of fashion and therefore relate usually to the detailed features rather than to the fundamental character of the goods demanded. Even this element of uncertainty, however, is less important than is sometimes supposed, because a shift in taste due to a change in fashion relates chiefly to the later stages in the productive process and affects the earlier stages only slightly. Hence, the prediction of these detailed changes need be made only for the relatively short period of time elapsing between the final stages of production and consumption. For example, it is hardly necessary to predict the style of shoes when deciding upon the production of steel for the manufacture of shoe machines or the production of brick for shoe factories. Thus the scope for error as a result of sudden variations in consumer tastes is greatly restricted.

Rapid changes in the supplies of the factors are similarly unlikely. The determinants of factor supplies, the size of the population, customs regarding the division of time between leisure and labor, and rate of saving are largely controlled by forces that are deeply imbedded in the culture. Moreover, since any one year's increment to the total supply of labor or of capital is usually very small in comparison with the size of the total supply in existence, violent changes in the total supply are not ordinarily to be expected. More significant are the uncertainties associated with technical invention, unexpected legislation or governmental decrees, war, or weather changes. At times these may occur suddenly and without warning, and are therefore not often (at least under the present state of knowledge) susceptible of prediction. These constitute, therefore, important sources of error in the plans of decision makers. But even here the changes in most cases are sufficiently slow or sufficiently restricted in application for "reasonable" capital adjustment to be possible.

It is, of course, most unlikely that a society could ever attain the perfect foreknowledge that would be essential to the attainment, or even approximation, of economy. Yet, the fact that the present is linked with the future through the continuity of the culture means (1) that investment plans can be based upon reasonably dependable predictions of the future, and (2) that through a process of unending adaptation, the supplies of capital goods can be "reasonably" adjusted to changing conditions. Though perfect adjustment can perhaps never be reached, it can be approached. Moreover, any reduction in the rate of change in the basic conditions of economic life or any improvement in the ability to forecast future changes tends to reduce the degree of error.

Investment in the Training of Human Beings

The stock of capital goods in a society consists not only of material things, but also of the learned attributes of human beings. These are of two classes: [4] (1) those attributes which are

---

4 See p. 88–89.

produced as a step in the provision of transferable goods, i.e., occupational skills, and (2) those physical and personal qualities of human beings which are desired not for their contribution in the form of transferable goods but rather for their direct contribution to the future welfare of the individual or of the society, e.g., well-adjusted personalities, desirable civic and religious attitudes, knowledge of the world of art and letters, etc. The production of either type of nonmaterial capital goods involves the use of labor and land, directly or indirectly, in the training or "improvement" of human beings, for the purpose of providing goods in the future. In other words, it is investment. Thus, the principles governing the process of investment must be broadened to include nonmaterial capital goods. Let us first approach the problem with reference to investment in human beings for the purpose of producing transferable goods, i.e., the training of workers.

Since individuals differ in their aptitudes and capacities, economical investment in labor personnel requires the proper selection of individuals for various occupations, and then the proper kind and amount of investment in each person. This will be accomplished if three rules are followed. First, investment must be distributed among different persons so that the marginal return will be equal for all persons. Otherwise it would pay to increase the investment in those classes of persons yielding a relatively high rate of return and to reduce it in those yielding a low rate of return. Second, the marginal rate of return from investment in human beings must be equal to that obtained from investments in material capital goods. Otherwise it would pay to change the proportions of investment as between persons and things. Third, the *type* of investment made in each individual (i.e., the occupation for which he is to be trained) must be suited to his capacities in the sense that his total product must be the greatest possible—consistent, of course, with the two preceding principles. This rule is necessary to provide for the fact that a given individual might be trained for any one of a score of different occupations in which the return would justify the investment. Toscanini, for example, might have been an excellent maître d'hôtel or watchmaker. The problem, then, is to select that occupation in which the value of the individual's total product will be at a maximum so long as the marginal return on the investment in him is not less than the going marginal return on other forms of investment. Any other arrangement would mean that the total productivity of society would be less than maximum, since a reshuffling of the occupational structure would increase the total product.

Through application of these three rules, the economical selection of personnel and the economical distribution of investment in human beings would be accomplished—except for inevitable errors due to imperfect foresight or to inadequate ability to measure the potentialities of individual human beings. Such errors, incidentally, cannot be quickly or easily remedied because it is not easy to transfer persons from one occupation to another. If, for example, a person is selected and trained to become a dentist, it is not a simple matter to transfer him to the field of engineering or accountancy. These adjustments in modern society are made largely as a result of the death or retirement of persons wrongly placed, and the training of new personnel to fill up the ranks of occupations requiring expansion.

So long as investment in human beings results in the future production of transferable goods, the product can be marketed and price can be utilized as a criterion of the value of the return. When, however, the investment is designed for the creation of attitudes, beliefs, values, and other human qualities which are desired in and of themselves, so that no transferable product emerges, the price system is of no use as a guide. Though the principle of equi-marginal returns is applicable in principle, there is no objective criterion available for deciding what proportion of the social productive power should be devoted to this class of investment. Decisions regarding the allocation of labor and land to civic education, to the development of music appreciation, the inculcation of religious doctrine, or to similar purposes must be based upon nonpecuniary evaluations. In some cases the problem can be solved by providing these capital goods in response to the free choices of the individuals in whom the investment is to be made. This, however, cannot be relied upon completely for the reason that much of this type of investment must be made when the individuals are immature and unable to render capable judgments as to what is "good" for them in the long run. Consequently, it is necessary for many of these choices to be made by persons other than the beneficiaries—by parents or by public officials. And to guide such persons, there are no objective criteria available for determining how much of the social productive power should be invested in the "improvement" of individuals. The problem can be solved only through some form of social valuation.

Investment in Research and the Arts

A peculiarly strategic type of investment consists in the application of labor and land to scientific investigation, invention, and artistic creation. Such investment results in additions to the body of knowledge, the development of new technical methods of production, the discovery of commodities not previously available, and the creation of works of art. The amount of investment to be carried on in this field should be guided in accordance with the familiar principle of equi-marginal returns, i.e., the marginal rate of return on investment in research and artistic creation should be equal to that in any other field. There is a special problem, however, in evaluating the returns from knowledge and works of art since these things, once made available, are not *scarce* in the usual sense of that word. Awareness of an idea, knowledge of technique, or appreciation of a work of art by one person does not lessen the possibility of similar experience on the part of other persons. Therefore, no purpose is served in limiting the use of ideas, techniques, and works of art by charging a price for the use of them.[5] This means that the price system does not afford a criterion for evaluating the product of investments in this field, and that some form of collective demand must be substituted for individual demand.

The Utilization of Nonreproducible Natural Materials

Whereas the provision of capital involves the sacrifice of the present in favor of the future, the use of nonreplaceable

---

[5] There may be an exception in the case of painting and sculpture, where a price may be necessary in order to restrict the size of the throngs who may wish to view these objects. This, however, is not usually a problem. It is seldom that the appreciation of an object of art by any one person interferes in the slightest with similar appreciation by other persons.

natural materials, chiefly minerals, robs the future in favor of the present. Thus the problem of how rapidly capital should be accumulated is matched by the obverse problem of how rapidly natural resources should be exploited. This, like many other questions, must of necessity be decided collectively.

The rate of exploitation of natural resources, if determined in accordance with the choices of individual consumers, would surely be much more rapid than if the rate were determined by collective decisions. This discrepancy between the individual and the social point of view can easily be explained by the fact that no individual has any material incentive to be sparing in the use of natural resources, however seriously he may consider the interest of future generations, because his efforts to conserve will be negligible in effect. For example, I see no sense in my driving my car sparingly in order to conserve the petroleum supply unless I can be sure that other persons are doing likewise. Therefore, significant conservation waits upon some form of collective action—which will provide incentives or will require individuals to pursue the policy which is regarded as socially desirable. Economic theory offers no help, however, in deciding what rate of exploitation is most desirable. This must ultimately be decided in terms of the way in which the group evaluates the interests of the present in comparison with those of the future. Their judgment in the matter is likely to be tempered by the realization that future changes in technology may render valueless certain natural resources which are highly prized today and by the belief that the future will take care of itself according to the theory that "necessity is the mother of invention."

Chapter 23

SOCIAL ECONOMY:
RECAPITULATION

The preceding several chapters have been devoted to the discussion of principles and problems in the theory of social economy. The purpose has been to discover criteria for determining the "best" use of economic resources under the assumption that the aim of economic activity is maximum aggregate satisfaction. The purpose of the present chapter is to draw together the various portions of the argument into a concise summary and to comment briefly on the significance of the principles.

The theory of economy may be summarized as follows:

1. Given supplies of the factors of production will be used more economically if they are allocated in response to the free choices of individual consumers and in conformity with certain pricing rules:

    a. A uniform price shall be placed on all units of each factor.

    b. The price of each good shall be equal to its average cost of production.

    c. The factors shall be organized in the least costly manner.

    d. The price of each factor shall be set so that the demand for it is equal to the available supply.

    Rules *b* and *c* may be alternately and more simply formulated in this way: The quantity of the various factors used in producing each good should be adjusted so that the value of the marginal product of each factor will be equal to its price. These rules, whichever formulation of them is used, are sufficient to guide production of individual (as distinct from social) goods which are produced in industries where the factors are sufficiently divisible for constant or increasing cost to obtain.

2. For industries of decreasing cost, output must be adjusted so that price is equal to marginal cost—provided the gain from this procedure is not offset by any undesirable redistribution of income resulting from the taxation necessary to cover the deficit.

3. In applying the pricing rules to the production of social goods, ideal output is that at which "total marginal satisfaction" is equal to average (or marginal) cost. In this case voting and other devices for expressing individual preferences may serve as the counterpart of free individual consumer choice.

4. The above principles are adequate to guide the allocation of resources only provided incomes are distributed "correctly" and consumers (or voters) make the "right" choices. Unfortunately there are no simple and definite criteria of "correctness" in the distribution of incomes or "rightness" in consumer choices. At the present state of knowledge, conclusions in these areas are based upon tenuous hypotheses or upon common-sense judgments.

5. Moreover, the above principles are relevant only to the problem of determining the best use of given supplies of the factors of production. They offer no guidance in determining the optimum supply of the factors. The supply of labor must be regulated, on the whole, through collective decisions concerning the amount of leisure and the intensity of labor. Similarly, the supply of capital and the rate of exploitation of natural materials must be determined through collective decisions regarding the relative value of goods at different dates in the future. The supply of different kinds of capital goods, material and nonmaterial, must be adjusted so that the marginal (value) product of capital is equal in all of its uses.

Substantial parts of the theory of economy are ambiguous. The pricing rules, to be sure, are reasonably definite, but there are many important problems relating to the distribution of income, the guidance of consumer choices, production under decreasing cost, production of social goods, and supply of the factors which, for better or for worse, cannot be resolved through the mere application of a system of pecuniary rules or by the manipulation of variables in a set of equations. There is no substitute for human judgment in determining the "best" use of resources. This, however, should not detract from the importance of whatever explicit rules and criteria can be devised, and should stimulate effort to enlarge the number and scope of such rules, so that the conditions of social economy, instead of being matters of conjecture and unfounded opinion, can become more exact and objective.

The fact that pecuniary calculus is limited in its application to certain relatively narrow problems in the theory of economy has led to two divergent tendencies among economists. On the one hand, certain writers (e.g., Carlyle, Kingsley, Ruskin, Emerson, Schäffle, and Hobson) have tended to repudiate altogether the possibility of measuring satisfactions in terms of price. As Hobson has said, "To perform with scientific precision the task of translating economic values into ethical or human values is manifestly impossible. For economic values in their first intent are quantities of money, while ethical or human values are qualities of life." [1]

On the other hand. another more numerous group of writers have virtually abandoned all effort to analyze the conditions of economy, and have been content merely to concentrate attention on the problem of describing and explaining the operation of the existing economic order and developing a theory of welfare based exclusively upon pecuniary calculus. It has been held either that all other problems lie beyond the proper scope of economics or that nothing useful can be said beyond the realm of "price theory."

The position taken here is (1) that pecuniary calculus is highly significant and should be applied wherever possible, (2) that constant attempts should be made to discover new criteria of economy, whether pecuniary or nonpecuniary, in order to enlarge the area of definite knowledge and reduce the area of "unfounded opinion and common-sense judgments," and (3) that such investigations fall clearly within the proper

---

[1] John A. Hobson, *Economics and Ethics,* New York, 1929, p. vii.

scope of economics (in the sense that the economist, by training, is best suited to the task).

The theory of economy is no more than a set of principles and criteria to be followed by any society that wishes to use its economic means for the purpose of attaining maximum aggregate satisfaction. The theory tells us nothing about the specific institutions that would be required to give effect to these principles. It makes no recommendations concerning the relative merits of various types of economic systems, e.g., capitalism, socialism, syndicalism, fascism, or their modifications. The theory requires, it is true, that production be carried on in response to the free choices of consumers and that valuations (prices) be placed upon all goods and factors. It also requires that goods be offered to consumers in a market so that individual choices can be made known.[2] These elementary requirements, however, place no serious limitations on the character of the economic system. Free consumer choice in a market is a condition which could be readily fulfilled in any of the leading types of economic systems.

In any society aiming at maximum aggregate satisfaction, the problem of economic policy is to arrange its economic institutions so that the conditions of economy will be attained. This is, of course, a problem of politics and of directed cultural change.

The theory of economy can be used not only as a guide to economic policy but also as a set of criteria for judging the effectiveness of any given economic system. The remainder of this book is an appraisal of the capitalistic system from the point of view of its performance in the achievement of human satisfactions.

---

[2] It is possible, however, that some device other than a market might be used for this purpose.

PART V

Capitalism

Chapter 24

THE CAPITALISTIC SYSTEM

Earlier parts of this book have been concerned with some of the essential features of economic life that are common to all societies wherever located or however organized. Part II was devoted to economic institutions, Part III was a discussion of the physical aspects of economic life, and Part IV expounded in general terms the theory of economy on the assumption that the social objective is maximum aggregate satisfaction. The remainder of the book, Part V, will present an analysis of a particular kind of economic system, namely, *capitalism*.

The purpose of Part V will be to evaluate capitalism in terms of the theory of economy. The questions to which we shall try to find answers are these: (1) How does a capitalistic economy function? (2) To what degree is it possible for a capitalistic system to achieve an economical use of resources?

Definition of Capitalism

Capitalism is here defined as a particular type of economic system having the following essential characteristics:

1. *Private property:* Each individual has, within broad limits, the right to control, use, or dispose of any land or capital goods which he has acquired through production, exchange, gift, or inheritance.
2. *Free labor:* Each individual has the right to control, use, sell, or otherwise dispose of his own labor, but not that of any other individual.
3. *Free enterprise:* Production is carried on within firms under the direction of managements [1] that are free to

---

[1] The term "management" is intended to refer to those persons who jointly perform the functions of promotion, policy formation, and administration. The older term was "entrepreneur," but this term implies that these functions are

246

acquire factors by purchase, rental, or hire and are free to organize the factors so acquired in any way or for any purpose they choose, and are free to sell their products in any market they choose. For purposes of formal analysis, the government may be regarded as a firm which organizes the factors of production for the purpose of "producing" governmental services, which pays out incomes to the factors it employs, and which "sells" its products for a "price" in the form of taxes.

4. *Functional distribution of income:* The income of each individual is received as compensation for the services of the factors which he owns.

5. *Free consumer choice:* Each individual is endowed with the right to use his income as he pleases not only in the purchase of goods offered on the market but also in the division of his income between savings and consumption and in the decision to add to or draw upon his cash balances.

6. *Advanced technology:* Production is carried on under relatively indirect or capital-using methods and with a relatively high degree of specialization and division of labor.

7. *Money economy:* Money is in common use as a medium of exchange, as a measure of value, and as a store of value. Transactions are commonly carried on with the use of money as a medium of exchange and with prices expressed in the standard monetary unit.

8. *Complete competition:* A large number of consumers are competing for each type of good, a large number of firms competing in the sale of each good, a large number competing for each type of factor, and a large number of individuals supplying each type of factor. In each case "large number" means a number sufficient for the contribution to demand or supply of each buyer or seller to be a negligible part of the total demand or supply— so that each exerts no more than a negligible influence upon price or quantity traded.

combined in one person, which is seldom the case. "Management" is a term of increasingly common usage. It refers to all those who exercise the entrepreneurial functions.

9. *Limited government:* Government is restricted to such activities as protection of property rights; resistance against foreign invasions; establishment of weights, measures, and the monetary unit; provision of a few public works such as roads, schools, and aids to navigation. Especially, government does not regulate or influence prices or production.

This is an imposing array of characteristics. Surely there is not now and never has been an actual economic system that would qualify as strictly "capitalistic" under this definition. Yet, with generous qualifications the definition roughly fits the economy of the nineteenth-century Britain, or of the United States before World War I.

Operation of a Capitalistic System

The general mechanics of the capitalistic system are these: The use of resources is determined as a resultant of the separate and independent decisions and actions of individuals who function as suppliers of the factors, as consumers, and as managers of firms. The factors are hired by the firms which pay the owners for them; the income received in this way by the owners is then used to buy the products of the firms; the money received by the firms for the sale of their products, in turn, is used to pay for the factors employed. Thus a constant stream of money passes (1) from firms to owners of the factors (via the market for the factors of production), and (2) from owners of the factors back to firms (via the market for goods).

In this process the firms are middlemen who buy the factors, convert them into goods, and sell the goods to the consumers. (Of course, in addition to the transactions between factors and firms and between firms and consumers there are numerous inter-firm transactions arising from the specialization among firms in various parts of the productive process).

In a completely competitive system, the influence of each individual upon the prices of goods and of factors is negligible; consequently, each assumes that the prevailing system of prices, whatever it may be, is a given datum, and attempts to adjust his consumption, the disposal of his factors, and his managerial decisions in the light of these prices so as to maximize personal net advantage. In adjusting to any given system of prices, however, the combined effect of the separate actions of many individuals is likely to bring about changes in the prices. These price changes will in turn lead individuals to alter their actions, which will bring about still further price changes. This apparently endless succession of changes ceases only when a system of prices is established which induces no further changes in the actions of individuals and which, therefore, tends to be stable. When such a price system has been established and actions of individuals have been adjusted to it, the economic system is said to be in *equilibrium*. As will be shown, the economic relationships in capitalism are such that the system tends toward a position of equilibrium; and once equilibrium is established, any departure from it is likely to set in motion forces tending to restore it.

In short, capitalism may be characterized as an automatic self-regulating system motivated by the self-interest of individuals and regulated by competition.

For many generations it has been almost axiomatic among Western democratic peoples that capitalist equilibrium is synonymous with *economy* or *maximum aggregate satisfaction*. Accordingly, the dominant economic philosophy has been the philosophy of *laissez faire*. It has been vigorously argued by some, and assumed by many more, that if the capitalist system were allowed to operate unfettered by "artificial" government controls, the resulting equilibrium would produce the most economical allocation of resources and the best distribution of product. This view is perhaps less widely accepted by the present generation than by its forefathers, but is nevertheless a powerful element in the modern war of ideologies.

The purpose of the remainder of the book is to examine the philosophy of *laissez faire* in terms of the theory of economy as previously outlined. In the next chapter we shall discuss the process by which equilibrium is approached in a capitalistic system. Then we shall compare conditions under capitalist equilibrium with the conditions that are prerequisite to economy. Later we shall examine some of the difficulties encountered by capitalistic systems in achieving equilibrium and some of the limitations of the theory of economy as applied in practice.

Chapter 25

EQUILIBRIUM

The forces that lead a capitalistic system toward equilibrium may be described most clearly if we start with an economy that is thoroughly disorganized, and trace the process through which equilibrium would be established. Let us assume, therefore, a society (a) consisting of a given population with certain definite physical and cultural characteristics, (b) occupying a particular land area, and (c) possessing certain definite quantities of various capital goods. Let us suppose, further, that this society has been visited by some form of catastrophe, say abject military defeat, which has caused a breakdown of production and has upset all economic relationships and calculations. The experience of Germany or Japan at the end of World War II suggests that this assumption is by no means preposterous. Next, let us assume that our hypothetical society has decided to adopt a kind of capitalism that would conform to the definition outlined in the preceding chapter and, accordingly, has transferred all productive property to private ownership—except for the relatively small amount needed by the government. Finally, let us assume that the money supply is given and that it is held by private owners.

In this setting it is possible to trace the movement of the economy toward a position of equilibrium and thus to explain the mechanism by which the use of resources is determined under capitalism.

At the particular moment in time when the capitalist system starts to operate, the supply of factors available in the society would be given and fixed. The supply of land, of course, would be fixed once and for all. The supply of labor would be fixed since it is determined by such slowly changing elements as the size and character of the population, the previous training which the members of the group have received, and the decisions of the group regarding the apportionment of time between labor and leisure. Similarly, the supply of material capital goods, resulting from previous productive efforts, would be given. The *immediate* problem, then, would be: How will these given resources be used?

The Rental or Hire Market for the Factors of Production

In the chaotic situation assumed, the people (1) in the role of consumers would be eager for goods, (2) in the role of suppliers of factors would be desirous of income, and (3) in the role of businessmen would be keen for profitable business opportunities. Businessmen would presumably begin to organize firms and thus to mobilize the factors into producing units. As a result, the market for the factors would become active—firms seeking suitable factors, and individuals attempting to obtain employment for their factors, i.e., their labor, their capital goods, and their land.

Each firm coming into the market would have tentative plans for the production of one or more goods. These plans would be based largely upon the estimates of the managers regarding the prospective prices of these goods. Since the price of each good would depend partly upon its market *value* relative to other goods, and partly upon the *value* of money, the managers would be required to prophesy (1) the relative demand of consumers for their products and (2) the general value of money. In the disorganized state of the economy these estimates could be little more than "best guesses" based primarily upon past experience and partly upon an analysis of any new relevant circumstances.

A firm would be inclined to carry out its plans only if the prices of the necessary factors were low enough for the anticipated unit cost of the product not to exceed (with allowance for uncertain contingencies) the expected price of the product. Thus, in general, the lower the prices of the required factors, the more likely would the firm be to undertake the contemplated production. Within any industry the managers of different firms would be likely to differ in their appraisals of opportunities, no two viewing prospects in precisely the same way or with precisely the same degree of confidence. Consequently, the lower the prices of the factors used in the industry, the more firms would be encouraged to start up and the greater would be the demand for these factors.

In still another way the prices of the factors would affect the demand for them. Once the various firms had decided to begin production, each would attempt to achieve the least costly combination of the factors and scale of output. In so doing, it would be guided by the relative prices at which the various factors could be obtained. Generally, the lower the price of any given factor, the more generously it would be used in combination with others, and the higher the price of any factor, the more sparingly it would be used.

It may be concluded that the demand for any factor would be inversely related to the price because (1) a lower price would tend to encourage more firms using this factor to start up, and (2) a lower price would induce firms to employ the factor more generously. It would be possible to draw up a schedule for the market showing the total demands of business firms for the various factors at each combination of prices.

By hypothesis, the supply of the factors for the time being is given. Consequently, it may be assumed that the individuals supplying the factors would offer their respective resources on the market for the highest prices that could be obtained. This supply would then be confronted with the demands of business firms that are seeking factors.

At first no one in the market would be aware of what prices of the factors would equate the demand with the supply. Firms would begin, however, to make price offers for the various factors. Since under complete competition all firms would be acting independently and without knowledge of the plans of others, the offers of the different firms might vary widely at first. In due time, however, there would be a tendency toward uniform price offers. Those firms offering a high price for any given factor would be besieged with suppliers of that factor wishing to obtain the high price. The managers of these firms, recognizing the ease with which the factor could be obtained at this price, would tend to lower their offers. Conversely, those firms offering a relatively low price for the factor would have difficulty obtaining any and would be tempted to increase their price offers. The price offers of various firms for each factor would thus tend to converge upon a single price.

The question still remains: What would this price be? The answer is that the price of each factor would tend to be established at a level such that the demand for the factor would be equal to the available supply. This price may be termed the *equilibrium price.*

The demand for each factor would depend upon its price in relation to the prices of other factors. Other things being equal, the lower the price of a factor, the greater would be the demand for it. Thus, to reach the equilibrium price, the price of each factor would be lowered to a point where demand would be sufficient to take over the available supply. If the price were higher than this, some units of the factor would be without employment. The owners of the unemployed units, in order to move them into use, would offer these units at less than the prevailing prices. This would induce firms to hire only those units offered at low prices, thus forcing down the price for *all* units. The reduction in price, at the same time, would induce firms to employ more units of this factor. When the equilibrium price had been reached, the demand would have increased to absorb the entire supply. On the other hand, if the price of the factor were less than the equilibrium price, the demand of firms for the factor would exceed the available supply—firms would attempt to hire more units than could be supplied. As a result, a shortage of the factor would appear. Owners would hesitate to dispose of their factors at the prevailing price, and firms desiring additional units would tend to make increased price offers. Other firms, in order to retain their supply of the scarce factor, would match these increases. Consequently, the price would tend to rise until there were no longer any "unsatisfied buyers."

With uniform prices on the factors adjusted so that the demand for each factor would be equal to the supply, the employment of *all* available factors would be provided for. At the same time, through the pricing of the factors the incomes of the owners of the factors would be determined.

In the process of arriving at the equilibrium prices, some of the factors would be disposed of at higher and lower figures. These "errors" in the trial-and-error process of reaching market equilibrium would tend, in time, to be corrected. Assuming that the factors were hired for short periods (e.g., by the day), these errors would be corrected when bargains were being struck for the second day. In practice, however, many of the factors might be contracted for longer periods. "Errors" in the pricing of such factors could not be corrected until the expiration of the contracts.

The Purchase Market for the Factors

The above discussion is based upon the assumption that firms obtain all required factors by hiring or renting them. But it is also possible for them to obtain the use of land and capital goods by outright purchase rather than by rental. (This would not be true of labor under the assumption of no slavery.) In practice, the use of land and durable capital goods would be obtained partly by rental and partly by direct purchase; and the use of rapidly depreciating capital goods (including those which are capable of only a single use) would always be obtained by purchase, since rental would be impracticable. Let us examine how the prices of land and capital goods would be determined in the purchase market.

In the case of rapidly depreciating capital goods not subject to rental—for example, raw materials, partly finished goods, or supplies, the price of each would tend to be established at whatever level would be necessary to equate the demand of firms and the given supply.

For land and durable capital goods the solution is slightly less simple, since the purchase price and the rental price of each durable asset are interrelated. The two prices are connected *via* the interest rate. In order for a firm to purchase a durable asset, it must obtain the money; the *interest* on the money becomes part of the cost of purchasing the durable asset and must be taken into account when a firm is choosing between purchase and rental. Similarly, when an owner sells a durable asset, he acquires money which can be lent out at interest, and the possible income from interest must be taken into account when he is choosing between sale and rental.

Let us first take up the case of nondepreciating assets (land). Suppose a firm wishes to obtain a particular type of site, the annual rental on such sites being $1,000 and the purchase price $18,000. Assuming that the firm can borrow money at 5 per cent, purchase will clearly be preferable to renting, since the annual interest cost will be only $900 as compared with the $1,000 rental.[1] Consequently, the management will elect to rent instead of to purchase. Other firms similarly placed will make similar decisions. Only those firms which are unable to borrow for less than about 5½ per cent would prefer to rent instead of to purchase. As a result, the demand in the rental market would be relatively active, but in the purchase market sluggish; the rental price would tend to rise and the purchase price to fall; and these changes would induce more and more firms to rent and fewer to purchase.

Similar results are obtained if the same situation is viewed from the standpoint of the owners. Assuming, again, that the rental price is $1,000 and the purchase price $18,000, an owner who would be able to lend money at not more than 5 per cent would clearly prefer to rent rather than sell his site, since if he sold, his interest income would be only $900 as compared with the $1,000 rental. Only those owners who would be able to lend money at 5½ per cent or more would prefer to sell. At these original prices, however, rental would be extremely difficult and sale relatively easy. Thus the owners wishing to rent would tend to lower their rental offers and those wishing to sell would raise their selling offers.

In equilibrium the two prices would tend to be established so that the demand and supply in each of the two markets would be equalized. The ratio between the two prices would then be approximately equal to the rate of interest on money loans. Any deviation from this ratio would tend to cause inequality between the demand and the supply in the two markets. If the ratio between the rental price and purchase price should increase, the demand in the purchase market would increase and the supply would decrease; whereas the demand in the rental market would decrease and the supply would increase. This would tend to bring about a restoration of the original ratio, since under these conditions the price would tend to rise in the purchase market and to fall in the rental market.

---

[1] This ignores the possible effect of taxes or other expenses paid by owners and not applicable to tenants.

It may be concluded that the rental price and the purchase price of any nondepreciating asset will be determined according to the following two principles: (1) The ratio between the rental price and the sale price will tend to be equal to the rate of interest on money, and (2) Each of the two prices will tend to be established at such levels that the demand in each market will be equated with the supply. When these conditions are satisfied, the entire supply of the asset will be at the disposal of firms either through purchase or rental.

We turn now to the relation between the rental prices and purchase prices of depreciating assets (capital goods). The principles applicable to the market for capital goods are similar to those for land, except that the decisions of firms between rental and purchase are significantly influenced by the fact that depreciation must be borne by the owner of the asset. Consequently, the ratio between the rental price and the purchase price will depend not only upon the rate of interest but also upon the estimated length of life of the asset.

Suppose a firm is choosing between the purchase or rental of a machine which is estimated to have a life of ten years. The choice lies between the payment of a large sum immediately or a series of smaller sums at periodic intervals during the next ten years. The decision of the firm will depend, then, upon the rate of interest. Assuming that the machine can be rented for $100 per year and that the firm can borrow money at 5 per cent, it would pay the firm to purchase the machine provided the purchase price were less than $810.78, but if it were above this figure it would pay to rent. The amount, $810.78, represents the present value of an annuity of ten annual payments of $100 each (assuming that the rate of interest is 5 per cent and that the rental is to be paid in advance at the beginning of each year).[2]

Since the rate of interest available to different firms may vary, and since various managers will place different estimates on the probable life of particular assets, the ratio between the rental price and the purchase price is not perfectly definite. However, any increase in the ratio would induce more firms to purchase and fewer to rent; and any decrease in the ratio would have the reverse effect.

---

[2] Consult any standard annuity table on the present value of a ten-term annuity at 5 per cent.

In view of the influences determining the decisions of firms regarding rental or purchase, the rental price and purchase price in the market for any capital good would tend toward a ratio such that the purchase price would approximate the present value of the future rents, discounting at the average rate of interest and taking depreciation into account. Moreover, in equilibrium the two prices would tend to be established at such levels that the demand in each market would be equated with the available supply.

These conclusions (regarding both nondepreciating and depreciating assets) were reached on the assumption that funds to purchase land and capital goods are derived from loans of money. The conclusions are not substantially altered, however, if the funds are obtained from individuals who are given equities (e.g., common stock) instead of creditor claims (e.g., bonds). In order for the firm to sell stock, the prospects of return on the investment must be at least equal to that which the individual owner of money could obtain by lending his money; otherwise, he would prefer to lend rather than to purchase proprietary interests. Thus, in order for the firm to secure money through the sale of stock, it must offer prospects of a return sufficient to pay all expenses and in addition leave a surplus to remunerate the stockholders. Although the firm may have no *legal* obligation to pay returns on proprietary capital, the prospective return (either in cash, in kind, or in increased equities) must be sufficient to attract such money. In this sense, the securing of money through the sale of equities involves an interest cost.[3]

The Money Market

Thus far in the discussion, it has been assumed that the rate of interest is given. It is subject, however, to market determination and must itself be accounted for. The market in which the

---

[3] Moreover, once the money is in the hands of the firm, another reason exists for regarding interest as a cost of using equity capital. This lies in the fact that the *firm* as well as the individual has the option of lending the money rather than using it for the purchase of land and capital goods. The use of money for the purchase of assets involves the sacrifice of the possible interest which could have been obtained by lending the money. Hence, interest must be included as part of the cost of acquiring assets and must be reckoned with in deciding upon the relative advantages of purchasing or renting durable assets.

rate of interest is determined is usually called the *money market*. We now turn to an examination of that.

At the inception of our hypothetical economic system, it may be assumed that the available supply of money would be in possession of many different individuals. Each person would wish to retain a certain minimum cash balance for day-to-day use, for protection against unforeseen emergencies, and for use in snapping up "bargains." Many would have surpluses which they would be glad to turn over to business firms provided some return could be expected for the use of the money.

These surpluses would constitute the potential supply in the money market. They could be used either for loans to business firms or for the purchase of equities, the difference between the two uses being of significance chiefly in relation to the distribution of profits and losses. The actual supply of money offered in the market would likely vary to some extent, depending upon the expected rate of return from investments. At low rates individuals would tend to hold their money and offer relatively less on the market; at high rates they would tend to hold less money and offer more on the market. Thus the supply of money at any time would tend to vary directly with the interest rate.

The demand for money, on the other hand, would come from firms requiring funds to purchase assets, to make advance payments of wages and other expenses, and to provide working cash balances. The demand would thus be dependent upon the decisions of business managers, which would depend mainly upon: (1) their expectations regarding the profit to be derived from the contemplated uses of money, and (2) the conditions upon which money could be obtained. Business managers would be inclined to borrow provided the anticipated return from the use of the money would exceed the contractual interest cost. They would seek equity funds if the prospective return from the use of those funds was sufficient to induce investors to place their funds, i.e., at least equal to the interest rate. Under these conditions any rise in the interest rate would tend to reduce the demand for money, since possible uses for money previously attractive to business managers would now be unprofitable. On the other hand, any decline in the interest rate would tend to increase the demand for money, since new projects, formerly unprofitable, could now be undertaken. Thus, assuming the expectations of all business firms to be given, the demand for money would vary inversely with the rate of interest.

The rate of interest would tend to be established at the level equating the demand for money with the supply. A rate higher than this would unduly restrict the demand, leaving individuals with surplus funds which they would seek to invest by offering them at a lower rate. On the other hand, a rate lower than this would cause an expansion of demand beyond the supply, and the competition of firms for the limited supply of money would lead to a rise in the rate.

Up to this point the discussion of interest has ignored the element of uncertainty and the cost of administration involved in lending money.

The market rate of interest, therefore, must include not only a return for the use of the money, but also compensation for uncertainty and remuneration for the necessary administrative costs to the investor. Since the different investments available to lenders at any time vary both in risk and in administrative cost, it is clear that there cannot be a single rate of interest applying to all investments. Investors would tend to avoid the relatively uncertain or costly investments and to seek those which are safer and less costly. As a result, the supply of funds for the former would tend to be relatively small, so that the interest rate for them would tend to be high; and for the latter the supply of funds would be large and the interest rate low. It is a well-known fact that in all money markets securities tend to be classified according to risk and cost, and that the market rate of interest on the various types of securities varies accordingly. Instead of a single interest rate, a whole complex of rates tends to be established. Thus the rate on each loan may be thought of as a composite of three elements: (1) remuneration for uncertainty, (2) compensation for cost, and (3) net return for the use of the money.

The Market for Goods

Once the factors had been assembled by the various firms, production could be started. At the outset each firm would produce at a given rate according to its prearranged plans (e.g., one thousand pairs of shoes per week, five thousand yards of cloth per week, etc.), and each would pay out income to the factors employed at a regular rate per week.

The demand of consumers for these products would depend upon three elements: (1) the wants of the consumers, (2) the incomes of the consumers, and (3) prices of the products.

In a capitalistic system characterized by complete competition, the wants of consumers would be regarded by business firms as given. The product of each firm would be exactly like that of its many competitors; therefore no firm would have any incentive to incur costs in attempting to influence the wants of consumers. On the other hand, the incomes of consumers would be, at least temporarily, determined by the outcome of negotiations in the market for the factors. Hence the significant and only remaining variable determining consumer demand would be, for the time being, the prices of the goods offered to consumers.

Under different price configurations the demands of consumers may be expressed as a schedule showing, for each combination of prices, the amount of each good that will be purchased. In general this schedule will have the characteristic that the demand for any one good (other things being equal) will vary inversely with the price of that good. However, it must be remembered that the demand for any good is also complexly related to variations in the prices of other goods.

Having decided upon their rate of production, business firms would be faced with the problem of obtaining the funds with which to remunerate the factors employed. These funds, of course, would be derived from the sale of the product to consumers. Hence the price at which these products are to be sold would have to be set. Each firm would wish to set its price as high as possible. However, the actual price it would ultimately be able to set would be determined competitively.

At the outset no one would be able to predict the equilibrium price for any good; each firm would be inclined to set its price more or less arbitrarily. Since the various firms would be acting independently, one may be sure that similar goods would at first be offered at widely varying prices. The price of each good, however, would soon tend toward uniformity. Purchasers would tend to buy at the lowest possible price. As a result there would be an intense demand for the goods offered at low prices, with no demand for those offered at high prices. Thus the sellers offering goods at high prices would be forced to lower their askings; whereas the strong demand experienced by those offering to sell cheaply would induce them to raise their prices. As a result the prices on all units of each good would soon tend to become uniform.

The question remains as to what would be the equilibrium level of each of these uniform prices. If the price of any good was too high, it would not be possible to sell the entire output. Firms having unsold surpluses would lower their price in order to clear their shelves, and other firms would be forced to follow suit in order to retain their customers. This price reduction would continue until the price was just sufficient to make possible the disposal of the entire output. On the other hand, if the price of any good was too low, the demand would exceed the output, causing an apparent shortage in the market. In view of the brisk demand, firms would be induced to raise their prices (or unsatisfied buyers to raise their offers) until the demand was compressed to the dimensions of the available supply. Equilibrium in the market for goods would be established when the prices of all goods were such that the demand of consumers for each good would be exactly equal to the available output.

When equilibrium had been realized, the prices of goods would be adjusted so that the entire current output could be purchased with the income available to consumers. Thus, in the determination of many prices it would be necessary not only that the *relative* prices of different goods be adjusted, but also that the average level of prices be generally consistent with the level of incomes. If prices on the average were too high, income would be insufficient to buy the current output of goods, and firms would be induced to lower their prices. On the other hand, if prices on the average were too low, consumer demand would be so intense that current output would be insufficient. Recognizing this, firms would be motivated to raise their prices.

Temporary vs. Longer Run Equilibrium

So far, we have discussed equilibriums in the rental or hire market for the factors, in the purchase market for the factors, in the money market, and in the market for goods. But these would be only temporary equilibriums. The prices ·of factors would soon be subject to change because business firms would find it advantageous to alter their demands; and the prices of goods would be subject to change (even assuming constant consumer demand) because business firms would be inclined to alter their outputs.

We must now turn to a consideration of these longer-run adjustments.

The Tendency of Price to Equal Average Cost

During the early operation of the system, the output of each industry would be determined by the original decisions of separate business managements, each acting without actual market experience and without knowledge of the number of other firms planning to enter the same industry. It is inevitable that serious errors would have been made. The number of firms entering some fields would be so great and their combined output so large that the market price would fall far short of covering the average cost per unit of even the most efficient firm. Firms in these industries would, therefore, be exposed to significant losses. In other industries, however, the number of firms and amount of product would be so small that market price would exceed cost and make possible large profits.

In industries where all or a majority of the firms were incurring losses, the weaker and less efficient firms would tend to withdraw or to be forced out of business. The output of the industry would thus diminish and the price of its product would rise (assuming demand to remain constant) until price would be sufficient to cover the average costs of remaining firms. On the other hand, in the profitable industries, existing firms would continue operating, or even expand, and new firms would be encouraged to enter. The output of these industries would consequently grow and the market prices of their products fall until average costs and prices would be equal.

As a result of these variations in output, factors would be disemployed in the unprofitable industries and employed in the profitable industries. To the extent that both classes of industries utilized the same factors in the same proportions, this would have no effect upon the relative demands for the various factors. But, as is more likely, if the one class of industries should require the factors in proportions somewhat different from the other, the net effect would be a change in the relative demands for the different factors. Some would be in greater demand and others in smaller demand.

Variations in the demands for the factors would lead to changes in their prices. These price changes, in turn, would lead to two types of repercussions. In the first place, changes in the prices of the factors would induce many firms to alter the combinations in which the factors were employed. They would be inclined to use more sparingly the factors for which the prices had risen and more generously those for which the prices had fallen. This, of course, would cause costs to rise in some industries and to fall in others, leading to profits in some and losses in others, and finally causing the expansion of the profitable industries and a fall in their prices, and the curtailment of the unprofitable industries with a rise in their prices. Complete adjustment would be reached only when a new system of prices on the factors had been established, which would equate demand and supply and under which every firm would be satisfied with the combination of factors it had achieved. In the second place, variations in the prices of the factors would alter the incomes of many individuals, which, in turn, would tend to alter their demands and hence the prices of goods.

The outcome of all these adjustments would be: (1) Uniform prices would be established on all units of each factor and of each good; [4] (2) The supply of each good would be adjusted so that the price per unit at which it could be sold would just equal the average cost per unit of producing it; and (3) The price of each factor and of each good would equate the demand

---

[4] In connection with the many adjustments in the output of various goods, the value of the marginal product of each factor in each of its uses would become equal to the price of that factor. Whenever the value of the marginal product of a factor in any use exceeded the price of the factor, it would be evident that more of that factor could be profitably employed in that use. As a result, the total demand for the factor would increase—raising the factor price—and the output of the product would increase—lowering the product price. When the adjustment had been completed, the price of the factor and the value of its marginal product would be equal. Conversely, whenever the value of the marginal product of a factor was less than the price of that factor, the resulting loss would indicate the need for reducing the employment of the factor and output of product until the price of the factor and its marginal product would be realigned.

and the supply. These conditions conform to three of the four pricing rules discussed in Chapter 15.

Concerning the second of these conditions, namely, that price and average cost would tend to be equal, further discussion is required to explain the meaning of the term "cost" in this context.

The Meaning of "Cost"

During the early operation of the system, many firms would discover, either through experience or through the example of competitors, that production costs are higher than need be. Since any reduction in cost would lead to an increase in profit (or a decrease in loss), such firms would set about to rearrange their productive organizations by altering the combinations of the factors employed.[5] In order to achieve less costly combinations they would seek to increase their employment of some factors and to reduce that of others. This would tend to alter the relative demands for the different factors, with resulting changes in the price of the factors, in incomes, in the demand for goods, etc.

With widespread decreases in production costs, applying to many different industries, it would be possible to maintain the rate of output for the economy with the employment of fewer factors than were previously required. In consequence, employment would be reduced. The owners of the disemployed factors, however, would attempt to secure their re-employment by offering them at less than the going prices. This would tend to force down the prices of the affected factors, tempting businessmen to organize new firms which would absorb the unemployed factors. The output of the economy would thus be increased. In order to make possible the sale of this increased output, the prices of goods would tend to be reduced in conformity with the lower cost.

In the generalization that the price of each product tends to be equal to cost, the cost referred to is *least cost*.

Assuming the prices of the factors to be given, there would be one particular combination of the factors that would involve the least cost in the production of each good. In attempting to

---

[5] Part of the problem faced by each firm in striving to attain the least costly combination of the factors is to achieve the optimum *scale* of output. See pp. 265–266.

minimize their costs, individual firms would aim at achieving this unique combination of the factors; consequently there would be a tendency for the costs of all firms in each industry to approach this minimum level. Through the influence of competition, the firms having costs in excess of the practicable minimum would be forced either to achieve minimum cost or to drop out. The cost of production of all firms in each industry, then, would tend to become approximately equal at the minimum level. This conclusion perhaps requires clarification.

Suppose that each firm in a given industry has reorganized its productive facilities in order to attain minimum cost but that some firms have been unable to produce as cheaply as other firms. Their failure might be due to one or both of two conditions: (1) inefficient management, or (2) inability to secure factors as efficient (for a given expenditure) as those available to competitors.

If the cost differential is due to inefficient management, there would be a tendency either for new management to replace the old within existing firms or for entirely new firms to supersede the existing ones. The owners of the firms in which there were managerial weaknesses might simply oust the present managers in favor of more efficient ones. As a result, cost would presumably fall to the level of that in the more efficient firms. Or the inability of the firms to produce at minimum cost might cause their downfall. They could continue to exist only so long as price was in excess of minimum cost. But such a price would be an open invitation to new firms under more efficient management to enter the field, expanding output and lowering price until continued losses forced existing inefficient firms to withdraw. In other words, the price would tend to approach equality with minimum cost, making untenable the position of any firm unable to achieve minimum cost. In effect, new efficient firms would have replaced old inefficient ones, and the costs of all surviving firms would have become identical.

If a firm is to attain the least costly combination of the factors, one thing among others that it must do is to achieve the optimum *scale* of output.[6] Scale of output makes a difference because the factors are frequently not divisible into small units,

6 See pp. 157–161.

but are obtainable only in relatively large "lumps." Consequently, to achieve an efficient combination of the factors when some of them are lumpy would require a sufficiently large scale of output to make possible adoption of the optimum ratio between lumpy and divisible factors, i.e., ensure full utilization of the lumpy factors. On the other hand, an excessive scale of output would lead to increased unit costs, partly because beyond a certain point managerial costs per unit of output tend to rise and partly because increased output necessitates a widening of the periphery of the geographic market area with increased transportation costs. Between the two extremes of small and large output would lie the optimum scale of output for a firm, where the least costly combination of the factors could be attained. When it is argued that all firms in a competitive industry would tend to produce at minimum cost, it is implied that all would operate at the same level of output. Any firm failing to achieve this output or exceeding it would be forced into line by competition or would be eliminated. In the competitive struggle of firms only the "fit" (i.e., firms producing at minimum cost) could survive.

The fact that different firms in the same industry might temporarily have different costs would be due not only to variations in managerial efficiency but also to the inability of some firms to secure the most advantageous factors. Some firms might have access to the "finest" land or to the "best" managerial talent, and thus be able to produce at lower cost than other less favored firms. Such an advantage, however, would be short-lived. As soon as the advantage was discovered by competing firms, they would seek to bid away the advantageous factors by offering higher prices for them. In order to retain them, the firms now hiring them would be forced to increase their prices. The competitive bidding for these factors would continue until their prices were so high as to offset any special advantage accruing through their use. Under the revised system of factor prices, the costs of all firms would then be equal.

Replacement of Capital as a Cost

At the time when the hypothetical economic system under discussion started operation, the supply of capital goods, material and nonmaterial, would be given. The immediate problem would be to arrange the use of these available resources. As production got under way, however, various types of capital goods, especially inventories of raw materials, goods-in-process, and supplies, would be quickly used up; durable capital goods such as machines and buildings would depreciate; and even the available trained personnel would slowly become depleted through disability, retirement, death, etc. The continuation of production, then, would require that new capital goods, material and nonmaterial, be produced to replace those being worn out. Consequently, in order to prevent the abrupt collapse of the productive system, a substantial portion of the current productive activity would necessarily be devoted to the provision of capital goods; that is, to the earlier stages in the production of future goods.

As a result of all the adjustments discussed above, the price of each final good would be equal to the cost of producing it. Part of the cost, however, would include the outlay necessary to obtain the use of capital goods. It was assumed that this element of cost would be determined by the market prices upon capital goods or upon their use, and that these prices would be set at whatever levels would equate the demand with the *given* supply. The fact that capital goods are both producible and depreciating means, however, that it is inadmissible—except for short-run analysis—to assume that the supply of capital goods is fixed. Hence, an additional problem must be faced: What are the influences determining the supply of capital goods?

The capital goods required by a firm if it is to maintain production may be acquired from two sources: the firm may (1) produce its own, or (2) buy from other firms. In practice, most firms rely upon both sources. In either case, the acquisition of capital goods by a firm can occur only if the owners or lenders are willing to maintain sufficient capital in the enterprise. Should they withdraw money from the venture as rapidly as its capital goods depreciate, then the firm would be unable to acquire any new capital goods and would be forced to quit business as soon as the existing supply was exhausted. The actions of owners and lenders would depend largely upon their estimates of the profitability of the venture.

In the preceding sections it was pointed out that the price

of each good would tend to equal its cost and that the costs for all firms in any industry would tend to be equal. Under these conditions all industries and all firms would be equally profitable; i.e., profits would be zero in all industries. When the time came, however, to replace worn-out capital goods, this would no longer be true, since the rental or purchase price of newly produced capital goods would likely be higher or lower than the original prices. For example, if the original purchase price of a capital good were $1,200 and the cost of producing a new one $1,500, no firm could afford to undertake this production. As the existing units were worn out, the supply would thus be reduced and the price increased, until finally at $1,500 newly produced units would be forthcoming. On the other hand, if the original price of a capital good were $800 and the cost of production $600, the profitability of producing new units would lead to an increase in supply and a fall in price. These changes in supply would also, of course, similarly alter the rental prices of these assets. Thus the costs of obtaining various types of capital goods, and hence total costs, would tend to vary in many industries—increasing in some and decreasing in others. This would cause some industries to become highly lucrative and others to become unprofitable. Capital would be attracted to the former and repelled from the latter. This would lead to an expansion of the profitable industries and an increase in the demand for the capital goods used there, and to contraction of the unprofitable industries and a reduction in the demand for the capital goods used there. In equilibrium the output of each industry would be adjusted so that price and total cost would again be equal.

The part of this total cost applicable to the use of capital goods would now be determined, not merely by the relation between the demand and the *given* supply, but rather by the cost of producing the capital goods. Since the production of a capital good may be regarded merely as one of the early stages in the production of a final good, we reach the conclusion that *in equilibrium the price of any good is equal to the sum of the costs incurred at all stages in its production.*

Before final equilibrium would be reached, a still further adjustment would be necessary. Changes in the prices of capital goods during the process of adjustment would induce firms to vary the combinations in which the factors were employed. There would be a tendency to economize on the capital goods whose prices had risen and to increase the use of those whose prices had fallen. This, in turn, would have repercussions on the relative profitability of different industries and would affect the ultimate outcome of the adjustment.

Problems of adjustment would also be encountered in connection with the supply of nonmaterial capital goods, i.e., culturally produced human traits—human training.

At the outset, the supply of labor as regards both hereditary and cultural capacities would be given, and the rate of wages of each type would depend solely upon the relation between the demand and the given supply. The wages for some types of labor, however, might be so low as to discourage the entry and training of new persons into these fields. As a result of the death, disability, retirement, or withdrawal of persons from these fields, the supply would be diminished and the rate of wages would be increased.

On the other hand, the rate of wages for other types of labor would likely be so high as to attract new recruits, with the result that the supply would be increased and the wages reduced. In equilibrium wage rates would tend to be adjusted, so that the supply of each type of labor would be stabilized.

In capitalism, as we know it, however, there would be no necessary tendency to carry out investment in human beings, so that the expected rate of return on all investments would be equalized. This is true for two reasons: (1) Investments in human beings are made largely by persons other than the one who is to enjoy the return, namely, parents, taxpayers, and philanthropists; (2) The investment is seldom made purely for the purpose of promoting future production, but has ulterior and nonpecuniary objectives. Investment in human beings is, in other words, to a considerable extent a form of consumption for parents, and the enhanced productive power of the person in whom the investment is made is only a secondary objective.

Chapter 26

EQUILIBRIUM vs. ECONOMY

It has been shown that in a capitalistic system, where economic resources are allocated by means of the spontaneous choices of individuals, the system would tend toward a position of *equilibrium*. In equilibrium, the following conditions would be realized:

1. A uniform price would be placed upon all units of each factor.
2. The price per unit of each good would be equal to its average cost of production.
3. The factors would be organized for the production of each good, in the least costly manner.
4. The price placed upon each factor would equate the demand for it to the available supply.

These conditions correspond exactly to the pricing principles for social economy as set forth in Chapter 15. (A review of this chapter would be helpful at this point.)

Largely on the basis of the fact that the conditions of equilibrium correspond to the pricing principles for economy, it has been argued for generations—especially during the latter part of the eighteenth century and during the nineteenth century—that economy can be achieved through the untrammeled operation of a capitalistic system—or more assertively—that capitalism is the only way by which economy can be attained. Perhaps the greatest exponent of the doctrine was Adam Smith, whose great book, *An Inquiry into the Nature and Causes of the Wealth of Nations*, was designed primarily as a polemical treatise in support of capitalism. He wrote in 1776:

. . . every individual who employs his capital in the support of domestic industry, necessarily endeavors so to direct that industry that its produce may be of the greatest possible value.

The produce of industry is what it adds to the subject or materials upon which it is employed. In proportion as the value of this produce is great or small, so will likewise be the profits of the employer. But it is only for the sake of profit that any man employs a capital in the support of industry; and he will always, therefore, endeavor to employ it in the support of that industry of which the produce is likely to be of the greatest value, or to exchange for the greatest quantity either of money or of other goods.

But the annual revenue of every society is always precisely equal to the exchangeable value of the whole annual produce of its industry, or rather is precisely the same thing with that exchangeable value. As every individual, therefore, endeavors as much as he can both to employ his capital in the support of domestic industry, and so to direct that industry that its produce may be of the greatest value; every individual necessarily labours to render the annual revenue of the society as great as he can. He generally, indeed, neither intends to promote the public interest, nor knows how much he is promoting it. By preferring the support of domestic to that of foreign industry, he intends only his own security; and by directing that industry in such a manner as its produce may be of the greatest value, he intends only his own gain, and he is in this, as in many other cases, led by an invisible hand to promote an end which was no part of his intention. Nor is it always the worse for the society that it was no part of it. By pursuing his own interest he frequently promotes that of the society more effectually than when he really intends to promote it. I have never known much good done by those who affected to trade for the public good. It is an affectation, indeed, not very common among merchants, and very few words need be employed in dissuading them from it.

What is the species of domestic industry which his capital can employ, and of which the produce is likely to be of the greatest value, every individual, it is evident, can, in his local situation, judge much better than any statesman or lawgiver can do for him. The statesman who should attempt to direct private people in what manner they ought to employ their capitals would not only load himself with a most unnecessary attention, but assume an authority which could safely be trusted, not only to no single person, but to no council or senate whatever, and which would nowhere be so dangerous as in the hands of a man who had folly and presumption enough to fancy himself fit to exercise it.

The idea that the conditions of capitalist equilibrium are identical with the conditions of social economy (therefore that capitalism results in economy) has been and is a powerful intellectual force in modern war of ideologies. If it is true that the pursuit of private interest by free individuals can give us an economical allocation of resources—if individual self-interest, restrained by competition, conduces to social advantage—then does it not follow that capitalism is the best of all economic systems?

The question of whether capitalism can achieve economy under modern conditions is perhaps the most crucial social issue of our age. In the chapters to follow we shall consider this question. Specifically, we shall try to appraise the feasibility of attaining economy within a capitalistic system. But too much must not be promised. The tools of economic analysis are far from adequate for the satisfactory completion of this task. Nevertheless, it is worth while to attack the problem from this standpoint. We shall approach the task in two steps. First, we shall consider some of the difficulties or obstacles that sometimes prevent a capitalistic system from reaching equilibrium. Second, we shall consider the performance of a capitalistic system in regard to those matters which lie outside the realm of price equilibrium.

Chapter 27

PREDICTING THE FUTURE

Any kind of economic system—whether capitalism, socialism, or any other—must adjust itself to changes in the supply of the factors, in the tastes of its consumers, in the aims of its government, in the technical methods of production, in weather conditions, etc. Such changes are constantly taking place; hence the system is always in process of adjustment to new basic conditions. But such adjustments usually can be made only over long periods of time. Sometimes, for example, adjustments in the supply of specialized capital goods or of specialized types of labor take generations. Thus, it frequently happens that before a society has completed its accommodation to one change in fundamental economic conditions, another change has occurred requiring a different adjustment. Before this one is completed, a still different adjustment is required, and so on. The economic system may be compared to a donkey in a treadmill striving to grasp a wisp of hay (equilibrium) dangled temptingly close to his nose but which he can never quite touch.

Because of the time required for adjustment to change, no economic system can ever be expected actually to attain equilibrium or economy. There is merely a tendency toward equilibrium which is an ever-changing goal. In recognition of this, many theorists, in discussing economic equilibrium, have *assumed* a static state in which all fundamental conditions remain constant. In such an unchanging environment, complete accommodation to the basic conditions could be achieved. Incidentally, one of the conditions of the assumed static state would be not only that the economy would in fact remain unchanged but also that people would *expect* it to remain unchanged. The system would not come to rest if people expected things to change from their present position. Their false

273

expectations would give rise to adjustments away from—rather than toward—equilibrium.[1]

But the real world is not static. It is characterized by a continuous series of changes in supplies of the factors, in consumer tastes, and in technology. Moreover, decisions regarding the use of resources must be made long prior to the outcome of these decisions. Therefore, these decisions must be made—not merely on the basis of past or present conditions—but in terms of *expected future conditions.* Hence, an important problem of economy in a changing world is to make as accurate predictions of the future as are possible.

It is not given to mankind to discern the future perfectly. In all societies, therefore, uncertainty regarding the future is an obstacle to the best use of resources. The problem in capitalism, however, is greatly accentuated by the fact that the function of decision making is diffused among many individuals who are more or less out of touch with one another. Hence, in addition to the uncertainties related to possible changes in the supplies of the factors, in demands, and in technological change, each individual firm or supplier of factors is confronted with an additional and a very important uncertainty, namely, the actions of *other* firms or *other* suppliers of factors.

If a business firm is planning to undertake or to expand the production of a given commodity on the strength of an expected increase in demand, the decision may result in disappointment if a large number of other firms make similar plans at the same time. Even assuming that the expected increase in demand does materialize, the simultaneous decisions of the several firms may cause total output to be extended beyond the appropriate level. As a result, all firms in the field—even those whose production remains unchanged—will suffer losses because the output at the new capacity cannot be sold at a price sufficient to cover cost. Similarly, if many firms expect a decrease in demand, the ensuing reduction in output may be excessive. Moreover, the correction of such errors is by no means assured, because the adjustments involved require individual decisions involving the future. Consequently, these decisions are likely

---

[1] Equilibrium requires not only that present prices and costs be equated but also that expected prices and costs be equal.

to be inappropriate to the extent that the forecasts upon which they are based are inaccurate.

The failure of appropriate adjustment is particularly likely if firms are accustomed to planning on the supposition that *present* prices and costs will continue into the future. When the price is high, various firms will plan to enter without considering the effect upon price of an increase in output by other firms. When the new output reaches the market, the price will fall. At this new price production will be unprofitable; hence many firms will plan to withdraw. Subsequently, the resulting shortage of the commodity will cause a rise in price which will encourage an increase in output. And so on, perhaps indefinitely.

A special and highly theoretical case of this type of instability has been formulated as the "cobweb theorem," so called because the diagram used to illustrate the theorem resembles a cobweb. Assume: (1) that production is in the hands of a sufficient number of firms so that each firm acts without reference to the effect upon the market of changes in its output, (2) that individual entrepreneurs are uninformed regarding the decisions of other entrepreneurs, (3) that a more or less definite period of time must elapse between the making of entrepreneurial decisions and the resulting changes in supply, and (4) that decisions are made on the supposition that present prices and costs are likely to prevail in the future. With these conditions and given supply-and-demand schedules as indicated in the left-hand portion of Figure 10, suppose that the industry is in a state of disequilibrium so that the output is at Q_1 and the price at P_1. At this price, entrepreneurs will plan to produce quantity Q_2. When the new increased output appears on the market, the price will fall to P_2. At this price, however, entrepreneurs will plan to offer Q_3, but at this restricted output the price will rise to P_3. At this price, firms will plan to increase output to Q_4, etc. If, as shown in the left-hand portion of Figure 10, the demand curve has greater slope than the supply curve, the oscillations will theoretically tend always away from, rather than toward, equilibrium. On the other hand, if the slope of the demand curve is less than that of the supply curve, as shown in the right-hand portion of Figure 10, the oscillations will theoretically lead successively toward equilibrium. If the

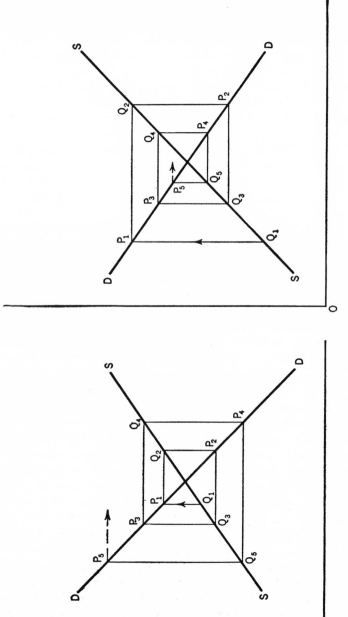

FIGURE 10

276

slope of the two curves is equal, the oscillations will presumably be perpetual, with no tendency toward or away from equilibrium. The cobweb theorem is, of course, highly idealized and would seldom apply in practice.[2] It is, however, illustrative of possibilities.

The failure of equilibrium in the market for goods, due to the inability of entrepreneurs to predict each other's plans, is paralleled in the market for the factors, particularly labor. For example, if an individual anticipates a strong demand for machinists and on the strength of that prediction trains himself for that trade, his expectations may be disappointed by the fact that many other individuals have entered the occupation at the same time. As a result, machinists' wages will fall below what is necessary to retain the given supply of persons in the trade. Moreover, the resulting low wage may drive individuals out of the trade and discourage entry into it to the extent that wages would later rise well above what would be necessary to maintain the existing supply.

The diffusion of decision making in capitalism introduces a special source of error into the allocation of resources. Individuals are unable to know the plans or to predict the behavior of other individuals. Hence there is no assurance of consistency in the plans of various decision makers. This type of uncertainty appears to be inherent in the capitalistic system. It is possible that agencies for the systematic and comprehensive collection and dissemination of trade information can reduce the extent of errors from this source.[3] But the collection of statistics on the *plans* of businessmen represents some difficult problems, not only because of the complexity of the statistical procedures but also because the very nature of the profit system requires that businessmen conceal their plans.

---

[2] Mordecai Ezekiel, "The Cobweb Theorem," *Quarterly Journal of Economics,* 1938, p. 270; N. S. Buchanan, "A Reconsideration of the Cobweb Theorem," *Journal of Political Economy,* February, 1939, pp. 67-81; N. Kaldor, "A Classificatory Note on the Determinateness of Equilibrium," *Review of Economic Studies,* February, 1934, pp. 122-136.

[3] This is the theory underlying much of the work of the United States Department of Commerce and of the President's Council of Economic Advisers.

Chapter 28

MONOPOLY

O ne of the basic features of a capitalistic system, as that system has been defined, is *complete competition,* i.e., pure competition among buyers and sellers in the markets for all goods and for all factors throughout the system. Only with complete competition would the equilibrium attained in a capitalistic system necessarily result in an economical allocation of resources.

Consequences of Restrictions on Competition

Without complete competition, allocations would be distorted so that price and average cost would not always be equated. The value of the marginal product of the various factors would then not be equal in all cases to their respective prices and the value of the marginal product of each factor would not be equal in all its uses.

Such distortions might occur if competition were deficient among (1) sellers of goods, (2) buyers of goods, (3) sellers of factors, or (4) buyers of factors.

First, the case of deficient competition among sellers of goods. Suppose that in the market for shoes the competition among producers would for some reason be restricted. The firm or firms in that industry would then be inclined to limit output so that the price of shoes would rise above the average cost of producing them. To do so would increase their profits. The industry would then no longer satisfy the condition that the value of the marginal product of the factors employed should be equal to the prices of those factors. Instead marginal product would exceed factor prices. With the restriction in the output of shoes, fewer workers (and land and capital) would be employed in the shoe industry. Some would be forced to seek employment in other industries. But the entry of the displaced shoe workers into these other industries would increase output there and these industries would be forced to reduce their prices. Thus, the marginal-value product of these displaced workers would be reduced to less than that when they had been employed in the shoe industry. And, of course, their marginal-value product would be less than that of the remaining workers in the shoe industry. Since it is uneconomical for workers to produce less outside the shoe industry than they could produce in it, the allocation of factors resulting from deficient competition in the shoe industry would be clearly uneconomical. Economy would be restored only by transferring these workers back to the shoe industry, i.e., by eliminating the restrictions on output in this industry.

Second, deficient competition among buyers of goods would occur, for example, if consumers should band themselves together into buying clubs or cooperative societies to purchase collectively, or in cases where a single firm uses most or all of a given raw material. If any one buyer or group of buyers should represent a large part of the demand for a given good, its decision to buy more or less would affect the price of the good and the amount of it which could be profitably produced. Under these conditions, the buyer might prefer to buy less at a lower price than to buy more at a higher price (assuming increasing cost). Output of the good would then be curtailed, and the factors employed in its production would have to be shifted to other uses. But the value of their marginal product in these other uses would be less than in their former employment, and as a result the new allocation would be uneconomical.

Third, deficient competition among owners of factors would occur if a group of workers, printers, for example, banded together to place restrictions on the entry of additional workers into their trade. The restriction on the supply of printers would reduce the supply of their product and increase both the price of their labor and the price of their product. But the workers excluded from the union would be forced to seek employment in other trades where their marginal product would be less than in the printing trade. Again, this would represent an uneconomical allocation.

Finally, the deficient competition among buyers of the factors would occur, for example, if one employer hired all the labor of a given type. Since his demand would influence the wage of that kind of labor, he might prefer to hire fewer workers at a lower wage than more at a higher wage. The displaced workers would then be forced to seek employment with a lower marginal product than obtained for those remaining in the industry.

Although deficient competition among buyers is probably not uncommon, the principal "monopoly" problem in capitalistic countries has been the deficiency of competition among sellers of goods and among sellers of factors. Hence, in the remainder of this chapter the discussion will relate to competition among sellers. The question that will be considered is this: To what extent is it possible or practicable in a capitalistic system to achieve pure competition among firms and among owners of factors?

Basic Conditions of Competition among Firms

The basic conditions of pure competition among the firms in an industry are two: (1) the presence of a large number of noncollusive firms, and (2) the free and easy entry of new firms. Regarding the second condition, new firms must be free to enter, not only to enlarge the product in response to an increase in demand, but also to displace the less efficient existing firms.

When the number of firms in an industry is large, the contribution of each firm to total supply is negligible. Each disregards the effect of changes in its output upon the price of the product. Hence, each assumes that the price is beyond its control and simply adjusts its output to the given or expected price, whatever it may be. In short, there is no deliberate restriction of supply in order to increase price. At the same time, the existence of a large number of firms makes collusion extremely difficult.

On the other hand, if the number of firms in the industry is small, each firm is conscious of the effect of its policy on the price of the product and on the behavior of competitors (if any). Deliberate restriction of output in order to raise price or to prevent price from falling is a probable result.

A large number of firms, however, is not sufficient to assure competition within an industry. Nor does the existence of only a few firms inevitably lead to monopolistic behavior. The second important factor determining the degree of competition is free and easy entry of new firms into the industry.

If the entry of new firms is restricted, the mere presence of a large number of firms in an industry will not necessarily prevent price from rising above average cost. For example, if an industry were to experience an increase in demand and new firms were prevented from entering to serve the expanded market, existing firms would increase output only to the extent that marginal (not average) cost would equal price. In this case, price would exceed average cost. On the other hand, a monopolist would possess singularly little power, if he were readily vulnerable to the competition of new firms.

Because there are *two* essential conditions of competition—conditions which are not necessarily concurrent—there are four combinations, ranging from complete competition to monopolistic competition and monopoly (with of course every gradation between). These four are:

1. Number of firms large and entry of new firms easy.
2. Number of firms small and entry of new firms easy.
3. Number of firms large and entry of new firms difficult.
4. Number of firms small and entry of new firms difficult.

Although some considerable deficiency in competition occurs under combinations 2 and 3, the really important and serious deficiency occurs under the fourth combination, i.e., number of firms in the industry small, and the entry of new firms restricted.

This situation is likely to exist in industries in which the demand for the product does not exceed several times the optimum output of a single firm. In such industries production tends to gravitate into the hands of one or a few firms. Moreover, these firms tend to be protected from the entry of additional firms for two reasons: (1) The output would usually be produced less cheaply if one or more firms were added to the industry, and (2) Existing firms are usually so firmly entrenched that it is difficult for new firms to supplant them.

Cost Function of a Firm

As the first step in the analysis of this case, it will be useful to review briefly the effect of changes in the output of a *firm* upon its average *cost of production*.[1] (1) Since some of the factors can in practice be obtained only in relatively large increments, average cost tends to fall as output of the firm is increased until these lumpy factors are fully utilized. (2) Since the advantages of division of labor are attainable only as the scale of output is increased, average cost tends to fall as output is increased until gains from division of labor have been fully realized. (3) After a certain output is reached (undoubtedly very large), average costs per unit for management tend to rise. (4) As the quantity of output increases, it may become necessary to draw upon raw materials from a wider geographic area or to serve a wider market, so that increases in output may involve greater transportation costs. When these diverse influences are combined, the net result for the typical firm is as follows: Increases in output are associated with decreases in average cost up to a certain point, but beyond this point further increases in output are associated with increases in average cost. When the cost function is plotted, with output on the horizontal axis and average cost on the vertical axis, the curve becomes somewhat U-shaped. (See curve AC in Figure 11.) The output which can be produced at minimum average cost is called *optimum output*.

Demand Small Relative to Optimum Output of a Single Firm

Let us now examine an industry in which the demand for the product is small relative to the optimum output of a single firm.

Assume that the total demand for the product is as shown in Figure 11 and that production is divided equally among four different firms, the cost curve for each being like that shown in Figure 11. If the demand curve for this *industry* is plotted with the average-cost curve for a *firm* (Figure 11), the demand curve

[1] See pp. 158–161.

(*DD'*) will cut the average-cost curve (*AC*) at a point (*K*) to the left of the point of minimum average cost (*L*).[2] In this situation, the entire production would sooner or later fall into the hands of a single firm. This can be demonstrated by showing the untenability of having more than one firm in the industry.

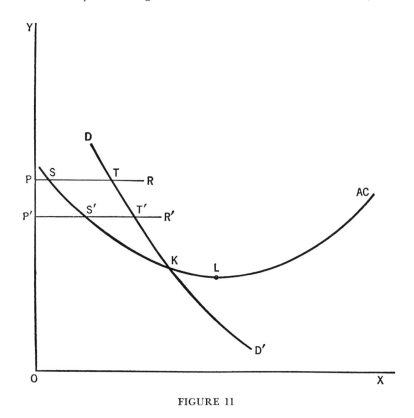

FIGURE 11

If there were four firms, losses would be incurred by each firm unless an output could be attained at which price would be sufficient to cover its cost when it is producing one fourth of the total output. This would be possible, and conceivably might occur, if from some point (*P*) on the *Y* axis (Figure 11), a horizontal line could be drawn (*PR*), intersecting the cost curve at *S* and the demand curve at *T*, such that *PT* is equal to, or

2 The distance from the *Y* axis to *L* represents optimum output for a firm.

greater than $4PS$.[3] On the other hand, if the price were OP', then PT would be less than $4PS$. In this case, no one of the four firms would be able to cover its cost, and some would inevitably be eliminated. The question of which ones would be forced out would be determined by the relative financial resources of the several firms and the relative tenacity of the several managements.[4] But sooner or later, as a result of the process of elimination, the number of firms would be reduced to a point where the surviving firms could achieve a sufficient output to bring costs into line with price, i.e., to a point where PT would be equal to or greater than PS times the number of firms. At price OP', $P'T'$ is twice $P'S'$, indicating that in this industry two firms might possibly be able to survive.

The mere reduction in number of firms to a point where the surviving firms could conceivably make ends meet would give only precarious and temporary balance. It would hardly bring durable stability so long as more than one firm remained. For example, the situation indicated in Figure 11 where four firms might meet their costs would be highly unstable. Each firm would be tempted to cut price in order to draw business away from its rivals and thus to reduce its own costs and reduce theirs.

It is true that if all the firms were of about equal financial strength and of equal skill in strategic maneuvers, each might be reluctant to upset the existing balance.[5] To do so would lead to corresponding or greater price cuts by the rival firms and to losses all around. Losses would continue until (1) only one firm remained, or (2) a truce was declared and the original situation restored. But if the several firms were of unequal strength and cunning, as would usually be the case, the boldest firms might deliberately reduce price as a means of capturing the field. In the resulting price war, one or more firms would be

---

[3] In case the four firms were producing at different outputs so that each had a different average cost, then in order to make possible the survival of all firms, the price would have to cover the average cost of the firm having the smallest output.

[4] If some firms are producing at a smaller output (consequently at a higher cost) than others, these firms would suffer greater losses than those which had achieved larger output, and would likely be forced out, leaving the field to the latter.

[5] Cf. G. W. Stocking and M. W. Atkins, *Cartels in Action*, New York, 1946.

eliminated. Eventually, except with most unusual restraint or collusion, one firm—presumably the toughest and strongest one —would be the master of the industry. Thus, in the long run and perhaps by a devious course, an industry of the type under discussion would gravitate into the control of a single firm. Obviously, it is in the interests of productive efficiency that it should do so, since the entire output could be produced more cheaply by one firm than by several.

Once the industry was in the hands of a single firm, a stable situation would have been achieved. New firms would not likely be attracted into the industry. A new firm would venture to enter only if (1) it expected to be able to oust the present firm and itself to become the sole firm in the industry, or (2) it expected to force the monopolist to curtail his output and allow price to rise to a point where $PT = 2PS$ so that both firms could survive.

Under the first of these two alternatives, the new firm could succeed only if it were financially stronger than the monopolist. In order to supplant the monopolist it would be forced to cut prices ruthlessly until the losses inflicted upon the monopolist would force him from the field. But when this had been accomplished, the industry would again be in the hands of a single firm.

Under the second alternative, the new firm would enter only if it believed that the monopolist would prefer to retreat rather than engage in cutthroat competition. The monopolist would, of course, make this choice only if he believed that the challenger was possessed of greater financial resources so that price cutting for him would be a futile strategy. But the resulting duopoly would be more or less unstable and at some time would probably give way to monopoly.

It is sometimes argued that if the entrenched single firm were to exercise monopoly powers by restricting output and raising price above cost, the entry of a competitor would be facilitated. This, however, is largely wishful thinking. The managers of the prospective new firm would be aware that the monopolist could, without loss, reduce price to the level of his cost. Indeed, the monopolist, if threatened in this way, might find it worth while to maintain excess capacity and thus be able on short notice to enlarge output and lower price. So the prospective competitor would be unlikely to attempt to enter unless he felt able to supplant the monopolist.

It may be concluded, then, that an industry in which demand is small relative to the optimum output of one firm will, in all probability, fall into the hands of a single firm. This firm will be rather effectively insulated from the potential competition of new rivals. It will be able to limit output and so to charge a price in excess of average cost without undue fear of attracting competitors.

Industries in which demand is small relative to the optimum output of a single firm are generally of two types: (1) those in which the advantages of large-scale production are marked, i.e., in which the firm attains least cost only with large output; and (2) those producing for an extremely small demand. The first type is exemplified in the modern world by the railroads and the electric power industry. The second type is exemplified by firms producing seldom-used goods such as Alpine equipment or certain kinds of scientific apparatus. In either case, the demand is small *relative* to the optimum output of a single fim.

Entry of a Second Firm

Let us now analyze the conditions under which a second firm might be added to an industry of the type we have been considering. We have seen that it would not be feasible so long as the demand curve for the *industry* intersected the average-cost curve of a *firm* at a point less than optimum output, i.e. (referring to Figure 11), so long as K is to the left of L. Suppose, then, an increase in demand, so that K is now to the right of L. The addition of a second firm would still be infeasible, unless demand should increase so much that production could be carried on as cheaply by two firms as by a single firm. More specifically, the second firm could be successfully added only when a total output could be found which (1) could be produced as cheaply by two firms as by one, and (2) could be sold at a price sufficient to cover the cost when produced by two firms.

Let us assume, for simplicity, that the cost curve for the prospective new firm is identical to that for the existing firm.

Then AC in Figure 12 represents the cost curve for *either* firm. Intersecting the cost curve is a demand curve D^1D^1 which represents the original demand, and a series of demand curves D^2D^2, D^3D^3, etc., showing successive increases in demand. The entry of the second firm would be possible when the demand had increased sufficiently for production to be carried on as

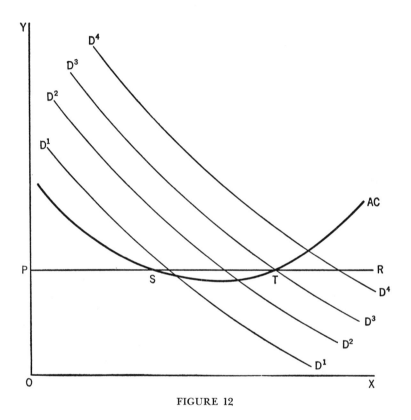

FIGURE 12

cheaply by two firms as by one. This would occur when a horizontal line PR could be drawn through a point T where the demand intersects the cost curve so that PT is equal to, or greater than $2PS$. In the figure, this condition is satisfied when demand is at D^3D^3. At this demand, product PT could be produced by two firms, each producing PS as cheaply as the same total output could be produced by one firm, i.e., $PS = ST$.

If demand were increased to D^4D^4, with only one producer the cost of producing the entire output in a single firm would be greater than the cost if output were divided between. two firms.

Assuming demand at D^3D^3, a new firm wishing to enter the industry would merely arrange to offer on the market at price OP any amount of the commodity which could be disposed of at that price.

The monopolist, if not already selling at this price, would now be forced to it. But the sales of the new firm at this price would be about as great as the sales of the old firm,[6] so that the two firms would divide the market, each producing PS units of the commodity with a total output of PT and with price at OP.

The entry of the new firm would, of course, be distasteful to the monopolist, and he might make strenuous efforts to cripple the newcomer. For example, he might reduce the price to less than cost. If the new firm met the price reduction, the market would still be divided equally between the two firms, and both would be losing money. The monopolist, if financially stronger than his rival, might in this way force him out. But even so, he would always be vulnerable to the entry of a new firm having sufficient financial strength to withstand his cut-throat tactics. However, it must be recognized that the temptation to drive out a rival by "ruinous" price cutting would always be present, so that one cannot conclude that the situation described would be completely stable when the field had been divided between two firms. As the demand increased, however, the position of the monopolist would become increasingly tenuous and the industry would become steadily more inviting to businessmen in quest of opportunities.

With two firms established in the field, the entry of another new one would be difficult without further increases in demand. Its entry would reduce the sales of the established firms and force an increase in cost. The resulting situation would be unstable, and perhaps sooner or later one of the three might be forced out. If the newcomer was financially stronger than one of the established firms, he might survive. In practice, however, the entrenched firms would usually have advantages protecting

---

[6] Assuming no product differentiation.

them from the rivalry of new firms. With this protection, they would be able to manipulate price and output in the manner of duopolists. However, their powers along these lines would be less than those of a monopolist, since any adjustment of output or price by either would be dependent upon cooperation on the part of the other. There are many situations in which such cooperation would be possible even without overt collusion. Moreover, the possibility of collusion is very great when the industry consists of only two firms.

Three or More Firms

With two firms well entrenched, what are the conditions under which a third firm could successfully enter? Here we apply the same principles as in the preceding case. A third firm could enter when demand had increased so that the two existing firms have each expanded production beyond the point of least cost to the extent that a total output could be found which (1) could be produced as cheaply by three firms as by two, and (2) could be sold at a price sufficient to cover cost when produced by three firms.[7] Further increases in demand would permit the entry of the successive additional firms.

In each case the entry of a new firm would become possible only when the demand were so large that existing firms were producing under increasing cost, i.e., beyond the optimum output.

When the demand would permit of only a single firm, a considerable extension of output into the range of increasing cost would be possible before a second firm could successfully enter the field. The position of a monopolist in such an industry would likely be very strong. When the industry was composed of two firms, the possible extension into the range of increasing cost before entry of a third firm would be somewhat less, and the protection against the entry of new firms would be correspondingly less. And with the entry of each successive new firm, the smaller would be the possible extension of output into increasing cost, and the easier the entry of new firms. Finally,

---

[7] Referring to Figure 12, a third firm could enter when the cost for a firm at one-third PT is less than the cost at one-half PT. A fourth firm could enter when cost at one-fourth PT is less than at one-third PT, etc.

when the number of firms in the industry became very large, only a small increase in demand would be necessary, to attract one or more new firms, and the margin of protection against the entry of new firms would be very small.

Similarly, when the demand would permit of only one firm, the entry of a new firm to displace the existing one would be difficult since the entrenched firm, fortified by monopoly profits, would likely be able to withstand the competition of any newcomer. When the industry was composed of a few firms, their displacement would be somewhat less difficult than in the case of the monopolists' industry, but nevertheless far from easy. But as the number of firms increased, the power of resistance to the entry of new firms would become progressively less, until, when the number of firms was very large, there would be a constant turnover in which new firms would be continuously entering and old firms continuously withdrawing. Also, as the number of firms increased, the possibility of collusion would become less. It would be clearly more difficult to reach collusive agreements among thousands of firms than among two or three.

Conclusions

We have seen that fully competitive conditions are not likely to prevail in an industry where the demand for the product is small relative to the optimum output of one or a few firms. In such an industry, the entire product will be produced by a small number of firms who may be able to restrict output and so raise price above cost. Moreover, these firms may be more or less insulated against the entry of new firms, they may be able to manipulate output and price, and they may be able to practice collusion.

Under modern technology, the capacity of the single firm has been steadily growing until today only a relatively few industries are adapted to small-scale methods. In many industries efficiency requires firms of enormous size. Moreover, developments in the field of business organization such as the chain store and the branch plant have increased the advantages and the scope of the large firm. Thus, under modern technology and modern methods of business administration, the most efficient size of firm has become so great that production of many—perhaps most—commodities tends to be concentrated in the hands of one, or a few, giant organizations which tend to be more or less protected from the entry of new firms. The automobile industry, the steel industry, the tire industry, the public utilities, and the railroads are a few examples of the industries in which the advantages of large-scale operations are so great that only a few firms can survive. The technical superiority of large-scale methods is so great that competition is unattainable in a substantial, probably major, portion of a modern economy.

The primary difficulty in attaining complete competition within capitalism is due to the fact that the ratio between demand and the optimum output of a single firm is relatively small in many industries—especially under modern technology.

Other Limitations upon Competition

There are certain other limitations on competition among sellers of goods which have been and are important in the actual world. These, however, may not be necessarily inherent in capitalism.

First, new firms may sometimes be effectively excluded from an industry by social, legal, or technological barriers to the geographic mobility of capital, labor, management, or goods. Thus, producers in a given local area may be immunized against the rivalry of those in another. The importance of this has been lessened by institutional changes increasing the mobility and adaptability of the factors and of management. On the other hand, all manner of legal restrictions on the free flow of the factors and of goods have been deliberately imposed by nationalistic governments and by the guardians of local interests. These artificial legal barriers are, however, directly antithetical to the theory and spirit of capitalism. They are anything but inherent in that system.

Second, new firms may be prevented from entering an industry by action of the state (aside from restrictions on geographic mobility)—for example, special prohibition laws, charters, licenses, patents, copyrights, and taxes. It is doubtful if even product differentiation would be an effective monopolistic device without the legal protection of trade names, patents, etc.[8] Action of the state to restrict competition may be justified on grounds of providing incentives for innovation, as in the patent system. The broad problem of economy, in this case, is given priority over the narrow pricing principles. But aside from the giving of encouragement to innovation, the governmental barriers to the entry of new firms are contrary to, rather than consistent with, the spirit of capitalism.

Third, entry of new firms may be impeded by lack of knowledge on the part of potential entrants. They may not know of the opportunities, they may not realize that existing firms are enjoying profits. In capitalism, as in all systems, there is a profusion of ignorance. Indeed, lack of knowledge may be somewhat more prevalent in capitalism since it is to the interests of existing firms to conceal their profits in order not to attract competition. Yet it is doubtful if ignorance on the part of potential entrants can long constitute an effective barrier to the entry of new producers.

Fourth, existing and entrenched firms may conspire to prevent the entry of new firms or to force other existing firms out of business through intimidation, violence, threats of price cutting, and other "unfair" practices. As has been indicated, this is more likely to occur when the number of firms is small than when the industry is composed of many firms. All proponents of capitalism would agree, however, that such practices are not consistent with the spirit of capitalism and that it is the duty of government to suppress them.

It must be recognized, however, that a condition prerequisite to complete competition is "ethical" conduct on the part of all individuals and firms. There must be no intimidation, deception, or fraud, and there must be no attempt through temporary price cutting below cost, secret rebates, and other devices to prevent the entry of new sellers into any market or to drive out existing sellers. There must be no collusion among

---

8 Without such legal protection, the attempt of any one firm to insulate itself from rivals would be frustrated, since at the moment of its triumph other firms would be free to duplicate the product of this firm, so that its advantage would be largely lost. The only remaining source of product differentiation would be "secret" processes. In this day of research, such secrets would be highly ephemeral.

independent sellers. Moreover, since the discouragement and regulation of such practices is generally left to the government, there must be no attempt on the part of any firm, individual, or group to influence political decisions in order to increase their particular commercial gains. And since the government can do no more than reflect the ethical attitudes of the people, the existence of competition rests, in the last analysis, upon "general prevalence of strong and strict feelings in favor of impartial justice, of liberty for all and special privilege for none, of the nearest possible approach to the maintenance of full equality of opportunity, of perfect honesty, in all private and governmental transactions, and the like. . . ." [9]

For the game to go on, it is necessary that there be a set of rules well understood, accepted, and lived up to by all the players. If a tackle insists on kicking the opposing lineman or if a catcher throws dust in the batter's eyes, the game can go on only if the rules are changed or if the violators are coerced into obeying the rules. This coercion will be possible only if there is strong social sentiment among teammates, opponents, and spectators in favor of "fair" play. If interest in winning becomes greater than the desire to play the game, the game tends to break up.[10]

Experience would give credence to the view that capitalism does not breed the type of ethical attitudes necessary to its own existence. The dollar becomes so important, not only as a means to the attainment of goods but also as a source of power and a symbol of success, that there is a constant temptation for individuals to violate the rules of the game in order to advance their own "scores." The efforts of government to curb these violators have resulted in the attempt by interest groups to control the government. The scene of battle has merely shifted from the field of business to the field of politics.[11] Yet we have no reason to believe that the ethical attitudes necessary to the enforcement of the rules of the game are impossible of attainment.

We have briefly considered four obstacles to competition

---

[9] O. H. Taylor, "Economic Theory and Certain Non-economic Elements in Social Life," in *Explorations in Economics: Notes and Essays Contributed in Honor of F. W. Taussig,* New York, 1936, pp. 389-390.

[10] F. H. Knight, *Ethics of Competition,* New York, 1935, pp. 292-293.

[11] O. H. Taylor, *op. cit.,* pp. 388-389.

which are commonly found in capitalistic societies. These were:
(1) social, legal, or technical barriers to geographic mobility of
the factors or of goods, (2) governmental action, (3) lack of
knowledge, and (4) unethical conduct. It was concluded that
each of the four was not inherent in or unique to capitalism.
In fact, it is a primary function of government in a capitalist society to lessen these obstacles so far as practicable and so far as
consistent with other objectives.

Competition in the Market for Factors

We have explored the conditions necessary for competition
among sellers of goods. In a general way, the same principles
apply among sellers of the factors although there are special
circumstances in the market for each factor.

In the market for the use of land and natural resources, the
number of sellers is in most cases reasonably large. Entry of
additional sellers is, however, almost absolutely restricted since,
by definition, the supply of land can seldom be increased. The
degree of competition among sellers of land use is determined,
then, mainly by the number of persons among whom ownership
of the given supply is divided. If ownership is concentrated in
the hands of one person, his position will be that of a monopolist. If it is divided among two or several persons, the market
for the factor will be less than purely competitive. If the ownership is diffused among numerous persons, the market will be
relatively but not purely competitive, since entry of additional
sellers will not be possible even in case of an increase in demand.

The market for liquid capital tends to be one of the more
highly competitive markets since the number of sellers and
buyers is large and the entry of new sellers and buyers is relatively easy.

In the absence of collusion in the market for most kinds of
labor, the number of sellers tends to be large and the entry of
additional sellers easy. There are a few kinds of labor for which
the demand is so small that only one or a few workers are required—such workers may obtain a degree of monopoly power.
There are also some occupations for which the prerequisite
training is so costly or lengthy, that only the well-to-do or their
children can enter. Moreover, the hereditary capacities required

for certain occupations may be absolutely limited to a few persons. Such limitations on supply tend to restrict competition. These cases are, however, exceptional. In the great majority of occupations, the number of workers is very large and the entry of additional workers relatively easy. In all capitalistic countries, however, the rise of trade-unions has tended to give labor a degree of monopoly power. In some cases the union can raise wages above the level for other comparable occupations, and thus limit the number of persons who can find employment in the trade, or sometimes it can restrict entry of additional workers into the occupation and thus make possible a relative rise in wages.[12] It must be emphasized, however, that trade-unions are no more consistent with the basic tenets of capitalism than are restrictive price agreements among producers.

The net conclusion is that in the absence of collusion and government controls, each of which is inimical to the spirit of capitalism, reasonably active competition would exist among the sellers of most factors.

Conclusions

The question to which we are seeking an answer in this chapter is this: Is it possible or practicable in a capitalistic system to achieve complete competition among sellers of goods and among sellers of factors?

The answer we have reached is that reasonably active competition is possible under the basic premises of capitalism, except among sellers of goods in industries where the demand for the product is no more than several times the optimum output of a single firm. Under modern technology this situation is so widespread as to throw considerable doubt on the efficacy of competition as a device for preventing prices from exceeding costs. For example, all available studies of the concentration of industry in the United States indicate that a few hundred giant companies account for major portions of the total product of the country. Although this degree of concentration may be far

---

12 A clear distinction must be made between the effect of a rise in wages in one occupation above the going rate for comparable occupations and a general rise in wages affecting all occupations. The latter may not necessarily restrict employment. See pp. 302–304.

beyond technological and managerial requirements, yet there can be little doubt that in many important industries very large firms are technically superior to small firms, and that the attempt to impose complete competition upon our economy would be very costly in terms of productive efficiency.

Chapter 29

UNEMPLOYMENT

A second feature of capitalism—much more important than the errors arising from faulty prediction of the future and from monopoly—is its frequent failure to satisfy the condition that the demand for the factors should be equal to available supply. As is well known to anyone who has lived through the 1930's, or who has studied the history of business fluctuations, demand is sometimes insufficient to employ all of the factors. The result is idleness of labor and capital goods.

There are many who argue that much of the unemployment of resources in our time is not an inherent result of the operation of capitalism—as that system has been defined. Rather, it is held that unemployment has been the result of the failure to achieve the basic conditions of a capitalistic system. Unemployment has been attributed particularly to incompleteness of competition in the markets for factors and goods, to government intervention, and to manipulation of the money supply. According to these views, if the basic tenets of capitalism had been observed, fluctuations in employment would have occurred only as a result of errors in prediction and would have been of moderate—even negligible—amplitude.

Another view—in my judgment a more valid one—is that wide fluctuations in employment are inherent in capitalism—even when all of its basic conditions are fully realized. It may be freely conceded that unemployment is sometimes caused and often prolonged by failure to observe the "rules" of capitalism. Yet the preponderance of evidence would lead to the view that instability and unemployment are inherent features of capitalism itself.

This is not the place for a full-scale discussion of the theory of employment. Yet the basis for the view that fluctuations are inherent in capitalism can be briefly indicated.

It is useful to distinguish three types of unemployment.

Seasonal unemployment refers to the disuse of the factors occasioned by regular annual variations in weather, holidays, etc. There is no need to discuss this type of unemployment in the present connection except to say that it would be present in all types of economic systems.

Frictional unemployment refers to the disuse of factors resulting from the process of economic adjustment to new conditions or resulting from the need to correct errors in the allocation of resources. This type of unemployment occurs when factors are freed from productive activities that are being curtailed and are not absorbed immediately into other uses. The delay might be due to lack of immediate alternative employment opportunities because the availability of these unemployed resources was not foreseen. In capitalism the amount of frictional unemployment may be relatively large because of the difficulties of prediction mentioned above. The number of errors in allocation is likely to be large, and somewhat more shifting of resources from one use to another may be necessary than in a type of system where prediction is less difficult. However, frictional unemployment is not ordinarily serious. It has been estimated that in the United States of the late 1940's frictional unemployment of workers totals 2 to 2½ million persons or 3 to 4 per cent of the labor force.[1]

The important type of unemployment to which a capitalist society is subject—the type which is peculiar to capitalism—is *cyclical unemployment*. This is the unemployment associated with the broad sweeps in total business activity with which we have become so familiar.

One of the characteristics of capitalism is the free choice of the individual and of the business firm in the use of their incomes. This implies not only free choice in decisions as to how to spend their incomes for goods and services, but also free choice in *whether or not* to spend them at all.

Once an economy is operating at full employment, it can stay at that level only if (1) consumers spend their incomes for newly produced goods and services at the same rate as they are receiving these incomes, and (2) business firms are paying out

---

[1] *Monthly Labor Review,* January, 1947, pp. 1-10.

income to the factors at the same rate as the receipts from the sale of their current product are flowing in.[2] If consumers and business firms decide not to spend a portion of their incomes, then aggregate demand will turn out to be less than aggregate supply. Production will be curtailed and unemployment will result. Thus, the analysis of cyclical unemployment centers upon the conditions under which individuals or business firms may decide to refrain from spending a part of their receipts.

The current product of a society may be divided into two categories: consumer goods and capital goods. Also the incomes of individuals may be divided into two parts: that which is used for consumption and that which is saved. The demand for the current output of consumer goods derives, of course, from the expenditures of individuals for consumption. And the demand for newly produced capital goods derives, directly or indirectly, from the savings of individuals.

It happens, however, that individuals can save without using their savings to buy new capital goods. They can do this simply by holding part or all of their savings in the form of money.[3] In this case the demand for capital goods declines without a corresponding increase in the demand for consumption goods. The result is unemployment.

Individuals will not choose to hold their savings in the form of money so long as attractively profitable investment opportunities are available. To hold their savings idle in the form of money will yield no (prospective) return,[4] but will merely conserve principal. Whereas, to invest the money, i.e., to use it to buy newly produced capital goods, will result in a positive (prospective) return on their money capital over and above principal. But, on the other hand, if there are no opportunities for investment which are considered attractively profitable, i.e., if the prospective return from available investments is zero or less (after allowance for risk and incidental costs), then they may choose to retain their savings in money—with unemployment as the result.

---

[2] In a growing society the stream of expenditures must rise at the same rate as the growth of production.

[3] Another possibility is that they may use part of their funds simply to buy and sell securities or previously produced capital goods or land.

[4] Even a negative return if the risk of its being stolen, of bank failure, or of a decline in its purchasing power is taken into account.

In a capitalist society the tendency to save is strong, partly because of the unequal distribution of income and partly because of the personal uncertainty and insecurity inherent in capitalism. This means that the demand for capital goods is large and that a high proportion of the social productive power tends to be devoted to the production of capital goods. On the other hand, in a capitalist society the opportunities for investment are limited largely to those which are profitable according to fairly restrictive pecuniary standards. The investment must be one which promises to yield a product that can be sold in the market for a price to cover all costs of production. Because consumers and business firms act individually and because the scope of governmental activities is restricted, it is not possible to invest for broad social (nonpecuniary) objectives or to expand decreasing cost industries beyond the margins of profitability. Thus, the range of practicable investment is narrowly limited.

When the high rate of saving associated with the unequal distribution of income is combined with the limitation of opportunities for investment implicit in pecuniary standards of profitability, a capitalist system tends toward a condition of capital saturation in which all *attractive* investment opportunities are filled up. At this point, savers prefer to hold their savings in the form of money, instead of investing them in capital goods, since capital goods are expected to return a yield of less than zero (after allowance for risk). Thus crisis occurs, and the system is then plunged into depression. It can recover only when new profitable investment opportunities appear or when the tendency to save becomes less strong.

This description of capitalist crisis is greatly oversimplified and must be qualified and amended in certain respects if it is not to be misleading.

In the first place, certain complexities in the capital market arising from its institutional structure have been ignored. Individuals are not the only source of savings. In every modern capitalist society a large amount of savings are diverted directly from business profits into the purchase of capital goods without their ever being paid out to individuals. Moreover, between the individual saver and the firm which employs capital goods are many middlemen, such as savings banks, insurance companies, investment banks, etc. The commercial banking system also has an important role in the capital market. The organization of the capital market is such that the function of saving tends to be separated from the function of investing. Despite these complexities, however, the fundamental principle remains that the failure of saved funds, from whatever source, to be used for buying new capital goods, directly or via middlemen, is the basic source of capitalist crisis.

Second, the initial impact of a decline in investment gives rise to secondary repercussions which accentuate its effects. For example, an initial decline in investment of $1 billion will at first reduce national income by $1 billion. But at this reduced rate of national income, consumers will curtail their purchases and such investment plans as remain will be curtailed. These changes will reduce income still more and will further curtail consumer spending and investment, etc. This downward spiral will end only when the decline in income has sufficiently curtailed saving for all remaining savings to find an outlet in investment, i.e., when total demand is again equal to total supply. As a result of these secondary effects, an initial reduction in investment of $1 billion will result in a decline in income of a multiple of $1 billion. The multiplier in advanced capitalistic countries is said to be of the order of two to four.

Third, although the crisis is precipitated by the inability of all current savings to find profitable investment outlets, it does not follow that when all the forces have worked themselves out, actual savings will exceed actual investment. It is true that the holding of saved funds in cash by some individuals will result in a decline in aggregate income as indicated. But it is not necessarily true that the decline will be limited to the incomes of the particular individuals who wish to remain liquid. The effects will be widespread, and all who are affected by the decline in income will be unable to save as much as before. As a result aggregate savings will be reduced. A stable situation can be reached only when incomes are reduced sufficiently for current savings to be compressed to a point where they are equal to current investment. At this point savings and investment are of necessity equal.[5] This equality of actual savings and actual in-

---

5 Another way of showing that savings and investment are equal is through the following relationships: (1) total output is equal to the output of consumption goods plus the output of capital goods; (2) total income is equal to consumer

vestment is formally true by definition. Yet the decline in income associated with capitalist crisis is due to the fact that *planned* savings are in excess of *planned* investment. As a result of the inconsistency between savings plans and investment plans, income is reduced, which reduces savings, etc., etc. But when the adjustment to this situation is complete, savings and investment are in fact again equal—but at a lower rate of savings, investment, and income.

Fourth, the savings-investment theory of capitalist crisis is sometimes criticized on the ground that it would not be true if prices were flexible and could be adjusted readily to the reduction in aggregate demand. In terms of the critics, unemployment results not from the disequilibrium between planned savings and planned investment, but to price rigidities which inhibit appropriate economic adjustments. This point of view has only partial validity.

If, when unemployment occurred, all prices (both of goods and factors) were to fall in unison, then there would be no change in anything but the value of money. The relation between the prices of goods and of factors would be the same as that which prevailed before the crisis. Hence, there would be no change in the scope of profitable investment opportunities. Also the tendency to save (after correction for changes in the value of money) would be as strong as before. So a general reduction in all prices would not restore prosperity.

If there were a reduction in factor prices without a corresponding reduction in the prices of goods, cost-price relationships would be revised favorably from the point of view of potential investors. The margin of profitability of capital investment would be extended and new investment opportunities would be created. Such a reduction in factor prices would, however, curtail consumption. It would involve a reduction in the incomes of landowners and (chiefly) workers, and would hence reduce their demands for consumer goods. Since workers are usually in the lower income brackets and use most of their

---

expenditures plus savings; (3) total output is equal to or identical with total income since everything that is produced must be distributed to or owned by someone; (4) the output of consumption goods is equal to consumer expenditures (any consumption goods produced but not purchased by consumers are added to inventories and are classified as capital goods); therefore, (5) savings are equal to investment.

incomes for consumption, the reduction in the demands of workers would be nearly equal to the decline in their incomes. On the other hand, the change in cost-price relationships would increase the incomes of the owners of capital, and would hence increase their demands for consumer goods. But most capital is owned by persons in the upper income brackets who would use for consumption only a fraction of their added incomes. As a result of the entire transfer of income from workers to the owners of capital, there would be a net reduction in total demand for consumer goods and a corresponding increase in the rate of saving. Thus, although the change in cost-price relationships might stimulate investment, it would also increase the tendency to save and hence would increase the amount of investment needed to maintain full employment. But this is not the end of the story. The reduction in demand for consumer goods resulting from the cut in factor prices would have an unfavorable effect upon investment because capital goods are used ultimately to produce consumer goods. So when the effect of this dampening of investment is added to the effect of the increase in saving, it is doubtful if a reduction in factor prices can be depended upon to prevent the onset of unemployment. It may be that in some situations and under certain special conditions, a reduction in factor prices would have on balance a stimulating effect on investment, especially in the very short run. Generally speaking, its effect would be the opposite.

Since cutting wages would usually not prevent, but rather accentuate, a capitalist crisis, it may be argued that the reverse solution, namely, raising wages, would overcome the problem of capitalist crisis. By raising wages, saving would be reduced, consumption would be expanded, and, as a result of the increase in consumption, investment would be stimulated. Thus, unemployment would be prevented. Theoretically, this might be an adequate solution, but it is not a practicable one within the framework of capitalist institutions.

Each enterprise in a capitalist system represents a negligible part of the total economy. It does not and cannot be expected to consider the effect of its actions on total demand. Any one enterprise, therefore, could hardly be expected to raise wages in order to forestall unemployment. To raise wages would appear to the management as merely an increase in cost without any resulting benefits and as a harm to its competitive position. The effect of its raising wages upon the demand for its own product would be negligible, since the increased purchasing power would be diffused among many other firms. From the point of view of the individual enterprise, the action would be effective and desirable only if many other firms were pursuing the same policy at the same time. Only then would it avoid the risk of competitive disadvantage, and only then would the increase in purchasing power be effective for its products. But for the increase in wages to be general would require either social control over wages and prices or collusive agreement among firms, either of which would be inconsistent with the fundamental tenets of capitalism.

In recent years labor unions have espoused the philosophy of raising wages and distributing purchasing power to the masses as a way of combating depression and have attempted to impose wage settlements accordingly. Labor unions are, of course, collusive institutions which are not consistent with the condition of complete competition. However, even if one overlooks this, labor unions would probably not be successful in their efforts in this direction unless they could exercise strong influence over the prices of goods as well as over wages. That is, for an increase in wages to be effective it must not be accompanied by corresponding increases in the prices of goods. Otherwise, the original wage-price relationship remains unchanged and the increase in real purchasing power arising from the higher wages is dissipated in higher prices. On the other hand, if labor unions should become effective enough to control both wages and prices, I think all would admit that the system would no longer have the essential feature of capitalism.

The conclusions of our discussion of cost-price relationships in relation to the problem of unemployment are: (1) that to cut wages without cutting prices would likely not forestall unemployment, and (2) that to raise wages without raising prices would be an appropriate remedy but would require a degree of social control incompatible with the basic tenets of capitalism. This reinforces the general conclusion that tendencies toward unemployment are inherent in capitalism.

Chapter 30

BEYOND EQUILIBRIUM

In the preceding three chapters we have considered some of the obstacles faced by a capitalistic system in the pursuit of equilibrium. We have seen that there are problems of predicting the future, of deficient competition, and of unemployment. However, even if it could be shown that equilibrium is easily attainable in a capitalistic economy, yet that in itself would not guarantee the achievement of maximum aggregate satisfaction.

It was indicated earlier that the mere attainment of the basic pricing principles (as would happen in equilibrium) does not automatically produce maximum aggregate satisfaction. Other important problems are involved, among them the output of goods produced under conditions of decreasing cost, the output of social goods, the distribution of income, consumer choice, the supply of labor, and the supply of capital. Each of these subjects will be discussed in this chapter.

These topics were treated at some length in Chapters 17-22. Therefore only a brief application of these problems to capitalism is necessary at this point.

Decreasing Cost

The conclusions reached in Chapter 17 regarding decreasing cost were: (1) that the most economical output for an industry subject to decreasing cost is that which can be sold at a price equal to long-run marginal cost, and (2) that a decreasing-cost industry should be established whenever, at some output, the total satisfactions to be derived from the product are in excess of total cost of production. Under capitalism, neither of these rules can be applied because both involve operation at a loss. Moreover, as shown in Chapter 28, a decreasing-cost industry is likely to fall into the hands of a single firm (as it should from

305

the point of view of efficient operation). But the single firm, in pursuing its interest, may limit its output to an amount even less than that which could be sold at a price sufficient to cover cost. Thus, on two counts, the output of decreasing cost industries is likely to be less under capitalism than would be economically desirable.

Collective Choice

Even under the most extreme form of laissez-faire capitalism, demand must be exercised collectively for some purposes (See Chapter 18). This would be true, for example, in the production of elemental governmental services such as the maintenance of order, protection of property, and the provision of a generally favorable environment for economic life. These services are not salable on the market as commodities and, therefore, cannot be provided in response to individual demand growing out of free individual consumer choices. Rather, they must be provided in response to the choices of the group or of its leaders. Capitalism provides no special mechanism for arranging that the satisfactions from the marginal penny spent on governmental services will be equal to the satisfactions from the marginal pennies spent on other goods. But capitalism is no different in this respect from other types of economic systems. It has the great advantage, moreover, of reducing the area of collective choice to a minimum.

Capitalistic systems as we have known them, however, have probably tended to overemphasize pecuniary individual values and to underestimate social values. Group attitudes have tended toward the judgment that whatever can be produced in response to pecuniary demand of individuals is worth producing and that to produce anything which cannot be sold for a price and at a profit is more or less wasteful. Thus, in the capitalist context, people often consider inconsequential gadgets and momentary pleasures more significant than parks, schools, hospitals, conservation of natural resources, or other social amenities. But these evaluations—though perhaps fostered by the individualistic attitudes developed under capitalism—are not necessarily inherent in that system. It is true that a basic tenet of classical capitalism is that the activities of government should be held to a minimum. Yet, once it is admitted that there are *some* social values worth pursuing, there is nothing in the theory of capitalism which sets a definite limit to the number or extent of the social values which may be legitimately pursued. One might easily conceive a capitalistic system in which one fourth or one half of all resources are allocated in response to collective demands for social goods and yet in which the remaining resources are allocated entirely according to capitalistic principles.

Distribution of Income

In all capitalistic countries, the distribution of income has, in fact, been grossly unequal. This inequality is probably an inescapable consequence of capitalism, though perhaps the differences in individual incomes need not be so great as they have in fact been.

In capitalism incomes are paid as market prices for the factors. The amount of any individual's income is determined by the character and quantities of the factors owned by him and by the market prices of these factors. Accordingly, the distribution of income depends partly upon the ownership of the factors and partly upon the market prices of these factors.

The influences determining the distribution of ownership of the factors are, of course, different for each of the several factors. The quantity of labor (human services attributed to hereditary characteristics) in the possession of each individual is biologically determined. Although not all authorities agree on the extent of native individual differences, all concede that individuals differ to *some* degree. Since these differences undoubtedly affect individual productivity, any system which pays out incomes in the form of prices on the factors will be characterized by a noticeable inequality of incomes among workers.

That which is ordinarily regarded as *labor* includes not only services attributable to hereditary endowments but also those made possible by environmental influences—especially nutrition and training. In Chapter 1 these were defined as nonmaterial capital goods. Since the most important of these environmental influences occur during childhood and adolescence, they are of necessity invested in the individual through means more or less beyond his control. In the kind of capitalistic system where the functions of government are severely restricted, the provision of training and other environmental factors would be left almost entirely to parents. The amount received by young individuals would then be closely correlated to the incomes of their parents. Many parents would not be able to send their children to schools and to provide the type of wholesome physical, mental, and moral environment necessary to the development of productive workers. Thus, the distribution of income would be strongly influenced by inheritance—even without any actual inheritance of property. This extreme reliance upon parents for the training of youth is not, however, a necessary characteristic of capitalism (except under a radical laissez-faire view). Free public education, public scholarships for talented individuals, school lunches at public expense, and other similar provisions for greater equality of training and health are social goods which can be provided while otherwise maintaining the essential features of capitalism. However, so long as the environmental influences upon children are, to a significant extent, provided by parents, the distribution of training will be determined in part by the prevailing distribution of incomes, and will tend to perpetuate that distribution.

In capitalist societies the distribution of ownership of material capital goods and land is determined by the distribution of the power to save and by the institution of inheritance.[1] The power of an individual to save is measured by the amount of his income in excess of that required for the maintenance of a scale of living acceptable to the individual. The greater this excess, the greater the amount which he can save. Studies of individual behavior in the use of income always show that individuals having large incomes save a larger *proportion* of their incomes than those having smaller incomes. Thus, the power to save is related partially to the willingness of the individual to depress his scale of living, and, much more importantly, to the size of his income. Saving increases the capital of the individual, thus increasing the quantity of factors from which his income is obtained. The more an individual saves, the greater is his income; and the greater his income, the more he can save. Once an individual gets

[1] One might add, in the case of frontier societies, by the ability to appropriate natural resources or luck in acquiring the particular resources which later prove to be valuable. Speculation and fraud are also devices for acquiring capital.

started in the accumulative process, therefore, his income is likely to grow progressively.

An individual endowed with superior natural talents and superior training is likely to have more income than a less fortunate person, and he is likely, therefore, to be in a position to save more. As he saves, his income increases; this enables him to save more; etc. By this process, a relatively small initial advantage in heredity or training is magnified so that the ultimate distribution of income becomes far more unequal than the original distribution of personal qualities (hereditary or environmental).

In practice, the inequality resulting from differences in the power to save is further accentuated by the institution of property inheritance. When individuals are able to acquire the property accumulated during the lifetime of their parents, they start out with income from a quantity of factors sufficient to give them a superior power to save. Such fortunate individuals, even though not endowed with unusual personal talents, enjoy a decided advantage in the competitive race for fortune, and the inequality of income distribution is thus enhanced. The institution of property inheritance is perhaps not an integral part of capitalism. An essentially capitalist system might operate without it.

One additional source of inequality in income may be described by the word "connections." Frequently, opportunities for lucrative positions or advantageous investments are made available to individuals through the influence of relatives and friends. Thus, the "right" family connections or the ability to win influential friends may place an individual in a position to obtain more income than he would get on the basis of his mere ability and capital. Though this type of advantage is prevalent under capitalism, it is at least doubtful if it is confined exclusively to capitalism. One would suspect that the scope for personal favoritism might be considerable under any system. In capitalism, however, it would likely take the form of favoritism in the race for wealth and income; whereas in other systems, it might be directed toward the attainment of other sources of prestige and power.

To summarize, the unequal distribution of the factors of production in actual capitalist societies may be accounted for in the following ways: (1) the unequal distribution of hereditary characteristics of human beings, (2) the unequal distribution of nonmaterial capital, (3) the unequal distribution of the power to save, (4) the institution of inheritance, and (5) personal connections.

The effect of all five of these factors is to lead to an unequal distribution in ownership of factors. Since under capitalism incomes are received as payment for the factors, this inequality in ownership of factors leads to inequality in the distribution of income. Under any system, inequalities in the amounts of productive factors possessed by (or in control of) various individuals would prevail. But these inequalities would hardly affect the distribution of incomes unless the amount of individual incomes were related to the possession of the factors as is necessarily true in capitalism.

The distribution of income in capitalism is determined not only by the distribution of ownership of the factors, but also by the prices of these factors. The pricing of the factors, of course, is accomplished in the market. The price of each factor is set so that the total demand is equated with the total supply. Thus, other things being equal, those individuals have the largest incomes who possess the most valuable (i.e., scarcest in relation to demand) factors.

Part of the inequality of income characteristic of capitalist countries could be mitigated without destroying the essential features of the system—for example, by provision of greater equality of educational opportunity and by instituting graduated income and inheritance taxes. Even with these modifications, however, the payment of income as a return for the services of the factors almost inevitably leads to inequality in the distribution of income, and this inequality is likely to lead to a thoroughly uneconomical use of resources under which the relatively trivial wants of the well-to-do can be satisfied at the expense of necessities for the lower income groups. In the capitalist system, however, incomes constitute not only the means to individual satisfactions (through the acquisition of consumption goods, power, and prestige) but also the primary incentive to productive effort. Consequently, the desirability of the capitalist distribution of income must be judged partly in terms of its effectiveness in providing individual motivation.

It is frequently argued that the unequal distribution of income is well worth its cost, in that the possibility of achieving a fortune stimulates men to exert themselves in the interests of social welfare and progress to an extent far beyond what would be achieved under other types of motivation. In line with this, it is argued that the introduction of steeply graduated taxes on incomes and inheritances threatens the very foundations of capitalism, since it lessens the attractiveness of the possible prizes from success in the competitive struggle. Moreover, it is pointed out that Russia has been forced to revert to the use of wage differentials as a means of achieving even tolerable efficiency. Thus, the question of income distribution is presented in the form of a choice of evils: under the capitalistic system, the distribution of income is admitted to be uneconomic from the point of view of maximizing satisfactions from a given national income; but under a more equitable distribution of income, the amount of income to be divided would be smaller. Is it preferable to have a small cake divided equitably or a large cake divided inequitably? The answer depends, of course, upon how large the cake will be in either case and how inequitably it will be divided. With present knowledge, a categorical answer to this question cannot be made. Certainly, any evaluation of the capitalistic distribution of income must consider the problem of incentives. Particularly, it must not overlook the possibility that an alternative type of reward for productive effort might lead to the same inequalities and injustices associated with capitalistic distribution.[2]

Consumer Choice

One of the fundamentals of laissez-faire capitalism is that each individual shall be free to spend his income as he pleases, and the production shall be carried on in response to these free consumer choices. In Chapter 23 it was pointed out that free consumer choice is an imperfect device for guiding the allocation of resources unless consumers are (1) rational, (2) informed, and (3) desirous of those goods which will, in fact, give greatest satisfaction.

The first of the conditions may reasonably be disposed of

---

[2] For more extended discussions of these issues, see Chapter 19.

merely by assuming that individuals would probably be rational to a relatively high degree in a culture like capitalism, where the practice of pecuniary calculation is well developed. The remaining two conditions, however, require more detailed treatment.

In laissez-faire capitalism, where production is carried on for profit by firms whose interests are not always identified with those of consumers, the information available to consumers is likely to be less than adequate for intelligent choices. In the first place, business firms tend to be secretive regarding methods of manufacture and the ingredients of products. This secrecy may be designed to prevent the duplication of the product by rivals, or deliberately to conceal derogatory facts. In either case, the practice constitutes a barrier to the attainment of adequate knowledge on the part of consumers. Secondly, consumers must generally rely upon sellers as the principal source of information regarding the qualities of products offered on the market. The consumer himself is usually not qualified to judge the merits of different goods and is ordinarily unable to afford the advice of disinterested experts (except in a few cases, for example, medical advice or architectural service). Thus, in the absence of consumer organizations or governmental intervention, he has no place to turn except to sellers whose advice (in the form of advertising and salesmanship) is of questionable informative value. It is true that the desire of businessmen to win and hold customers impels them to reasonable accuracy in the advice given, but it by no means induces them to impart complete information, because that would often involve the literal driving of customers to competitors. Oddly enough, even repeated experience on the part of the consumer with a given product may not provide him with the required information, because in many cases adulteration or impurities or weaknesses cannot be discovered by a novice even through use of the product, and harmful effects from a particular good may appear so tardily as to seem wholly unrelated. In short, the individual consumer himself cannot hope to gain the knowledge necessary for intelligent decisions. His only hope lies in relying upon the information and advice of disinterested experts—advice which can be obtained only at great expense unless it is derived collectively through consumer organizations or the government. To the extent that this is inadequate, the consumer is "on his own," facing a battery of producers operating according to the principle of *caveat emptor*.

The problem of the consumer is made more difficult in capitalism by the bewildering variety of goods available. This tendency toward the proliferation of goods may be explained chiefly by the phenomenon of product differentiation and partly, perhaps, by the practice of premature obsolescence.

Each capitalist enterprise is under strong motivation to differentiate its product from that of its rivals. This can be accomplished by producing a good having actual properties different from those of competing producers, by adopting a unique container or trade-mark, or by employing special conditions of sale. The practice of differentiation increases manifoldly the number and variety of goods. The consumer is required not merely to choose from among several types of a commodity, but from among many brands of each type. The increased variety of goods resulting from product differentiation may be justified on the ground that greater variety makes possible a more perfect adaptation of the supply of goods to the varying requirements of different consumers. The argument, undoubtedly valid if the variety in goods does not greatly exceed the variety of tastes, alters in no way the conclusion that product differentiation tends to complicate consumer choice.[3]

Another factor extending the range of consumer choices and hence increasing the problems of the consumer is the tendency to encourage premature obsolescence. Individual firms or industries producing durable goods find that the chief obstacle to greater sales volume is the continued existence of goods they have produced earlier. Consequently, firms in such industries are interested in the early obsolescence of durable goods already in use. They are eager to encourage or stimulate rapid changes in fashion, and are thus inclined to produce new "models" or new "styles" at frequent intervals and to direct their sales promotion toward the adoption of these new creations. There may be some question as to the extent of their influence in this direc-

---

[3] Product differentiation is perhaps not an essential feature of capitalism, but rather is a result of legislation—common to all capitalist countries—which protects patents and trade-marks. The identification of the product of a given producer has the great advantage of fixing his responsibility and encouraging him to make his products acceptable to consumers.

tion, but to whatever extent they are able to hasten obsolescence, the consumer is confronted with new alternatives which must be considered in deciding upon his expenditure of income. It may be argued that frequent changes in style are not undesirable because they provide harmless satisfaction of a very real human longing, namely, the wish for new experience. However, even accepting the validity of this argument, great emphasis upon "doctrine of obsolescence for change's sake" multiplies many-fold the problems of consumer choice. For many goods, e.g., women's hats, the main determiner of choice is fashion. How simple, relatively, would be the process of selecting a hat if all that were required were a durable and effective head covering! Thus, if it is true that capitalism tends to place accent on style changes, consumer choice in that system is made relatively difficult.

Finally, we come to the problem of whether individuals in a capitalist society are likely to have the "right" wants; i.e., whether they may be expected to choose those goods which will lead, in fact, to maximum satisfaction. As pointed out in Chapter 20, consumer choices are, on the whole, culturally determined; they are cast in institutional molds. The question becomes, then, one of determining the extent to which a capitalist culture conduces to those consumer choices that will lead to greatest satisfaction.

The primary criticism of consumer choices under capitalism is based upon the excessive emphasis placed upon the acquisition of goods as a means of attaining recognition, or, negatively, of avoiding reprobation. As a result, resources are used for this purpose which, if the culture permitted them to be used for the attainment of other interests, would contribute more fully to the sum total of satisfactions. The explanation of this lies in the fact that within capitalism the possession of income and wealth tends to become the socially accepted symbol of intrinsic personal merit.

The reward for productive effort consists almost entirely of money income. Thus, the money income of an individual is a measure of his productive contribution and therefore of his social merit. Moreover, the possession of property which is obtained chiefly from income confers substantial economic and social power upon the individual, which in itself is a source of personal distinction. In short, the possession of income and wealth becomes an emblem of honor, and the extent of an individual's income and wealth a measure of his merit.

In a primitive society where individual relationships are on a personal, man-to-man basis, the mere possession of income and wealth is sufficient to confer honor and prestige upon an individual. In this situation he is rated according to the extent of his land, the size of his flocks, or perhaps the number of his wives. But in the modern world of rapid mobility and impersonal relationships, the possession of income and wealth confers little prestige unless it can be made known to passers-by and to casual acquaintances. Hence, to obtain the distinction associated with pecuniary importance, it is necessary to *display* one's wealth, and in a day of absentee ownership this can be most effectively accomplished through *conspicuous consumption*. Veblen said, "The signature of one's pecuniary strength should be written in characters which he who runs may read." But the tendency to conspicuous consumption is by no means confined to the richer classes. Individuals of less wealth will also attempt, through consumption activities, to attain the recognition which is *their* due. And even the classes of lowest income, in order to escape complete degradation, join in the effort to secure status through display. Moreover, the individuals within each class attempt to outdo the others and to rival the class just ahead. Life becomes a problem of "keeping up with the Joneses" and "catching up to the Smiths." Since, however, the activity is competitive, it tends to be self-defeating. No one really gains in the struggle to get ahead, yet no one can drop out of the competition without losing caste. The end result is that a large, perhaps preponderant, portion of social resources is devoted, futilely on the whole, to the attainment of recognition. Since recognition could be attained quite as effectively with smaller use of resources, a large part of capitalist productive effort must be regarded as uneconomic. It is directed in response to "wrong" consumer choices. In the words of Veblen, conspicuous consumption is "called 'waste' because this expenditure does not serve human life or human well-being on the whole, not because it is waste or misdirection of effort or expenditure as viewed from the standpoint of the individual consumer who chooses it."

Fashion is an important element in conspicuous consumption. The ability of an individual to follow (or lead) the fashions signifies that his pecuniary strength is sufficient to allow him to discard consumer goods before they are worn out. Thus, new styles are first adopted by the aristocracy or the wealthy, and through imitation by those of lesser rank become fashionable. But rapid adoption by those of lesser rank defeats the purposes of the more well-to-do, so that they must move on to new styles, and so on in an endless procession. Through fashion, women especially are enabled to play a significant role in the great social masquerade as expensive ornaments symbolizing the social status and economic strength of their husbands. However, fashion cannot be explained solely in terms of its part in conspicuous consumption. It provides a socially approved way for the individual to obtain variety and new experience and to express symbolically his personality and his relation to the social situation. Moreover, the character of the fashions that are prevalent at any given time cannot be explained merely as the outcome of an adventitious chain of circumstance. The fashions of any period of time tend to change according to relatively smooth trends, any one fashion tending to develop as an outgrowth of preceding fashions. Moreover, the direction of any trend is determined by the social situation, by the events, the interests, the problems, and the "spirit" of the time. The whole subject of *fashion* is a fascinating social-psychological phenomenon regarding which our knowledge is by no means complete.[4]

The argument that emphasis upon display represents a wrong consumer choice, or, perhaps more accurately, a wrong social valuation, is as old as recorded history. It has always been a favorite theme of philosophers and religious prophets that the striving for recognition through conspicuous consumption is a completely futile and unworthy effort. The Sermon on the Mount states:[5]

Lay not up for yourselves treasures upon earth, where moth and rust doth corrupt, and where thieves break through and steal . . . take no thought for your life, what ye shall eat or what ye shall drink; nor yet for your body what ye shall put on. Is not the life more than meat, and the body than raiment?

---

[4] Edward Sapir, "Fashion," *Encyclopaedia of the Social Sciences,* Vol. VI, pp. 139-144; Paul H. Nystrom, *Economics of Fashion,* New York, 1928; Georg Simmel, "Fashion," *International Quarterly,* October, 1904, pp. 130-155.

[5] St. Matthew 6:19, 25.

In modern times, the philosophies of Thoreau, Ruskin, and Hobson have emphasized the distinction between wealth and welfare and the futility of pursuing the good life by means of wealth. The judgment of the philosophers is accepted, on sober reflection, by a great majority of individuals. Yet within capitalism the pressure to maintain one's "standard of living" is so intense that few individuals have the fortitude of a Thoreau (who incidentally was unmarried) to forsake the endless paraphernalia and ritual involved in "maintaining one's position in society."

A second criticism of consumer choices under capitalism is based upon the assumption that these choices do not represent independent decisions of individual consumers, but rather that they are the direct result of advertising, salesmanship, and propaganda carried on in the interests of "business." The validity of this criticism depends upon the degree to which sales promotional efforts are effective in shaping the choices of consumers. A widely accepted view on this subject is that the consumer is merely a pawn in the high game of big business and that he can be made to respond in any way that may serve the interests of the business community. Careful analysis of the facts seems to indicate, however, that the sales promotion is of much smaller influence than is generally supposed. Business experience has repeatedly demonstrated that no amount of sales pressure can "force" the public to accept commodities for which they feel no real need or which are alien to their interests at the time. And there are equally numerous instances where new commodities have become widely accepted without any appreciable amount of deliberate sales effort on the part of business.[6] Moreover, it appears that sales promotion, on the whole, is more significant as a determiner of such trifling matters as the type or brand of a given commodity that shall be purchased rather than of the basic pattern of consumption. And even in the smaller details, the over-all effect tends to be lost since the activities of one firm or of one industry tend to be offset by the activities of other firms or industries.

Sales promotion is of significance as a molder of basic consumer choices when it is used to inform the public of the avail-

[6] Cf. Paul H. Nystrom, *Fashion Merchandising*, New York, 1932, p. 35.

ability of a good for which they already feel a need or to which the general social situation has made them receptive. The interests of a people and the accepted modes of attaining these interests are rooted so firmly in the culture, that arbitrarily imposed sales promotions can hardly be expected to bring about significant changes in the pattern of consumption. In short, sales promotion, though far from negligible in effect, can hardly be regarded as a fundamental determinant of consumer choices. Thus, the chief criticism of sales promotion in a capitalist society is that it involves a somewhat wasteful use of resources. Its principal role is as informant to consumers, but in this capacity it is inadequate and misleading, because it is prejudiced. Moreover, to whatever extent it is effective, it may also be instrumental in the creation of monopoly.

Supply of Labor

In Chapter 21 it was pointed out that the labor supply depends upon the manner in which human time is divided between labor and leisure and upon the intensity of labor during the working period. It was concluded that in any economic system employing modern technology, these matters must usually be determined through group decisions or customs that permit of little latitude for individual choice. Capitalism is no exception to this principle. Such questions as the length of the working day, the number of holidays, or the content of a "day's work" are and must be determined socially.

Experience has shown that in the absence of labor unions, governmental regulations, or a tight labor market, abuses develop in which people are worked for longer hours and harder than they would prefer to work and than is desirable from the point of view of their health and their long-term productivity. It is probable, therefore, that the supply of labor is a matter which must be subject to social regulation and cannot be automatically solved through the workings of the market.

Supply of Capital

As pointed out above (Chapters 22 and 28), the tendency to save in a capitalistic system is relatively strong. This is not a valid basis of criticism so long as additional capital yields additional product. As pointed out in Chapter 22, we have no objective or definite criterion for determining the most advantageous rate of capital accumulation except that capital should not accumulate beyond the amount that can be used productively The rate of capital accumulation is primarily a matter of judgment involving a comparison of the interests of the present against those of the future.

A basic weakness of capitalistic systems as we have known them is that they tend to apportion too much capital to so-called "self-liquidating" projects and not enough to social purposes. This is the same point that was made on p. 306 in connection with the discussion of collective choice. It was pointed out there that the emphasis on pecuniary values found in capitalist socie‧ ties tends to blind the group to the advantages of providing for social needs in response to collective choice. It was indicated, however, that this was not an essential characteristic of capitalism, and that there was no necessary limit to the amount of production that could be carried on in response to collective choice while still observing the capitalistic principles in connection with the remainder of the production. Nevertheless, the myopic disregard of social values is closely connected with the capitalistic problem of unemployment. Investment tends to be limited to those projects which promise a *pecuniary* return sufficient to cover replacement and a reward for risk. Insufficient attention is paid to the opportunities for investment which promise a nonpecuniary (but nevertheless adequate) return in the form of social goods. This is because most such social investments must be made by the state or by cooperative action of many individuals and must usually be financed, sooner or later, out of taxes or voluntary contribution. We have all witnessed the spectacle of a capitalistic country prostrate because of supposed lack of investment opportunities when at the same time the nation has inadequate medical facilities, housing, schools, churches, roads, parks, flood control, navigation facilities, and other social amenities.

One must reiterate, however, that this distortion in the flow of investments is not necessarily inherent in capitalism. It is only a feature of those capitalistic systems we have known.

Conclusions

The purpose of this chapter has been to appraise the solutions offered by capitalism to a variety of problems which lie beyond the scope of mere price equilibrium. The following conclusions were reached: (1) The output of industries subject to decreasing cost is likely to be considerably less than that dictated by considerations of economy. (2) Capitalism, historically but perhaps not necessarily, has tended to undervalue social goods of the type which must be produced in response to collective choice. (3) The inequality of income distribution under capitalism clearly leads to an uneconomical distribution of product among consumers. This distribution of income, however, has a bearing on incentives, and our knowledge of incentives is not sufficient to provide a definite conclusion as to the net desirability of capitalistic distribution of income. (4) Under capitalism intelligent consumer choice is made difficult by the lack of disinterested information, by product differentiation, and by premature obsolescence. Moreover, in capitalistic systems, the values have been such as to direct consumption into competitive and wasteful channels. (5) Capitalism itself provides no satisfactory mechanism for determining the hours and intensity of labor; hence some form of social control through government, collective bargaining, or social convention is required. (6) Because capitalist societies have in practice tended to undervalue social goods, they have diverted too little capital into the production of social goods.

Chapter 31

CAPITALISM AND
ITS ALTERNATIVES

In the preceding several chapters, we have discussed capitalism. First, the capitalistic system was defined in terms of its characteristic institutions of private property, free labor, free enterprise, functional distribution of income, free consumer choice, advanced technology, money economy, complete competition, and limited government. This definition of capitalism was not intended to correspond accurately to any actual economic system of the present or past. It was intended rather as a definition of "pure" or "ideal" capitalism. Second, the operation of such a hypothetical economic system was described. Finally, the allocation of resources achieved under capitalism was evaluated in terms of the theory of economy as developed in Part IV of this book. It was shown that the spontaneous choices of individuals—tempered and regulated by competition—would lead toward an allocation of resources in which most of the basic pricing principles of economy would be fulfilled. However, capitalism was found wanting in several important respects.

Capitalism vs. Socialism

The conclusion seems inescapable that pure capitalism (as defined) would be subject to grave deficiencies and inconsistencies. Such a system would have little justification under modern conditions and would stand little chance of survival. That pure capitalism is unworkable under modern conditions has, of course, long been recognized. In all countries where capitalistic institutions have prevailed, a long series of institutional innovations has greatly modified the system. Among these new developments have been: the graduated income tax and other progressive taxes, social insurance, labor unions, trade associations, regulation of public utilities, antitrust legislation, government ownership and operation of certain industries, countercyclical fiscal policy, and many others. Nevertheless, much remains to be done—especially in promoting economic stability, developing competition or controlling monopoly, enlarging the output of decreasing-cost industries, expanding the production of social goods, and improving the conditions of consumer choice.

In some countries which still adhere to the outer form of capitalism, the process of institutional change has gone farther than in others. Perhaps the United States remains closer to the original and pristine features of capitalism than any other country. Even here, the trend toward new economic institutions— clearly evident as early as 1890—moves steadily forward.

Pure capitalism is doubtless anachronistic. We are apparently moving toward new economic institutions in which economic decisions will be determined more largely by collective action than has been true heretofore. The great question of our age is: Toward what sort of economic system are we moving or ought we to move? What economic institutions would be most likely to produce an economical use of resources—taking into account modern technology, the modern temperament, and modern ethical values as they have evolved out of our past experiences? At the polar extremes are two opposing answers to this question: (1) turning back toward pure capitalism, or (2) moving ahead toward the more or less untried system of pure socialism where all property is owned by the state, production is planned and executed by governmental agencies, and distribution is determined directly by political decisions. Between these diverse proposals are many variants which include elements of both polar extremes. Most of these compromise solutions involve a retention of the form of capitalism (private property, etc.) but an increase in the degree of state control over economic decisions. The present economic system of every country in the world, with the possible single exception of U.S.S.R., is a variant lying somewhere between the two extremes.

The great ideological conflict between those who lean toward pure capitalism and those who want to move in the direction of pure socialism deeply affects the vital interests of all individuals, all classes, and all nations. Therefore, it is a subject freighted with deep emotion and violent prejudice.

Capitalist Dogmas

Throughout the history of the controversy, the exponents of capitalism have used successively three arguments to demonstrate the impracticability or undesirability of socialism (or even of its more moderate variants).

The first argument is the Malthusian theory of population. On the basis of the theory that population tends to outstrip the means of subsistence, it was held that an increasing scale of living was impossible of attainment and that any attempt to equalize incomes would merely reduce *all,* instead of the many, to the level of subsistence. The spread of birth control and the unforeseen rapid rate of technological progress has tended to weaken this argument. However, it is still used and it is not entirely without validity.

The second argument designed to demolish the position of the socialists (and of all "planners" as well) is that rational economic calculation is impossible in a socialist state. Since the state would exercise management over all industry, it would be the sole demander of the factors and the sole seller of goods. There would be no competitive market, and therefore no objective method for placing valuations on factors and on goods. And with all valuations arbitrary and unrelated to the demands of consumers, rational calculation regarding the allocation of the factors would be impossible. Thus a socialist society could not be expected to achieve an economical use of resources.[1] This line of argument has been attacked in a series of books and articles showing that economic calculation could be carried in much the same way and with similar results in a socialist state as in a capitalist state.[2]

---

[1] See: Ludwig von Mises, *Socialism;* Lionel Robbins, *Economic Planning and International Order,* London, 1937; Friedrich von Hayek, *The Road to Serfdom,* Chicago, 1944, and *Collectivist Economic Planning,* London, 1938.

[2] The following is a sampling of the more important literature on this subject: H. D. Dickinson, *Economics of Socialism,* Oxford, 1939; Barbara Wootton, *Plan or No Plan,* London, 1934; A. P. Lerner, *The Economics of Control,* New York, 1946; Oskar Lange and F. M. Taylor, *On the Economic Theory of Socialism,*

The argument of the attack is that under planning consumers would be allowed free choice, and that the system could adjust to these choices by a process of trial and error—just as in capitalism. Factors would be employed, the prices on the factors being set so as to clear the market. Industries in which the price of the good was insufficient to cover the unit costs would be contracted, and industries in which the price of the good exceeded the unit costs would be expanded, until equilibrium was approached.

The third argument—one that is widely discussed today—is that capitalism is the only economic system compatible with political freedom or democracy. This argument is in three parts. First, the rise of political democracy was historically coincident with the rise of capitalism. (The *bourgeois* class was in fact at the vanguard of the attack on feudalism.) Thus, there is a strong presumption that freedom flourishes within a capitalistic system. A second part of the argument is that in those countries which have moved the farthest toward state control of industry, namely, U.S.S.R. and prewar Germany, political freedom has been severely restricted. The third part of the argument is that the kinds of economic decisions which would have to be made under socialism could not practically be left to democratic processes. A delegation of power to a central authority would be required, therefore, to a degree which would in practice be the negation of democracy. It is held that democratic processes are slow, wavering in purpose, and not suited to solving complex and detailed questions. Thus, any attempt to operate an economic system through democratic processes would bog down. On the other hand, the delegation of economic power to some centralized planning agency would give that agency so much power as in effect to abnegate democracy.

The first argument, relating to the coincidental rise of capitalism and democracy, is not impressive. The rise of political democracy and capitalism were, to be sure, part of the same broad sweep of human history and no doubt the rise of capitalism contributed importantly to the spread of freedom. Yet it hardly follows that the acme of human freedom was achieved by the transfer of power from a landed aristocracy to a commercial

---

Minneapolis, 1938; A. C. Pigou, *Socialism vs. Capitalism*, London, 1938; R. L. Hall, *The Economic System in a Socialist State*, London, 1937.

class. It may well be that the next great advance in human freedom and dignity may occur through another shift in the locus of economic power.

The second argument, relating to political conditions in modern Russia and prewar Germany, is also less than conclusive. The cultural background in both these states was hardly conducive to democracy. Neither provided fertile soil for the flowering of individual freedom. Postwar England may present a fairer test of the effects of increasing governmental regulation of economic life upon democracy and freedom, since it is a country with ancient and vigorous liberal traditions.

The third argument, i.e., the danger of concentrating great powers in a central planning agency, is the most telling of the three. There are indeed difficulties in regulating the details of economic affairs by the ballot and there are great dangers in delegating power as great as that which would be exercised by an independent central planning board. However, the problem is not necessarily an impossible or hopeless one. Indeed, one can visualize that the sum total of human freedom may be greater if economic affairs are regulated by a powerful *but responsible* planning authority than they are today with diffusion of authority but also with the instability and insecurity created by this diffusion. Freedom from want is surely an important member of the four freedoms. In any case, the issue may be largely academic. We are apparently in the midst of a world-wide drift toward greater governmental control of economic life as one country after another attempts to overcome the actual or supposed weaknesses of capitalism. The real problem may be to find a formula for combining planning and democracy. This is a task which requires the best thinking of our social scientists, our experts in public administration, and our politicians. Even more important, it is the task which requires clear thinking and good sense on the part of all people during the crises that almost certainly lie ahead. We must not sell our birthright for the promises, however plausible, of a dictator who would solve our immediate economic problems at the price of slavery. At the same time, we must not be misled by spurious definitions of freedom on the part of those who would defend the *status quo* merely to protect their own interests. The appropriate question is always: Freedom of whom and to do what?

Socialist Dogmas

Just as some of the arguments advanced on the side of capitalism are perhaps dubious, so also are some of the arguments and assertions dinned into our ears from the left.

First, socialists tend to attack capitalism with exaggerated statements of its weaknesses and without sufficient regard for its points of strength—which, after all, are considerable. For example, capitalism provides highly effective motivation for individuals. It spurs them on to great personal effort in providing the goods needed by society. Also, it encourages experimentation, innovation, new ideas, and new ways of doing things. Moreover, it provides a fascinating and varied "game" in the form of a competitive race for fame, fortune, and economic power which anyone with the wit, the courage, and the stamina can enter. Finally, capitalism is one type of economic system which has *demonstrated* that it is compatible with free political institutions. That any other system is compatible with or conducive to political freedom is a theory and not a demonstrated fact.

More important, those on the left—especially the Marxists—hold that the only way to solve the problems of capitalism and to cure its abuses is through revolution. By revolution they mean the confiscation of private property and the forcible removal of all private owners and their representatives from places of authority. It is held that a revolution by force is necessary and inevitable because the owning classes would never relinquish their powers without attempting to defend them by force. This general line of argument suffers from several weaknesses.

First, it exaggerates what can be accomplished through revolution. The institutions of a people, even under the most dynamic impulses and under the most troubled conditions, change but slowly. The mere substitution of one ruling class for another and the transfer of property rights associated with revolution does not miraculously alter the underlying institutions, the ethical values, and the outlook on life of a people. It may dramatize certain objectives, it may hasten certain movements already discernible, it may result in the immediate correction of certain abuses, or it may impose others. But it does not revolutionize the fundamental folkways and mores of the people. This is amply demonstrated, for example, by the French or the Russian revolutions. History has shown conclusively, I think, that whenever a revolutionary group has attempted to move the clock ahead too fast, it has been checked by powerful reactionary forces.

Second, the revolutionary dogma tends to underestimate the costs of a revolutionary upheaval—costs in terms of human lives, suffering, thwarted personal plans, bitterness, and general social disorganization. The prospective gains must be enormous, and there must be no alternatives, if this cost is to be justified.

Third, revolution constitutes a great danger to free political institutions. For example, the risks of losing freedom would be infinitely greater if socialism were reached by revolution than if it were approached by the route of evolution.

Fourth, the method of revolution with its sudden taking away of property and its sudden upsetting of established social organization inevitably involves needless injustices. It takes away from many people the property and the rights which they have worked for and planned toward and which they had a legitimate expectation of preserving, while at the same time providing windfall gains to others. This injustice can be greatly mitigated—though not entirely prevented—if social change occurs through orderly evolutionary processes.

Fifth, the revolutionist's comprehensive blueprints for social organization are likely to be unrealistic and impracticable. It is not possible to design a workable social organization on the drafting table. The complexity and the dynamic nature of society preclude the practicability of synthetic social organization. The evolutionary process, on the other hand, permits the society to develop by a process of trial and error in one aspect of its life at a time. Mistakes and inadequacies in piecemeal plans of the social engineers are less disastrous than the shortcomings of comprehensive blueprints.

Sixth, socialists tend to evade problems by attributing every ill to the capitalistic "system." Their creed fosters the view that nothing important can be done toward mitigating our problems because these problems are inherent in the system and ineradicable without the extreme remedy of revolution. They live in a state of wishful utopianism where all problems are solved if only socialism can be attained but in which nothing can be solved so long as we are "shackled" by capitalistic institutions. They tend toward an "either-or" complex. They have a sort of occupational blindness to and impatience with middle-of-the-road solutions. They sometimes even foster confusion and disorganization in the hope that it will precipitate the conditions favorable to revolution.

Finally, socialists (capitalists as well) tend to overlook the fact that true progress toward human happiness—the true, the good, the beautiful—is something that must come from within the hearts of men as well as through new laws or new institutional patterns.[3] For example, capitalism might work very well if most individuals were motivated by a desire to serve social ends rather than by the desire for pecuniary gain, competitive advantage, power, and prestige. And a socialist country peopled by selfish, brutish, lustful, power-motivated creatures would hardly constitute a good society.

The Way Ahead

Merely reciting socialist dogmas does not dispose of the fact that capitalism has serious weaknesses—weaknesses which threaten its very existence. This applies to capitalism not only in its pure form but also in the form in which we know it today. The problem is to build upon what we have, by rational and evolutionary processes, in order to overcome or mitigate these weaknesses—but still preserving, so far as possible, the benefits and advantages of capitalism.[4] The problem is to follow the dictates of our rational processes—not flinching from the task of moving forward even when indicated reforms may interfere with vested interests or upset established ways of doing things which are comfortable because they are habitual. The task is urgent. The present weaknesses of capitalism are serious. They threaten to bring about its downfall by revolution and to submerge with it the considerable amount of political freedom we now enjoy. It is doubtful, for example, if the present form of capitalism could survive another depression like that of the 1930's. And

---

3 For a development of this theme one should consult the teachings of most great religious leaders. The later writings of Count Leo Tolstoy are also largely in this vein.

4 Cf. Henry Simons, *A Positive Program for Laissez Faire*, Chicago, 1934.

this is not a mere academic question, because there is every reason to expect just such a catastrophe—perhaps within the next decade unless practicable remedies are found and preventive action is taken.

There are many who shrink from a frontal assault on our economic problems—who think they find the answers in turning the clock back to the nineteenth century and to pure capitalism. By this attitude they actually do a disservice to their own cause. Such turning back—even if it were possible—could lead only to disaster. It is by willingness to accept, or even encourage constructive evolutionary change that the essentials of capitalism and freedom can be preserved.

On the other hand, the socialist revolutionary, who wants a violent and sudden change in our institutions, is asking far more than is justified by conditions in an advanced capitalistic country like the United States. Conditions here, though far from perfect and surely in need of much reform, are not so bad or so hopeless as to justify the extreme remedy. One does not submit to major surgery in order to cure nervous indigestion. On the other hand, nervous indigestion is a very trying complaint, and well worth taking the trouble to cure. But the cure should be attempted by means of appropriate and scientifically approved remedies rather than by resort to quacks and witch doctors.

In the United States today, the means to orderly and intelligent attack on the weaknesses of our system are at hand. We have a long and vigorous democratic tradition. We have institutions for effecting orderly institutional change. We have an educated, literate, emotionally stable, and adaptable populace. We have the greatest aggregation of professionally trained social scientists in the world. The problem is one of social engineering. It involves rational analysis of the problems in terms of defined objectives and the development of rational solutions. The solutions, of course, must take into account the subtleties of human nature and the traditions and ethical values of our society. Solutions appropriate for Russia, China, or Ethiopia—with their unique cultural backgrounds—would be quite different from those suitable to the United States.

Obviously there are great obstacles to the successful engineering of evolutionary social change. People resist social change of any kind since it involves adaptation and the development of new habits and attitudes. Perhaps more important, changes are also resisted because they almost always interfere with the established interests of particular groups. The affected groups use all possible means to protect their position. This resistance of vested interests is, of course, the basis of the socialist case that fundamental social changes can occur only through violent revolution.

To solve our problems intelligently will require more scientific social knowledge than we now have. One can be reasonably hopeful that social scientists will be able to provide this knowledge—especially in view of the great strides in this area of study within the past generation. But in addition to knowledge, statesmanship on the part of our political leaders will be required, and also—not less important—our people must understand the issues and must learn to view these issues in terms of the broad social interest. The technical findings of social scientists are of little consequence unless there is also receptivity to the findings among the people. The great tasks of our age are to develop social science and to bring about a widespread diffusion of knowledge and understanding about social matters to the end that we may develop a free society of plenty and justice.

*Afterword**

by Howard R. Bowen

E conomics has often been billed as the most self-confident, if
not most successful, of all the social sciences. It appears to
have an accepted body of doctrine, a reliable principle of quantification, sophisticated technique, and a seemingly secure place
in public policy making. Yet economists are increasingly nervous
about the state of the discipline. Their concern has been expressed in a remarkable series of presidential addresses given to
economic societies on both sides of the Atlantic.

In 1968 Professor Kenneth Boulding entitled his address
"Economics as a Moral Science," and said "Economics has made
its own attempt to solve some of the problems involved in the
moral judgment in what we know as welfare economics. I believe
this attempt has been a failure though a reasonably glorious
one . . . ." Then he went on to say that the Paretian optimum
which is widely accepted by economists "rests on an extremely
shaky foundation of ethical propositions." It implies, said
Boulding, that there is no malevolence or benevolence in the
system. "It assumes selfishness, that is, the independence of individual preference functions, such that is makes no difference
to me whether I perceive you as either better off or worse off.
Anything less descriptive of the human condition could hardly
be imagined. The plain fact is that our lives are dominated by

Reprinted from *Nebraska Journal of Economics and Business* Vol. 11, No. 4
(Autumn 1972) by permission.

* The C. Woody Thompson Memorial Lecture delivered at the opening ses-
sion of the Midwest Economic Association, April 20, 1972.

precisely this interdependence of utility functions which the Paretian optimum denies."[1]

In 1970 Professor Wassily Leontief of Harvard gave an address entitled "Theoretical Assumptions and Nonobserved Facts." His complaint was the "proliferating superstructure of pure or should I say speculative economic theory," and uncritical enthusiasm for mathematical formulation," without adequate empirical foundations.[2]

In 1971 E. H. Phelps Brown, President of the Royal Economic Society in Britain, spoke on "the smallness of the contribution that the most conspicuous developments of economics in the last quarter of a century have made to the solution of the most pressing problems of the time." He referred to the temptation of economists to play a kind of chess in the form of logical games played with unrealistic assumptions.[3] In the same year Professor G. D. N. Worswick's presidential address to Section F of the British Association was on the topic "Is Progress in Economic Science Possible?" He said "The standards are high, the intellectual battalions are powerful, but notwithstanding the appearance of formidable progress in techniques of all kinds the performance of economics seems curiously disappointing." Economics possess "a marvelous array of pretend tools which would perform wonders if ever a set of facts should turn up in the right form."[4]

That the leaders of the profession should express such views about modern economics is astonishing. One could add to the chorus of criticism a recent symposium on the state of economics in the *Saturday Review*[5] and also many complaints from economists of the New Left.[6]

---

[1] Kenneth Boulding, "Economics as a Moral Science," *American Economic Review*, March 1969, pp. 5–6.

[2] *American Economic Review*, March 1971, p. 1.

[3] "The Underdevelopment of Economics," *The Economic Journal*, March 1972, pp. 1, 3.

[4] *The Economic Journal*, March 1972, pp. 74, 79.

[5] Leonard Silk, Daniel R. Fusfeld, Robert Lekachman, Marc J. Roberts, Robert A. Solo, and Charles L. Schultze, "Does Economics Ignore You?" *Saturday Review*, January 22, 1972, pp. 33–57.

[6] Assar Lindbeck, *The Political Economy of the New Left: An Outsider's View* (New York: Harper & Row, 1971).

My paper is also in a critical vein. It is on a rather ambitious subject at the border between social philosophy and economics. The topic is related to welfare economics. Its inspiration is not the maximization of the national dividend as recommended by Pigou nor the optimality of Pareto but the writings of an assorted collection of philosophers, religious leaders, and literary figures whom I call the humanistic critics of economics.

A Critique of Welfare Economics

For thousands of years, at least since the time of Aristotle, economic thinkers have explored the connections between economic behavior and the good life. The boundaries between economics and social philosophy have always been fuzzy. Most economists, even those deeply committed to scientific purity, have had their philosophic moments and most have been willing to speak out on issues of public policy. During the past two centuries much of the discussion has centered on whether or not market price is a useful measure of value and on whether the outcomes of a free-enterprise economy are conducive to human well-being. In recent decades the esoteric subspecialty known as "the new welfare economics" has emerged.

The new welfare economics draws upon the fewest possible value judgments. Its goal is to state a purely *economic* theory of welfare and thus to avoid the murky, subjective, and contentious areas of value judgments and ideological commitment. Its basic postulate is simply that more is better than less. In measuring the more or the less, the yardstick is *value* as set objectively by the market in the form of prices. The goal is to maximize the sum total of those values as expressed, for example, in the national income; values not capable of being reduced to prices are simply omitted as outside the scope of economics.

This approach to welfare has engaged some of the best minds of the economic profession. Considering the confining scope of its assumptions, it has produced results of surprising interest and usefulness. In the past decade or two, however, it has lost some of its lustre. Many economists hold out little hope for it as a solid basis for economic policy. As Kelvin Lancaster has said, the theory demonstrates how to extract "a minimum of results from a minimum of assumptions."[7]

The theory has not really freed itself from entanglement with values. Rather, it is based on values that are patently naive and crass. Its underlying assumption that additions to economic goods without limit will enhance human welfare has been questioned since the dawn of civilization and is as dubious today as in the time of Buddha, Socrates, or Jesus. Its effort to isolate the aspects of welfare measurably by market price has lulled society into ignoring broader and deeper values. Welfare—even welfare in its narrow economic aspects—cannot usefully be separated from considerations of human relationships, freedom, justice, status, power, security, and other values which the market does not adequately recognize. Also, as the institutional economists tell us, welfare economics takes culture as given and has nothing to say about cultural change as an influence on choice and as a determinant of welfare.

In the effort to avoid value judgments, welfare economics has shunned interpersonal comparisons of value. Welfare can be said to be enhanced only when at least one person gets more without any other person getting less, and only those group decisions are clearly beneficial which have unanimous consent. The rejection of interpersonal comparisons implies that nothing can be said about the effects on welfare of income redistribution, one of society's most traumatic issues, or for that matter about any political decisions in which opinion is divided. Like most economics, welfare economics presents a misleading and simplistic relationship between means and ends in which production is considered the means and consumption the end. Finally, welfare economics takes no account of the many zero-sum games that are played by human beings in which economic resources are used for status and power and in which the gains of some are offset by the losses of others. Moreover, it places no value on the games themselves.

Though the new welfare economics may have its uses, the practical affairs of life call for a broader theory, one that looks at the whole of human welfare and provides a place for non-market values. This is especially so as the fraction of the economy governed by individual choice shrinks.

---

[7] *Journal of Political Economy* 174 (1966), p. 132.

The Humanistic Critics

My thinking about welfare is in the tradition of a long line of humanistic critics of classical economics. Among them, I would mention Adam Müller, Friedrich List, John Rae, John Ruskin, Thomas Carlyle, William Morris, Charles Kingsley, Henry Thoreau, John A. Hobson, Thorstein Veblen, C. H. Cooley, Frank A. Fetter, J. M. Clark, and many others.[8] One could add to this list several outstanding contemporary economists such as Kenneth Boulding, Gunnar Myrdal, and Walter Weisskopf,[9] as well as some younger economists of the New Left.[10] These people surely do not represent a clearly-defined school. Some of them have questionable credentials as economists or dubious political associations. But they have in common grave doubts about conventional welfare economics as a guide to human welfare. Regrettably, most of them have been content to serve as critics. They have not constructed systems of thought to compare with the ruling economic ideas. I have long believed that these critics, however unsystematic they may be and however misguided on technical details, deserve careful study. I have long pondered what kind of a theory of welfare economics would flow from their suggestive but often vague ideas. I shall try to sketch the bare outline of such a theory.

I have noticed that a central concept of some of the nineteenth century critics is the word "life." *Life* is for them the goal of economic activity, the ultimate value, the object to be maximized. The cost of any product or activity is the amount of life that is given up to produce or achieve it. Sometimes cost is equated with death, which is negative "life." Life and death in this usage are matters of degree. A given person can enjoy more or less life; and to whatever extent he fails to attain the potential fullness of his life, to that extent he suffers death.

---

8 A highly informative and interesting paper on some of these critics is: William D. Grampp, "Classical Economics and its Moral Critics," delivered to the American Economic Association, December 1970, to be published in a forthcoming issue of *The History of Political Economy*.

9 Walter Weisskopf, *Alienation and Economics* (New York: E. P. Dutton & Company, 1971), and "Economics and Meaninglessness," *infra*, p. 67.

10 The Marxist literature relating to the "early Marx" and the concept of alienation might be added.

John Ruskin uses this terminology in his book *Unto This Last,* which he subtitled "Four Essays on the First Principles of Political Economy." Ruskin said (and I am quoting here several disconnected excerpts), "To be 'valuable' . . . is to 'avail toward life' . . . I believe nearly all labour may be shortly divided into positive and negative labour: positive, that which produces life; negative, that which produces death . . . the prosperity of any nation is in exact proportion to the quantity of labour which it spends in obtaining and employing means of life. . . . Production does not consist in things laborously made, but in things serviceably consumable; and the question for the nation is not how much labour it employs but how much life it produces. For as consumption is the end and aim of production, so life is the end and aim of consumption. There is no wealth but life."[11]

Similarly, Henry Thoreau wrote, ". . . the cost of a thing is the amount of what I will call life which is required to be exchanged for it . . . ."[12]

Thomas Carlyle in *Past and Present* refers to the "inner fountains of life" which may with a radical change in the social values "irradiate and purify your bloated, swollen, foul existence, drawing nigh, as at present to nameless death!"[13]

Similar use of the word "life" is found in Albert Schweitzer's famous phrase "reverence for life." For him the highest good is "to preserve life, to promote life, to raise to its highest value life which is capable of development"; and evil is "to destroy life, to injure life, to repress life which is capable of development."[14]

The most celebrated use of the concept *life* is found in the words of Jesus who said, "For whoever would save his life will lose it, and whoever shall lose his life for my sake will find it. For what will it profit a man, if he gains the whole world and forfeits his life."[15]

---

11 John Ruskin, *Unto This Last* (London: George Allen and Unwin, Ltd., 1960), pp. 118, 142, 143, 155, 180.

12 *Walden,* ed. Sherman Paul (Boston: Houghton Mifflin, 1960), p. 21.

13 *Past and Present* (Sew York: Charles Scribner's Sons, 1918), p. 28.

14 Albert Schweitzer, *Out of My Life and Thought,* trans. C. T. Campion (New York: Henry Holt and Company, 1949), pp. 157–58.

15 Matthew 16: 25–26. One can also find many contemporary examples of the use of the word "life" as an all-embracing objective of society. For example,

For the humanistic critics, true economy consists of ordering all human experiences so that life is maximized. Among these experiences are what economists call production and consumption. But production is not exclusively a means nor consumption exclusively an end. Rather, both production and consumption are part of human experience and both can yield positive and negative returns in relation to the ultimate goal, which is life. For example, work may be toilsome and loathsome or it may be creative and exhilarating. Consumption may be vulgar, superficial, or excessive; or it may be directed toward true life enrichment. Some of the humanistic critics—notably William Morris—emphasized the positive or life-fulfilling aspects of work—especially of craftsmanship, art, and personal participation and responsibility; and virtually all believed that life would be enhanced partly through consumption emphasizing intrinsic values as contrasted with status and power. They also believed that life would be enhanced through equity in the distribution of opportunity and income.

A Humanistic Theory of Welfare

Can a coherent and useful theory of welfare be constructed on the basis of the thinking of Ruskin, Carlyle, Thoreau, and the other critics? Such a theory would start, of course, from the premise that *life* is the object to be maximized.

The first step in constructing such a theory would be to sort out the means and the ends. The life of a person occurs through time, and time is the basic means. It is a limited resource having alternative uses, and is therefore subject to familiar economic principles.

Life consists of a stream of experiences strung out through time like beads on a chain. These experiences include eating, sleeping, working, commuting, meditating, planning, learning, loving, playing, loafing, fraternizing, and so on. Some of these experiences are purely means to ulterior ends and some are

---

Benjamin De Mott refers to "the variousness and fullness of life"; and the columnist D. J. R. Bruckner states, "There is a great need . . . for a new definition of life, a new vision. If the politicians will not provide it, the professions—starting with the economists—and the colleges can inspire it."

purely ends in themselves; but most are both means and ends. For example, sleeping and eating may be regarded as ends; but they are also means to work. Work on the other hand is a means to income but it may also be an end in itself because of the sociability, creativity, interesting experience it yields. Learning may be a means to work, but it may also be an end in itself. Thus, in the experiences of life, the means and ends are intricately interrelated.

The ends or values may be grouped together into abstract categories to which life experiences add or detract. Examples of such values are survival, health and safety, physical comfort, security, love, friendship, learning, aesthetic appreciation, religion, creativity, new experience, status, power, justice, and others. Values such as these are the elements which determine the amount of life that is achieved. Maximization of life occurs when the life experiences are such that these values have been attained to the greatest possible degree.[16]

The framework of the formal theory is that life is at a maximum when human time, the basic means, is allocated for the achievement of the various values so that the values are attained to the greatest possible extent. The solution is to apply the equimarginal principle in the allocation of time to various values. Thus, when the marginal increment of time devoted to any one value yields as much return as the marginal increment devoted to any other, and time is being used efficiently in each of its uses, no further increase in life is possible by reallocating time, and a maximum has been reached.

These principles are, of course, the staples of conventional economic analysis. As Kenneth Boulding has said:

In the endeavor to explain the relationship of so-called 'economic' variables . . . the economist has been gradually forced into a much more general theory, so that now economics has become essentially the general theory of choice, that is, of the implications of scarcity. As such the conclusions of economics are relevant not only in the small sphere of so-called 'economic institutions' (money, banking,

---

16 This conception of life is brilliantly developed by Steffan Burenstam-Linder in *The Harried Leisure Class* (New York: Columbia University Press, 1970).

firms, and the like) but apply wherever choice is necessary; which means that they apply almost universally; to art, music, government, even to theology.[17]

And in another connection, Boulding has said: "There are production functions not only for grapes and figs, but also for goods and bads and indeed for ultimate good."[18]

The theoretical framework I am propounding must be qualified in three ways. First, the fullness of life does not necessarily mean maximum satisfaction or maximum utility in the hedonistic sense. The most noble and the most highly valued lives may well involve sacrifice, duty, risk, and hardship. Second, since experiences at any one point in a life may have consequences for later periods in that same life, the object to be maximized is the life as a whole—from birth to death—not arbitrary sections of it such as single days or years.[19] This makes room for the concept of planning and investment. Third, since the choices and behavior of each individual will be largely guided by his culture, by the way he has been conditioned or forced to behave, the economic problem is not only to achieve appropriate choices within a given cultural pattern, but also to adapt the culture itself so that individuals will be guided toward life fulfillment. Cultural change comes about in part spontaneously as people adjust to changing conditions or try to solve problems; it also come about through education, the suggestion of the media, example of leaders and elites, legislation, discussion, fiat of dictators, or revolution.

With these qualifications, the basic theory is that to attain fullness of life requires that a scarce resource, human time, be allocated to various values so that marginal returns are equalized and so that time is employed efficiently in each use. Thus all the conditions are present for conventional economic analysis *except* for so-called objective market prices.

17 "Is Economics Necessary?" undated mimeographed summary.

18 "Economics as a Moral Science," *American Economic Review,* March 1969, p. 11.

19 Cf. Juanita M. Kreps, *Lifetime Allocation of Work and Income* (Durham: Duke University Press, 1971).

The Question of Measurement

A welfare economics with gross national *life,* rather than gross national *income,* as the object to be maximized cannot use price as a universal measuring stick. Price does not adequately measure health or friendship or love or security or a beautiful landscape. At best the goods and services that can be priced are partial means to these values.[20]

In the past most economists have sacrificed a broadly inclusive theory of human welfare in order to achieve quantification in terms of market price. But it is not beyond the powers of human judgment to invent systematic procedures by which to estimate gross national life at various points in time and to decide how fuller life might be achieved by better allocation of human time and greater technical efficiency in its use. In everyday life—in our families, in our colleges and universities, and in our government—we are forced to make such judgments constantly, but we do so in a somewhat disorderly and hit-and-miss fashion.

For several reasons, economists are now being drawn into the use of new techniques of measurement, or new ways of rendering judgments, as they advise on resource use.

First, an increasing proportion of the economy is involved with choices and activities that lie beyond the market, for example, natural resource development, education, research, the arts, public health services, military power, zoning, taxation, income maintenance, and so on. Market price is only a peripheral guide, yet decisions must be made and economists are asked to help.

Second, the public is becoming crictical of growth in GNP as a chief measure of national welfare and a chief guide to public policy. People are increasingly conscious that price and value are by no means the same things. Economists may point out that

---

[20] Marketable goods are used in the quest of these and most other values. Friendship may be enlivened by food and drink; religion has its churches and icons and its tithing; courtship calls for engagement rings; and security requires insurance and jails. But on the whole values such as friendship or religious experience are not marketable.

GNP was never meant to measure welfare,[21] but for generations most economists as well as most political leaders have acted as though it were a measure of welfare and as though the prime object of policy were to maximize GNP. Now many people are sensing that the doubling and redoubling of GNP does not necessarily enhance the quality of life. They are asking for more inclusive and more relevant welfare measures.

Third, the country is recognizing as never before the importance of side effects and externalities—both positive and negative—which are not readily measurable in dollars.

To sum up, in the words of Carlyle, "Cash payment the sole nexus; and there are so many things which cash will not pay! Cash is a great miracle; yet it has not all power in Heaven, nor even on Earth."[22]

And so economists and others are seriously exploring new techniques for measurement and systematic judgment. For measuring the effects of incremental changes in particular uses of resources such devices as program budgeting, cost-benefit analysis, and operations research applied to complex social systems are being explored increasingly. Social indicators are being developed to measure progress over time with respect to various parameters of social welfare. Efforts are being made to measure resource inputs and welfare outputs by means of public opinion analysis, interpretation of voting, use of surrogate measures, various Delphi techniques, and the like. These methods are all related and overlapping. They all seek to measure, or to form judgments about, the more and the less with respect to values not readily convertible into price.[23]

The traditional way of reaching judgments where such values are present has been to use the political process of discussion and voting—with voting as a decisive technique of measure-

---

21 Cf. Arthur M. Okun, "Should GNP Measure Social Welfare?" *Brookings Bulletin,* Summer 1971, pp. 4-7.

22 Thomas Carlyle, "Essay on Chartism," *The Works of Thomas Carlyle,* Centenary Edition XXIX (New York: Charles Scribner's Sons, n.d.), p. 169.

23 For a splendid discussion of concepts and techniques of measurement, see Jati K. Sengupta and Karl A. Fox, *Operations Research and Complex Social Systems* (Chicago: Rand McNally, to be published).

ment. The political process is available to be used by small informal groups and organizations, as well as by the state. The role of measurements of the kind I have mentioned is not to supplant the political process but rather to inform the political process and also to help with administrative decisions within broad policies laid down by the political process. Clearly, the economist has a place in this kind of measurement, and he needs a general theory of welfare, perhaps based on maximization of life, as a framework.

As the economist moves into the unfamiliar region of nonmarket values, he tends to cling to price as a yardstick. Whenever possible he tries to convert nonmarket values into money terms. Especially is this so in cost-benefit analysis. He is comfortable with market values; they have an aura of objectivity and are reducible to numbers that can be manipulated arithmetically. But the tendency to fall back on price has it pitfalls. It tempts the economist to bend his problem to his customary technique and to distort the results by overlooking the limitations of the market. Sociologists and political scientists—who are less preoccupied with the market than economists—may well assert increasing leadership in decision making where nonmarket values are involved. We may see the gradual contraction of the scope and role of economics in social affairs unless economists can free themselves to consider nonmarket values.

I should like to comment further on social indicators. These strike me as having great promise in connection with a general theory of welfare economics. The idea behind social indicators is that for many elements of human welfare, change over time might be measured so that progress or retrogression could be estimated just as it is for GNP, industrial production, or new housing starts. Social indicators might be constructed for many parameters of welfare, such as health, safety, and longevity; education; knowledge; distribution of income and opportunity; social status of minority groups; social mobility; crime and delinquency; financial security; worker satisfaction; amount and use of leisure time; structure of consumption; family life; housing; interest and participation in the arts; aesthetic aspects of the environment; natural resource depletion and development; population growth; and alienation and social morale.

To collect data on various aspects of social change is, of

course, scarcely novel. Yet surprisingly little systematic information has been gathered to measure change in the basic elements
of human welfare. Generally speaking, our data tend to measure
resource inputs rather than outcomes. This is well illustrated by
the field of education, for which we have vast amounts of data
about personnel, enrollments, expenditures, and the like, but
very little about the true educational attainments of our people.
Efforts are being made, however, to improve the situation. For
example, Bertrand Gross has been writing in the field for ten
years or more. Congressional hearings have been held and one
notable compilation of social indicators has recently been made
in HEW under the direction of Mancur Olson.[24] Other recent
studies include one sponsored by the Russell Sage Foundation
under the editorship of Eleanor B. Sheldon and Wilbert E.
Moore,[25] and another published by MIT Press under the editorship of R. A. Bauer.[26] Other work is in progress, especially at the
Michigan Survey Research Center under the direction of Frank
M. Andrews.

It is by no means out of the question that statistics may be
produced some day on social change or social progress comparable to the statistics on national income and product. I do
not even shrink from the idea of an aggregated index of national
social progress—which might serve as a kind of surrogate for
gross national life.

Aggregation raises the question of weights. For example,
how much weight should be given to progress in reducing air
pollution as compared with progress in reducing crime or progress in adding to the stock of knowledge? The weights might,
of course, be derived through public opinion analysis or from
the judgments of some group of wise men. Another way, based
on money values, would be to use as the index for each element
of social progress the estimated deficit between the actual annual
outlays for that element and the annual outlays that would be
needed to bring that element up to a reasonable national standard by a selected target date. The sum of the deficits when

---

24 U.S. Department of Health, Education and Welfare, *Toward a Social Report*
(Washington, D.C.: U.S. Government Printing Office, 1969).

25 *Indicators of Social Change* (New York: Russell Sage Foundation, 1968).

26 *Social Indicators* (Cambridge: MIT Press, 1966).

computed year after year would be the reciprocal of an aggregated index of social progress; the smaller the sum of the deficits the greater the gross national life. Thus, if air pollution were to get worse over time, the deficit would increase; or if crime and delinquency were to be reduced over time, the deficit would decline. The sum of the deficits for all elements of social progress would then become an aggregated index of progress. What I am proposing is somewhat comparable to the results of a path-breaking study published in 1966 by Leonard A. Lecht of the National Planning Association under the title *Goals, Priorities, and Dollars.*[27]

I shall not dwell further on the problem of measurement except to concede that measurement of social values presents many difficulties and subtleties, and that we are only at the threshold of achievements in this field.[28]

Social Criticism

I am not suggesting that human welfare, or *life,* as I have called it, can ever ultimately be measured in any statistical sense. A human life is a work of art. It can only be judged, as a poem or a painting is judged, by sensitive and informed critics. Similarly, judgments about the life of a society are aesthetic and moral judgments. To evaluate life calls for social critics who have thought deeply about style, form, and technique, and also about meanings and purpose. The task of making such judgments falls to people of unusual wisdom and sensitivity whom we may call

---

27 (New York: The Free Press, 1966). In this study Dr. Lecht started with sixteen national standards or goals that had been established by President Eisenhower's Commission on National Goals. The standards referred to objectives for such elements of national welfare as health, education, natural resources, research, housing, and consumer expenditures. Dr. Lecht estimated the annual cost of achieving these standards by a given future year. The difference at any given date between the actual annual expenditures and the estimated annual cost of achieving the standards represented the deficit. Changes over time in the size of the deficit measured social progress. Dr. Lecht's study was conducted with the constraint that annual expenditures would be limited by national productive capacity. One of his useful conclusions was that the standards were impossible to fulfill within the limits of national productivity and should be revised.

28 Cf. Alice M. Rivlin, *Systematic Thinking for Social ctAion* (Washington, D.C.: The Brookings Institution, 1971).

social critics. They are the ones who examine our society, who try to understand it, and who judge the extent to which potential life is being achieved.

Criticism is far from an exact skill. Critics are human and are subject to self-interest and to biased perspective and may disagree. Before rejecting criticism as a way of judging life, however, it is well to remember that in the arts critical judgments of wide acceptability are in fact reached. The greatness of Shakespeare's plays or Beethoven's quarters or Picasso's paintings is almost universally acknowledged, and the lesser or even insignificant stature of certain other artists or works of art is equally agreed upon. And artistic criticism is useful in understanding and interpreting works of art even when evaluation is not intended.

Similarly, historians, who are in a sense social critics of past civilizations, are able to reach judgments or to provide interpretations about the quality of life in various societies. For example, they have managed to reach some fairly well agreed understandings about Fifth Century Greece or Elizabethan England or Hitler's Germany. In the final analysis, measurement of social welfare is a matter of critical judgment made by sensitive and informed persons and constantly reviewed through the accumulation of knowledge, discussion, and debate.

Measuring devices such as social indicators, even if the data were complete and refined and even if the system of weighting were rational, can never by themselves measure the fullness of life. At most, they represent some of the conditions of the full life, or surrogates for the full life, but not life itself. Life is more than health, just income distribution, leisure, worker satisfaction, and the like. The goodness or fullness of life can be judged only in its entirety as a work of art.

To explore values that transcend the market, however, as is done in the study of social indicators, carries us far closer to life and to a meaningful theory of welfare than can ever be possible through a theory limited to the market and to inferences from the market.

Equality

In conclusion, I should like to carry the argument one step further. The humanistic critics have to a man been suspicious of social arrangements that place some men above others in income, status, and power. To the humanistic critics, pride is a deadly sin. A basic postulate is that all human beings are intrinsically of equal value and are entitled so far as possible to equal amounts of life. Individuals may differ widely in personal traits and talents. They may be able to realize life only through quite different experiences. And inevitably they may not all be able to achieve life to the same fullness. Nevertheless, equality of life is a social objective to be sought if not fully achieved. To the humanistic critics the principle of equality requires that social policy work toward removing social and physical conditions that stunt the ability to reap the fullness of life—one way being to open up opportunities equally to all and another being to redistribute income.[29]

The question of equality brings up a host of familiar issues about incentives, freedom, and differences in need.[30] In practice these issues call for compromises. The question of equality also brings up the question of interpersonal comparisons. I think the taboo on such comparisons has been counter-productive. It has, more than anything else, inhibited economics from making the contribution to social welfare analysis that it might and should have made. All economists are aware of the philosophical issues. It would be convenient if the world were so ordered that we could penetrate one another's inner consciousness. Regrettably it is not so. Pragmatically, however, there is no alternative in the operation of society but to make interpersonal comparisons. We do so every day in the family, the school, the workplace, the social welfare agency, the clinic, the law courts, and the legislative

29 A brilliant exposition of the issues treated in this section is found in John Rawls, *A Theory of Justice* (Cambridge: Harvard University Press, 1971).

30 Redistribution raises the question of a possible incompatibility between maximization of gross national life and equality among persons. Maximization requires that marginal increments of life be equal for all persons (leaving out of account for the moment the units in which marginal increments could be measured). Under this condition, sensitive and talented people might be able to use more opportunities and goods than stupid and brutish people. Equality requires simply that opportunities and goods be apportioned equally among persons regardless of the margins. My opinion is that the case for equality is stronger when one considers *life* as the object to be maximized than when considering only income. *Life* is more inclusive and more significant than income.

assemblies. Having no alternative, we must rely on human capacity for communication in words and actions. Most of us believe such communication can give us reliable—though not precise—clues to inner states of consciousness, emotions, satisfactions, intentions, guilt feelings, and the like. The inescapable truth is that in all matters pertaining to social welfare, he who would insist on precision, on objective evidence, or on the complete facts—or for that matter on an unexceptionable theory—will never reach any decisions. In the area of social welfare we fly by the seat of our pants, not by computerized instrumentation.

In any case, most economists accept egalitarian premises. Other things equal, most of them will actively prefer a solution to a policy issue which reduces inequalities over one which increases inequalities. A humanistic economics would place even greater emphasis on equality than has conventional economics, but would be concerned about equality of life as a whole, not just about money income.

The principle of equality holds not only that lives are of equal intrinsic value at any given time, but also that lives being lived at different times are also of equal value. The rights and claims of any one generation are equal to those of another, and no single generation has the right to impair the patrimony of the next. This principle, which is an ancient one but which has somtimes been neglected in welfare economics, is based on the idea that the planet will be inhabited for thousands of years and that the goal is maximization of life over this extended and unforeseeable future, not merely within the present generation. It is an intergenerational and planetary concept of welfare.

The principle of maximizing life over time brings into focus three interrelated questions which every generation must face and which are agitating our society today.

These questions are: (1) How much may any generation reasonably take from nature's storehouse of materials and environmental amenities? (2) How much capital and knowledge is each generation obliged to accumulate for future generations? and (3) How rapidly should the population be allowed to grow?

Ordinarily, these questions are answered largely according to the interests of the present generation. Future values are discounted at rates that make slight provision for values to be realized beyond a few decades hence. For example, with a discount rate of 6 percent, a dollar 50 years from now has a present value of five cents! Questions of social policy would be answered quite differently if the amount of life on this planet were to be maximized not merely for the present generation but for all future generations, including the most distant ones. On such a principle, the life of a person living in the year 2072 would have value fully equal to that of a person living in 1972, and future values would not be discounted at anything like the rates that now prevail. Except for uncertainty, the rate of discount would be zero, which simply expresses the idea that a human life at one time is worth as much as a human life at any other time, and a dollar of income which is instrumental to life is intrinsically worth as much on one date as on another. Because of uncertainty, however, with respect to future technology, population, demand, natural resources, and the like, decisions for the distant future are likely to be less productive than decisions for the near future. More errors will be made. Thus a rate of discount that allows for uncertainty would favor the present generation over future generations. But this discount rate would undoubtedly be less than the rate now customarily in use when decisions are made primarily from the perspective of the present generation.

Conclusion

Throughout two centuries the quarrel between economists, with their elegant welfare theories based on market values, and the humanists, with their insistence that value transcends the market, has led only to futility. This has been so in part because the interests of Western society have been focused on market values and in part because the humanists have failed to produce coherent theories susceptible of even rough quantification. Today these conditions are changing. Large sections of the public are disillusioned about market values as an index of human welfare, and advancements in the social sciences are pointing the way toward measurement or indications of values that are closer than market values to the true ingredients of life. The times call upon economists to broaden their purview, to add new tools to their kits, and to develop useful theories of welfare that persons of humane sensibilities can respect.

It is time for economists to restore their position not only as political economists but also as social philosophers.

As Ruskin said, "The real science of political economy, which has yet to be distinguished from the bastard science, as medicine from witchcraft, and astronomy from astrology, is that which teaches nations to desire and labour for the things that lead to life: and which teaches them to scorn and destroy the things that lead to destruction . . . the great and only science of Political Economy teaches them . . . what is vanity, and what substance; and how the service of Death, the Lord of Waste, and of eternal emptiness, differs from the service of Wisdom, the Lady of Saving, and of eternal fulness; . . . There is no Wealth but Life."[31]

---

[31] Ruskin, *op. cit.*, pp. 119-20. 156.

INDEX